Reconstructing Patriarchy after the Great War

THE PALGRAVE MACMILLAN SERIES IN TRANSNATIONAL HISTORY

Series Editors: **Akira Iriye** (Harvard University) and **Rana Mitter** (University of Oxford)

This distinguished series seeks to develop scholarship on the transnational connections of societies and peoples in the nineteenth and twentieth centuries; provide a forum in which work on transnational history from different periods, subjects, and regions of the world can be brought together in fruitful connection; and explore the theoretical and methodological links between transnational and other related approaches such as comparative history and world history.

Editorial Board: **Thomas Bender**, university professor of the humanities, professor of history, and director of the International Center for Advanced Studies, New York University; **Jane Carruthers**, professor of history, University of South Africa; **Mariano Plotkin**, professor, Universidad Nacional de Tres de Febrero, Buenos Aires and member of the National Council of Scientific and Technological Research, Argentina; **Pierre-Yves Saunier**, researcher at the Centre National de la Recherche Scientifique, France; **Ian Tyrrell**, professor of history, University of New South Wales.

Titles Include:

Glenda Sluga
THE NATION, PSYCHOLOGY AND INTERNATIONAL POLITICS, 1870–1919

Sebastian Conrad and Dominic Sachsenmaier (*editors*)
COMPETING VISIONS OF WORLD ORDER: GLOBAL MOMENT AND MOVEMENTS, 1880s–1930s

Eri Hotta
PAN-ASIANISM AND JAPAN'S WAR 1931–1945

Martin Klimke and Joachim Scharloth (*editors*)
1968 IN EUROPE: A HISTORY OF PROTEST AND ACTIVISM, 1956–1977

Erika Kuhlman
RECONSTRUCTING PATRIARCHY AFTER THE GREAT WAR: WOMEN, GENDER, AND POST-WAR RECONCILIATION BETWEEN NATIONS

Forthcoming:

Matthias Middell, Michael Geyer, and Michel Espagne
EUROPEAN HISTORY IN AN INTERCONNECTED WORLD

Also by Erika Kuhlman:

A TO Z OF WOMEN IN WORLD HISTORY

PETTICOATS AND WHITE FEATHERS: GENDER CONFORMITY, RACE, THE PROGRESSIVE PEACE MOVEMENT, AND THE DEBATE OVER WAR, 1895–1919

Reconstructing Patriarchy after the Great War
Women, Gender, and Postwar Reconciliation between Nations

Erika Kuhlman

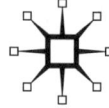
RECONSTRUCTING PATRIARCHY AFTER THE GREAT WAR
Copyright © Erika Kuhlman, 2008.
All rights reserved.

First published in 2008 by
PALGRAVE MACMILLAN™
175 Fifth Avenue, New York, N.Y. 10010 and
Houndmills, Basingstoke, Hampshire, England RG21 6XS.
Companies and representatives throughout the world.

PALGRAVE MACMILLAN is the global academic imprint of the
Palgrave Macmillan division of St. Martin's Press, LLC and of
Palgrave Macmillan Ltd. Macmillan® is a registered trademark in the
United States, United Kingdom and other countries. Palgrave is a
registered trademark in the European Union and other countries.

ISBN-13: 978-0-230-60281-6
ISBN-10: 0-230-60281-9

Library of Congress Cataloging-in-Publication Data

Kuhlman, Erika A., 1961–
  Reconstructing patriarchy after the Great War : women, gender,
and postwar reconciliation between nations / Erika Kuhlman.
     p. cm. — (Palgrave Macmillan series in transnational history)
  Includes bibliographical references and index.
  ISBN 0-230-60281-9
  1. Women and peace—Germany—History—20th century. 2.
Women and peace—United States—History—20th century. 3. World
War, 1914-1918—Women—Germany. 4. Reconciliation—Political
aspects—Germany—History—20th century. 5. Reconciliation—
Political aspects—United States—History—20th century. 6. United
States—Relations—Germany. 7. Germany—Relations—United States.
I. Title.

JZ5578.2.G3K84 2008
940.53'1—dc22   2007045892

A catalogue record of the book is available from the British Library.

Design by Scribe Inc.

First edition: June 2008

10 9 8 7 6 5 4 3 2 1

Printed in the United States of America.

For Danil

Contents

List of Figures		ix
Foreword		xi
Preface		xiii
Introduction		1
Chapter 1	American Doughboys and German *Fräuleins*: Securing Patriarchy and Privilege in the Occupied Rhineland	11
Chapter 2	Imperialism and Postwar Reconciliation: The International and Transnational "Rhineland Horror" Campaign	39
Chapter 3	"What to do with the Germans?": American Exceptionalism and German-American Reconciliation	71
Chapter 4	Women Activists in the Postwar World: Gender, Reconciliation, and Humanitarian Aid	105
Chapter 5	Binding up "Bitter Wounds": Gender, Nationalism, and Reconciliation on the Home Front in Germany and in the United States	139
Epilogue		173
Notes		179
Bibliography		221
Index		237

List of Figures

1.1	Map of the Rhineland occupation, 1918–19	19
1.2	"Time to Go Home, Sonny"	36
2.1	"Another Old Woman Tries to Sweep Back the Sea"	43
3.1	"The Hobble Skirt"	92
5.1	"He Will Come Back a Better Man!"	140

# Foreword

Transnational history may be approached in many different ways. What this volume offers is a study of wartime and postwar affairs through a focus on nonstate actors and themes, in particular women and gender relations. There are thousands of international histories of the First World War that examine interstate relations during and in the aftermath of the conflict. Such studies are of necessity based on perusal of official documents, diplomatic and military, and examine the behavior of, and interrelations among, nations. The nation (or the state) is the key unit of analysis. A transnational history of the war is quite different, as this book demonstrates. For one thing, it is much less concerned with states and governments than with members of such other categories of people as gender and race. An individual's national identity remains, of course, and the sense of nationalism would inevitably be enhanced when one's nation is at war. What is less predictable—and what has been much less systematically studied by historians—is the way in which ordinary men and women relate to one another across national boundaries. Sometimes, as this book shows, gender and racial identities become even more pronounced during and after a war.

As Erika Kuhlman shows, and as other scholars such as Petra Goedde and Naoko Shibusawa have demonstrated, in connection with the post-1945 occupation of Germany and Japan by U.S. forces, American troops engaged in the occupation of the Rhineland in the aftermath of the Great War established transnational relations with the occupied population, in particular women. These liaisons often involved prostitution, but some of them resulted in transnational marriages and offspring. Postwar reconciliation would have been unthinkable without the roles played by such women. There was little racial connotation at that time, in contrast to the situation after 1945, but elsewhere in the Rhineland, where France provided occupation forces, a racial crisis erupted as a significant portion of the troops consisted of African (mostly north African) troops from the colonies. The book shows how transnational categories like gender and race were impacting upon postwar international relations.

In addition to gender and race, transnational themes would include, as Kuhlman notes, such topics as hunger, exploitation, and, of course, peace. These are usually dealt with within national and international frameworks, but historians are beginning to recognize the importance of transnational organizations, above all international nongovernmental organizations, in dealing with such issues. Here again, the book is filled with instances where German, American, and other countries' organizations, many of them led by women, sought to promote an alternative world order, one that would be less oriented toward state-centered geopolitics than toward fundamental reconciliation and understanding among nations.

Events described in this book took place more than eighty years ago, but the perspectives it presents remain relevant today, for women then and now must ask the question whether they are better equipped than men to build transnational networks so as to promote a more enduring peace.

Akira Iriye
Rana Mitter

Preface

I began this project by thinking about marriage and its political and social roles in the aftermath of wars. Somewhere in the early stages of my research into the war brides of the Great War era, I discovered that there were an unusually high number of weddings between U.S. soldiers and German *Fräuleins* during the postwar occupation of the Rhineland, and that, coincidentally, the U.S. occupation had gone relatively smoothly. All this occurred in 2003 against the backdrop of the U.S. invasion of Iraq and its unhappy aftermath. Goaded on by the good-humored text and illustrations of the *Amaroc*, the newspaper of the U.S. Army of Occupation, I read about soldiers conspiring with *Fräuleins* to thwart the U.S. military's ban on fraternization. Soon, visions of rosy-cheeked German maids and suave American soldiers clinking glasses of freely flowing Mosel wine began dancing in my head. I started to wonder why relations between U.S. "doughboys" and German women had resulted so often in marriage, and what role these nuptials may have played in the occupation in general. Were there any similarities, I wondered, between the romance that sparked marriages between occupation soldiers and available women and reconciliation between formerly belligerent nations?

The Greek playwright Aristophanes seemed to think so. By the time the academic year ended in spring 2003, I discovered the *Lysistrata* Project, in which organizations around the country staged scenes from the play to raise people's awareness of the Iraq war and to encourage them to imagine how armed conflicts end. The temptress that Aristophanes imagined as the character he named Reconciliation in his play led to my own ruminations about what roles women have played historically in ending wars and why the term reconciliation is so seldom used to discuss relations among combatants after wars end. This book is the result of those ruminations, as well as the research and ideas of other scholars from which this volume has richly benefited.

I wish to thank Idaho State University for its generous funding of my research trips in the United States and Europe through a Humanities and Social Sciences Research Committee grant. In addition, two wonderful colleagues, Alison S. Fell and Ingrid Sharp, both of the University of

Leeds, secured funding for my trip to London for a fruitful and enjoyable conference on women's involvement in the First World War and further research in Coblenz, Germany.

The London conference opened up vast worlds of knowledge and collegiality with Kimberly Jensen of Western Oregon University. I have her to thank for her encouragement of my scholarship and for taking it in new directions. I would also like to thank editor Bruce Vandervort and two anonymous readers for the *Journal of Military History* for their insightful and book-changing comments on my essay. I received efficient help from archivists and librarians at the Hoover Institute at Stanford, the National Archives and Records Administration in Washington, D.C., the *Landeshauptarchiv* in Coblenz, the *Bundesarchiv* and *Stadtbibliothek* in Berlin, and the *Stiftung Archiv der deutschen Frauenbewegung* in Kassel. Jason Crouthamel of Grand Valley State University provided me with invaluable tips for navigating these facilities in Germany. Editors at Palgrave Macmillan, including Michael Strang, Alessandra Bastagli, and Christopher Chappell, have proven very helpful and efficient. I would also like to thank series editors Akira Iriye and Rana Mitter, as well as an anonymous external reviewer for very beneficial comments. Keith L. Nelson, author of the scrupulously researched book on the post–World War I occupation *Victors Divided*, permitted me to use his map of the occupied Rhineland. Paulette Meyer and Joan Birch helped with translations, and Don Amaroc McDonald offered his parents' doughboy-*Fräulein* marriage as an example of "international relations" after the First World War.

Finally, the best for last: I wish to think my family for their support and understanding through all of this business. My mother, though not a war bride, was reared in Germany, and she aided me at every turn with German language translations. My father kept asking me how it was going, which reminded me that I better make it go. Without my husband, Kevin Marsh, I would never have been interested in those international marriages to begin with (because our own has been such a happy dance).

Finally, this book is dedicated our little boy Danil, who will get his mother back on Thursdays again.

Introduction

The writer Ernest Hemingway wrote the definitive American Great War novel, *A Farewell to Arms*, after his own experience as an ambulance driver on the Italian front. In the story, mechanics with an army medical unit sit in a dugout and debate how and whether the combatants—rather than their political leaders—should stop the war, as the company awaits the start of an expected bombing campaign. The men, including the Italians Passini and Manera, and the American ambulance driver Lieutenant Frederic Henry, smoke quietly and drink rum together. Soon, the discussion turns to the various provincial Italian units—the Piedmont *bersaglieri* and the Nepalese *granatieri*—and which group would more likely attack than the others; male honor is clearly at stake. Soldiers refusing to attack were executed by the *carabinieri* (military police), reports Passini. But if not for such punishment, counters Manera, no one would attack. If no one attacked, he continues, the war would be over. Frederic Henry adds that the war would not end if one side stopped fighting, and that conditions could be worse if soldiers laid down their arms.

> "It could not be worse," Passini said respectfully. "There is nothing worse than war."
> "Defeat is worse."
> "I do not believe it," Passini said still respectfully. "What is defeat? You go home."
> "They come after you. They take your home. They take your sisters."
> "I don't believe it," Passini said. "They can't do that to everybody. Let everybody defend his home. Let them keep their sisters in the house."

Later, Henry comments that he knows that the war is bad, and that it must be finished. But the Italian says again that he believes the war will not end.[1] The stalemated trench warfare so characteristic of the Great War (the conflict ended in 1918 in the absence of a single truly decisive battle) had convinced Passini (and Hemingway) that claiming territory—the traditional way that wars were won—seemed no longer possible in modern combat, and that battles would only stop when soldiers refused orders to fight. For the ambulance driver, however, soldiers in retreat constituted a worse offense than continued fighting: it would be a humiliating reverse. The defilement of a warrior's women at the hand of the victors, in Henry's mind, would seal the dishonor of defeat. Ironically, after the calamitous 1917 Caporetto retreat, it is the U.S. lieutenant who deserts his unit and stops fighting to wrap a domestic cocoon around his fiancé Catherine Barkley, although he finds that he cannot escape the misery and destruction that the war has wrought. Hemingway's masterpiece fictionalized the dual forces tugging at the men and women who lived through the Great War years: the medieval warrior traditions, including chivalry, that soldiers had embodied as the war began; the chastity that women pledged as they sacrificed their male protectors to the heroic glory that warfare offered combatants; and the sense of disillusionment, cynicism, and irony that accompanied the upending of so much that the nineteenth-century world had deemed meliorative about human existence by the time politicians crafted the cease-fire and soldiers surrendered their arms in November 1918.[2]

How do wars end, and who determines how the belligerents will be reconciled in the peace that follows the war? How does the official peace process work to restore the home front to "normalcy," including normative gender roles and patriarchy, when the soldiers return from battle? What roles have women played in the reconciliation process (despite men's attempts, to borrow Hemingway's phrase, at keeping them "in their houses")? "Wars conclude," declared the rhetorician Kenneth S. Zagacki, "when individuals choose to construct rhetorical endings to them."[3] How did the official rhetoric formulated by presidents and diplomats representing their respective nations differ from that employed by private citizens and their organizations?

Postwar reconciliation is the process by which nations turn away from belligerency and toward friendly relations in part through agreed upon political settlements that address the disagreements that had resulted in war originally, and the atrocities committed by the defeated enemy during the war (the Treaty of Versailles did not address the wartime conduct of the victors). Reconciliation also refers to the process by which nations adapt to peacetime domestically (for example, by instituting employment programs for returning veterans). I chose the word reconciliation—rather than treaty or peace agreement—deliberately, because I did not want to limit this study to how elite heads of state declared the return of peace officially, on paper documents signed during elaborate ceremonies. Instead, I was interested to see how ordinary people—soldiers, housewives, business people, social workers, clergy, and especially women—conducted their lives in the face of a watershed international event such as the Great War and its aftermath. I wanted to explore how people living in belligerent nations changed their attitudes about, and their relations with, the enemy, and how (or whether) they reconciled themselves to peacetime in their homelands at the end of the war.

Official settlements such as the armistice, the Versailles Treaty, and the Treaty of Berlin represented the political avenues designed to right perceived wrongs and restore normal relations between belligerents. Events surrounding the signing and implementation of those agreements—such as the defeat of the Versailles Treaty in the U.S. Senate, the so-called "Rhineland Horror" campaign through which Germans condemned France's quartering of African soldiers in the occupied zone, the onerous reparations demanded of the defeated and the consequent Ruhr Crisis in Germany, the volatile nature of the revolutionary Weimar government and its shaky economy, and continued belligerent attitudes toward Germans in the United States coupled with the "cult of the fallen soldier" in Germany itself—all served to illustrate that the "friendly relations" conducive to peacetime would not be restored through the official peace settlements and that participants in those events often seemed to prefer war (or at least wartime rhetoric) to peace. The intense nationalism articulated in both Germany and in the U.S. (often expressed there as American exceptionalism), a holdover from the prewar era, hindered attempts at smooth official and unofficial reconciliations. On the other hand, a transnational perspective, in which people deliberately eschewed virulent nationalism, enabled some reconcilers to analyze the problems attendant to war and postwar that transcended imagined political boundaries (such as hunger, disease, injustice, and racial and sexual exploitation and violence) with an eye toward reconciliation. Transnational attempts at restoring peaceful relations, introduced by international women's organizations and others, represented the forces of modernity expressed in ideas such as universal human rights and female equality, ideas that were conceived rhetorically but rarely implemented practically. Instead, nations reinforced traditional, patriarchal relationships among men and women (in which masculinity remained privileged and femininity continued to be valued) by shunting women back to traditional female employment and by honoring women as mothers (and fallen soldiers as heroes) in Germany and in the United States.[4] At the same time, international relations among nations operated to ensure that the victorious nations retained their powerful positions in the postwar world.

Transnationalism has been defined as a school of thought that takes the interconnectivity of people around the globe and the flow of people and ideas across national boundaries as its starting point; in the process, its adherents reexamine ties that continue to bind humans to citizenship and to the nation. Transnational history as an approach within the discipline of history has been characterized by the desire among its practitioners to break out of the nation-state as the primary unit of analysis in reconstructing the past. It differs from comparative history in that in the case of a comparison between two or more nations, the principal unit of investigation remains the nation-state.[5] While this study necessarily looks at the nation and international relations and compares circumstances in the United States to those in Germany, it pays special attention to the ways in which transnational women activists identified goals for the postwar world—such as women's rights and peace (but also white racial solidarity, in the case of female Rhineland Horror campaigners)—that they thought required both international cooperation and cooperation among women around the world, irrespective of national allegiances.

This book is about the interplay between the events forming the official reconciliation process primarily between the United States and Germany, and the avenues chosen by ordinary Americans and Germans as they reconciled with each other across national boundaries. Marriages between protective U.S. soldiers and needy German *Fräuleins* contracted during the military occupation, the Rhineland Horror campaign (in which Germans tried to win the allegiance of Americans against their French allies), and U.S. citizens' humanitarian efforts in Germany all constituted ways in which Americans and Germans organized and crossed borders to try and "make up" with each other after the war. The intellectual and social currents of the day, including nationalism, American exceptionalism, racism, modernity, and normative gender roles, helped people interpret and give meaning to these endeavors. Visions of a new world order that would redeem the war's destructiveness lured men and women with promises of a fresh start, while at the same time traditional values, especially conventional gender roles and racial hierarchies perceived as "natural," continued to resonate in hearts on both sides of the Atlantic. David M. Kennedy's book *Over Here: The First World War and American Society* and Susanne Rouette's *Sozialpolitik als Geschlechterpolitik* (*Social Politics as Sexual Politics*) argue that "old order" values persevered during and after the conflict (as opposed to the war having ushered in modernity, as historians have argued based on their misreading of Henry F. May).[6] This study confirms Kennedy's and Rouette's views but offers a comparative look at the forces of tradition and change in both the presumed victorious and vanquished nations. I further complicate the continuity thesis with a survey of women's transnationalist ideas and organizations that were based upon notions of universal human rights and individual and national self-determination and self-determination for women. I wanted to see why these progressive ideas were not more successful, and why and how they were resisted. My title, *Reconstructing Patriarchy*, comes from Sheila Meintjes, Anu Pillay, and Meredeth Turshen's book *The Aftermath: Women in Post-Conflict Transformation*, in which the writers argue that "the rhetoric of equality and rights tends to mask the reconstruction of patriarchal power" as nations transition from war to peace.[7]

    This book also seeks to fill a gap in the historical literature surrounding postwar peacemaking. There are few histories analyzing the United States' role in the military occupation of the German Rhineland (with the notable exception of Keith L. Nelson's formidable 1975 work *Victors Divided: America and the Allies in Germany, 1918–1923*), and fewer still that discuss the "rhetorical endings" constructed by those outside Versailles diplomacy.[8] Most volumes dealing with the post–Great War period (valuable classics, in addition to Nelson's book, such as Sally Marks' *The Illusion of Peace: International Relations in Europe, 1918–1933*, and Klaus Schwabe's *Woodrow Wilson, Revolutionary Germany, and Peacemaking, 1918–1919*) focus on Wilsonian statecraft, diplomatic relations among European powers and the United States, and the forging of the cease-fire and treaties that ended the war. These works tell that history primarily from a national perspective; that is, they consider the policymakers and military men orchestrating the peace as diplomats and "top brass" representing the interests of their respective nations.[9] Indeed, at least since the nineteenth-century national revolutions, wars have generally been viewed as national, patriotic projects; multi-nation treaties form the compromises that resulted from diplomats' attempts at getting the most favorable settlement possible for their own countries.[10] However, the aftermaths of wars have seldom been told from a transnational perspective, even though the world's resources are spent prosecuting them, and regardless of the ways in which warfare results in humanitarian crises that transcend national boundaries.

Histories of the Great War's aftermath have seldom taken women's forays into foreign policy and peacemaking into consideration, despite literary traditions linking women to postwar healing.[11] In the Greek playwright Aristophanes' classic comedy *Lysistrata*, for example, the title character calls in Reconciliation, a beautiful naked girl, at the close of the Peloponnesian War and at the end of the sexual tug-of-war between Athenian and Spartan husbands and wives. Lysistrata then delivers a speech to representatives of each side of the conflict, in which she begins the process of reconciliation. She points out the similarities between the warring factions and then reproaches both sides for ruining Greece with their childish squabbles.[12] During the Great War, propaganda posters produced in all of the major belligerent countries featured angelic female nurses binding up soldiers' wounds.[13] Women in both the United States and Germany took the need for humanitarian relief for Central Europe to heart (in addition to their efforts to secure a just and lasting peace settlement); German women activists postulated that, indeed, *only* women were capable of performing such tasks (due to their presumed moral superiority and men's supposed depravity that they claimed was recently demonstrated in the war).[14] For transnationalists such as Jane Addams and Alice Hamilton, the humanitarian efforts of ordinary citizens stood in stark contrast to the allied governments' refusal to lift the disastrous economic blockade against Germany after the armistice.[15] By isolating themselves from the chaos that wartime and postwar policies engendered, the Allied and Central powers' heads of state widened the gap between the war they prosecuted and its ruinous social and economic consequences for both the combative forces in the field and for those remaining at home.

Women also, however, just as eagerly joined various nationalist organizations in both nations whose goals were to perpetuate wartime animosities, rather than heal international rifts. U.S. activists in the American Legion Women's Auxiliary pledged to uphold wartime allegiances—and their rhetoric did nothing to dispel wartime hatreds—while German women worked to commemorate fallen warriors for their heroism and foment international outrage over France's stationing of colonial troops in the Rhineland. While German women marrying American soldiers forged international ties, those involved in the Rhineland Horror campaign worked to dissolve cooperation between Germany and France that German and French members of the Women's International League for Peace and Freedom (WILPF) had constructed. A comparative history of the postwar period illuminates the ways in which nationalism, despite its typical patriarchal casting of women as valued—rather than equal—citizens, continued to lure women into its hold in both the presumed victorious and vanquished nations. A transnational analysis of women's roles in the reconciliation process, especially one that examines such cross-border factors as displaced populations, humanitarian relief, international marriages, and universal human rights, demonstrates the extent to which binary oppositions, such as victor-vanquished, war-postwar, and home-front—typically employed in postwar diplomacy, in the treaties that resulted, and in traditional postwar histories—are far too simplistic to tell the complicated history of postwar reconciliation between people and nations.[16]

The chapters that follow examine several aspects of reconciliation between the United States and Germany after the armistice, including the ways in which the U.S. military occupation of the Rhineland aided peacemaking, the Rhineland Horror campaign that endeavored to cut that occupation short, the ways in which U.S. politicians and pundits hoped to regenerate the Germans in order to be reconciled to them, reconciliation efforts by female reformers in the United States and Germany, and finally how Americans and Germans reconciled their respective home fronts to peacetime, all against the backdrop of the "big politics" of the postwar period.

In Chapter 1, I consider the ways in which the control of sexuality between American doughboys and German *Fräuleins* by U.S. army authorities and German men, and the occupation itself, operated simultaneously as systems of power and privilege to ensure male favor, on the one hand, and the perceived victor's advantage over the vanquished, on the other. Harnessing sexuality resulted in the relative stability enjoyed in the American zone, which in turn enabled the United States to mediate conflicts and operate as a reconciling influence among the other, more peevish occupying powers. The two systems of power and privilege—patriarchy and international relations—operated simultaneously to produce the hoped-for result of maintaining the American upper hand in the postwar world. The restoration of patriarchal power became one of the ways in which German and American societies returned to the status quo ante bellum; the return of patriarchy signaled that the peace would bring "normalcy," and not fundamental change, in gender relations (despite the fact that both nations rewarded women with suffrage after the war). Women made some gains, but also lost status; they could not be neatly contained in the oft-repeated categories of "victor" or "vanquished" in either country after the war.

Chapter 2 highlights an additional continuity between the pre- and postwar worlds: the maintenance of imagined racial hierarchies. The Germans responded to the perceived humiliation of the postwar occupation by trying to eliminate it through the Rhineland Horror campaign. The international crusade—and the extent to which it worked—demonstrated the steadfastness of previously developed assumptions of racial hierarchies and white superiority well into the supposedly "modern" twentieth century. As campaigners played upon the racialist ideologies prevalent in Europe and in the United States they hinted that the presence of armed African troops in Germany could foment a race war that threatened the entire world's white population. While patriotic groups in the United States, such as the American Legion, dismissed the propaganda as Germany's attempt to undermine the united Allies, they nevertheless did little to deny the essential assumption upon which the campaign was based: that Africans' heightened sexuality threatened white women's purity.

Chapter 3 explores the interrelations of the official peace negotiations in Paris with the unofficial, rhetorical ways in which Americans sought to reconcile with the former enemy. In addition, it analyzes German middle-class women's responses to the Versailles Treaty. The settlement that most Americans advocated reaffirmed longstanding traditions of what it meant to have fought a war: it confirmed the valor of the victors and the humiliation of the vanquished (indeed, the victor-vanquished duality required constant restating in the face of the horrendous carnage of the Great War), the right of the conquerors to spiritually redeem the losers in ways that affirmed American exceptionalism and reinforced the power that battlefield conquest had bestowed upon them, and finally it sought to restore traditional gender roles for men and women: it encouraged men to reassert their domination, while it promised to protect and defend women's vulnerability. In other words, most U.S. commentators interpreted the Great War as wars had historically been interpreted.

In Germany, female reformers staked out a claim for female participation in foreign policy, as representatives of the domestic sphere, since according to the *Bund Deutscher Frauenvereine* (German Women's Association), women were the only segment of the German population capable of uplifting the moral standards of their nation and of the world. At the same time, however, they vigorously supported traditional, patriarchal German society. Chapter 3 again demonstrates that newer ideas of equality and human rights could not in some cases surmount women's acceptance of their submissive place in a patriarchal society. In addition, notions of a new world order, in which all nations participated equally in shaping the postwar world, could not overcome traditional understandings of war and postwar—where the victors imposed penalties upon the vanquished—that most U.S. writers and political commentators accepted and reaffirmed.

In Chapter 4, I demonstrate that, despite the persistence of old ideas of racial hierarchies prevalent among white female reformers, women transnational members of the WILPF nevertheless offered an alternative for the postwar world. Women activists shaped international politics and peacemaking through rhetoric and action in an era when those touting proper gender roles for men and women—which they thought were well-defined and "natural"—sought to restrict women's activities to what they perceived as the private or domestic sphere. As postwar politicians reaffirmed time-honored links binding women as mothers to domesticity and to the nation, they also upheld the postwar tradition of rewarding the winners and damning the losers by extending the Allied military occupation of the Rhineland, by demanding war reparations, and by assigning Germany's former colonies to the Allied nations as mandates under the Treaty of Versailles. Male policymakers thus adhered to custom in both the domestic and the public, international realms. By barring women—the presumed chiefs of domesticity—from international politics, they in effect reinforced men's primacy in policymaking, thus reifying the old myth of "separate spheres." Women were excluded from diplomacy because affirming the privileges of the victors over the vanquished depended on keeping them isolated from worldwide policymaking since, as females were thought to be "naturally" dovish, ladies demanding access to international politics threatened to weaken the power and privilege of the conquering nations. Ironically, men (and women) denied female negotiators a role in the peace talks precisely because it was assumed that they would advocate peace, and not the national interest. Women reconcilers themselves fed nationalists' fears that women's involvement in politics would weaken national potency. Not all women activists were willing to completely undo traditional gender roles or relationships, and some eagerly applauded women's exclusive command of the domestic sphere. WILPF members glued themselves to their domestic roles when they glorified their positions as housekeepers and argued that women were inherently more pacifistic than men and therefore better suited to orchestrate a peaceful, postwar world than were their male counterparts. When women made essentialist arguments for the natural peacefulness of women, from the perspective of the nationalists they confirmed traditional views of femininity as the supposedly weaker sex, and weakness was anathema to the principle of nationalism just as nationalism, according to Eric Hobsbawm, had reached its hegemonic peak.[17]

Chapter 5 examines the gendered nature of how Germans and Americans reconciled themselves to peacetime in their homelands after the Great War. A comparative picture reveals that despite women's active patriotism during the war, patriarchy continued to dominate in both the triumphant and defeated nations. For example, as women were excused from their wartime positions in industry, American and German men and women began the work of venerating the male soldierly experience through myriad groups of "memory activists," as Jay Winter calls them.[18] While women's contributions to the national economy and war effort were loudly heralded in both countries during the war, that applause quieted as organizations such as the American Legion Women's Auxiliary and the *Volksbund Deutsche Kriegsgräberfürsorge* (People's Alliance for the Care of German War Graves) began valorizing the male soldier. Women's wartime contributions were largely forgotten as men retook their privileged positions in society after the war. At the same time, nationalism regained its strength in both the winning and losing nations. In the United States, nationalism took the form of isolationism, anti-immigration legislation, and the first Red Scare. Meanwhile, the events of the postwar years assured Germans that neither militarist ideology nor even the war itself had truly ended. Despite the efforts of women's transnational organizations to overcome zealous nationalism, renewed nationalism was the dominant thrust in both nations, regardless of whether victorious or defeated in the war, and it accompanied the return to gender normalcy.

1
American Doughboys and German *Fräuleins*
Securing Patriarchy and Privilege in the Occupied Rhineland

One of the ways in which nations make the transition to peace is by ensuring that there will be no more war. Postwar military occupations provide a means of securing a cease-fire so that in a relatively stabilized environment, politicians can begin to work out a peace agreement. In the post–Great War occupation, women helped midwife the needed social stability, in part, by creating domesticity with U.S. occupying soldiers. German *Fräuleins* formed romantic and sexual bonds with doughboys by collaborating with them to thwart the U.S. military's ban on fraternization between soldiers and German civilians, leading ultimately to the lifting of the ban; this in turn encouraged other collaborative efforts between the two former enemies to control female sexuality and achieve social stability in the Rhineland.

The United States' first major experience as a post–foreign war occupier came after World War I, and it was this experience that inscribed the patriarchal blueprint that was used in subsequent occupations. The following pattern unfolded after World War I and essentially repeated itself after World War II: the military attempted to enforce a complete ban on ordinary communication between Germans and Americans. American soldiers treated the anti-fraternization ban with contempt and repeated disobedience. German men responded by threatening not the soldiers but the German women who dared to consort with American men. Sex between soldiers and German women increased, prompting the military to acknowledge the failure of the anti-fraternization order. The army

---

This article first appeared in the *Journal of Military History*, vol. 71, no. 4 (October 2007): 1077–1106.

reluctantly began allowing marriages if the brides were pregnant and later if they could be shown to be of "good character," a euphemism meaning free of venereal disease (the soldiers were not subjected to examination). Within the first year of the occupation, the military lifted the ban on fraternization.[1]

In his review article "The United States as an Occupier," Akira Iriye noted that the person-to-person, victor-to-vanquished contacts established in the first two years of the U.S. presence in post–World War II Germany did more to ensure favorable German-American relations than the "geopolitical realities" of the cold war. The success of the occupation hinged on the ability of officers and soldiers to create collaborators among the native population, according to Iriye. In his article about the sexual behavior of American GIs stationed in occupied Germany, John Willoughby concurs with Iriye, adding that it was the military's successful channeling of GIs' sexual behavior that helped create a stable society, allowing the Germans to integrate into a Western alliance.[2] Neither scholar, however, considered the ways in which the control of sexuality in occupied zones and the occupations themselves operated simultaneously as systems of power and privilege to ensure male favor, on the one hand, and the victor's advantage over the vanquished, on the other, or the ways in which the two systems of domination are interrelated.[3]

About the post–World War I occupation, historian Keith L. Nelson has maintained that the United States and its allies undertook the project in order to "preserve the Allied advantage" confirmed by the armistice.[4] To secure his victory over the vanquished, U.S. Commander General John J. Pershing issued the ban on fraternization, preferring that his men strike an aloof pose toward German civilians because "familiarity breeds contempt," and contempt undercut the respect a contrite loser owed to the winner.[5] Patriarchy operates in a similar way: men sustain their power and privilege in society through women's acceptance of their subordinate status. Patriarchy is "the structural and ideological system that perpetuates the privileging of masculinity," according to Women Studies Professor Cynthia Enloe. "Patriarchal systems have been so enduring," she explains, "so adaptable, precisely because they make many women overlook their own marginal positions and feel instead secure, protected, valued." That marginalization has been accomplished, in part, through men's ability to define and control female sexual behavior, according to historian Gerda Lerner.[6]

Postwar occupations form a nexus through which two systems of power and privilege—patriarchal systems and international relations—can be examined side-by-side. Occupation, an endeavor involving two or more nations, constitutes "the temporary control of a territory by another state that claims no right to permanent sovereign control over that territory," according to Professor of Government David M. Edelstein. Edelstein identifies two types of occupations: comprehensive occupations, which seek stability and the development of a certain type of political system and economy in the occupied territory, and security occupations, such as the one that followed World War I, which seek only to prevent the occupied territory from becoming a threat to other states and to ensure that it does not become a destabilizing influence within its region.[7] Security occupations, like patriarchy, are conservative in nature: they midwife a militarily enforced stability in the territory in order to restore good relations between nations while maintaining the occupying power's military advantage. A return to traditional gender roles, in which the privileged are masculine and the protected feminine, characterized post–World War I German, French, and British societies, according to historians Susanne Rouette and Susan R. Grayzel, and are typical of all postwar periods. "The return to peace is invariably conceptualised as a return to the gender status quo," explain Sheila Meintjes, Anu Pillay, and Meredeth Turshen, "irrespective of the nontraditional roles assumed by women during the conflict."[8] In the American zone of the occupied Rhineland, gender "normalcy" resulted from the military's control of doughboys' and *Fräuleins'* sexuality (but especially women's illicit sexual activity), as well as through German men's shoring up of that control, helping to create the constancy needed to pacify the U.S. zone. The relatively benign, protective nature of the U.S. occupation in turn enabled it to operate as a reconciling influence among the other, more quarrelsome occupying powers;[9] this role as mediator (along with its economic power) girded the United States' privileged position in international affairs in the post–Great War era and beyond, despite its supposed isolationism (see Chapter 3).

The aim of this chapter is to investigate how the American reinforcement of patriarchy in its zone and arbitration of the occupation among its allies operated together to produce the desired result of maintaining American international advantage. First, I summarize the international context in which the occupation developed, and the diverse goals that each occupying power expected to reach from its participation in the venture. Next, I track the soldiers' march through areas previously held by the conquered enemy to the American army's headquarters in Coblenz, Germany. There the military established its authority by issuing, among other ordinances, the ban on fraternization. The next section deals with U.S. soldiers' responses to the anti-fraternization order. Soldiers chose to enter upon romantic and sexual relationships with local women because they were available but also in part because of their chauvinistic views of "the girl back home." The following section discusses the international marriages and the end of the fraternization ban. As the U.S. military took measures to control sexual activity in the Rhineland to ensure stability, the occupation became marked by a high rate of marriages between American doughboys and German *Fräuleins*. When the military finally sanctioned international nuptials, it facilitated American male protection of vulnerable German women, thereby allowing the victors to fulfill the needs of the vanquished, an important step in creating collaboration in the occupied zone that nevertheless preserved the winner's advantage over the losers. The next section looks at the rise in venereal disease and illegitimate births that resulted from the lifting of the anti-fraternization order. German men viewed German women's sexual indiscretions as a signal that the nation's morality—and indeed the *Vaterland* itself—stood at the brink of destruction (for German women's views of morality after the war, see Chapter 3). Officials primarily blamed women's uncontrolled sexuality for that moral decline, which they used to justify their control of female behavior. U.S. military personnel and their male hosts collaborated again to control female sexuality, and the crisis subsided in the American zone. As the heads of state of the occupying powers assembled to determine how the occupation would proceed and how to seal the fate of the defeated enemy, in many cases the United States was able to arbitrate most effectively because its zone had achieved the stability essential to a security occupation.

The Rhineland Occupation in International Context

The Allied parties involved in the Rhineland occupation—primarily France, Britain, and the United States—each desired different outcomes from the experience than the other two. Even before Versailles negotiations began, France's Premier Georges Clemenceau lobbied for a paring off of the Rhineland to serve as a buffer zone against future German aggression; when U.S. and British negotiators proposed a military occupation instead, Clemenceau determined to use it as a means of guaranteeing German payment of reparations. Early on in the occupation, France expanded its commerce on the left bank of the river and engaged in rampant blockade running between France and unoccupied Germany,[10] fomenting Rhenish separatism despite its allies' rejection of that pursuit (France's deeds were motivated by a sense that it had won the war but was losing the peace, according to historian Conan Fischer).[11] Each nation negotiated the occupation as a means to guarantee its own privileged position won militarily in the Great War and diplomatically through the armistice: the French, having lost the most in the war, intended to cripple Germany's economic and military might, thereby securing its own future; the British perceived French ambitions as equally threatening as the resurgence of German power and used the occupation as a means to check France's advantage, thereby maintaining the balance of power in Europe needed to keep its empire;[12] U.S. President Woodrow Wilson wanted to enhance America's prestige through acceptance of his Fourteen Points, which he hoped would form the foundation of the peace treaty; he viewed the occupation as the price to be paid for that peace.[13] The Allies' diverse and in some ways contradictory goals foreshadowed a rocky road ahead for the occupying powers.

Meanwhile, Germany's provisional government in Berlin fought to reconstruct society in the face of a variety of wolves at the door. Several political factions vied for power: the Spartacists (communists), Nationalists, the Center (Catholic) Party and the "Majority" Socialists. Internally, the government suppressed a Spartacist revolt in January 1919, and in February the assassination of the Bavarian premier led to several weeks of civil war in Munich. Externally, the Weimar Republic dealt with the threat of a separatist revolt in the Rhineland. Sensing that the occupational powers may be divisible, Foreign Minister Wilhelm Solf began pressuring the Americans and British to help the Germans protect the Rhineland against the French. Predictably, German officials reviled the occupation, but Wilson's Fourteen Points convinced them that the United States constituted the most benign of its foes.[14]

Economically, a multitude of challenges faced the fledging republic, including the continuation of the wartime blockade after the armistice, unemployment among returning soldiers, the reparations required by the treaty, and out-of-control inflation beginning in 1920. The British zone, headquartered in the industrial center of Cologne, withstood the harshest circumstances of the entire occupation. Food supplies were shorter there than in the agricultural U.S. and French zones.[15] One British visitor to the Rhineland remarked that while British public opinion "shed no tears" when a blockade stemmed the flow of supplies to Germany during the war, once British and American soldiers came into daily contact with German civilians, their attitudes changed profoundly (indeed, British civilians visiting the Cologne zone were astonished by the amiable relations between occupiers and occupied in the summer of 1919). Smaller industrial towns in the British zone, such as Solingen, bordered on the so-called Bolshevik "cholera area" of the Ruhr. The British military government in Cologne questioned its troops' loyalty and feared that its conscripts were themselves vulnerable to Bolshevik propaganda. British Prime Minister David Lloyd George remarked that the only bulwark against Bolshevism "was to feed Germany";[16] on the other hand, Germans reportedly feared that the British and Americans would not supply them "until all danger of a Bolshevik movement is past."[17] Although the blockade was not officially lifted until after Germany signed the peace treaty, American Relief Administration head Herbert Hoover and Lloyd George wheedled an agreement out of Paris negotiators to ship food to Germany in March 1919 (see Chapter 4).[18] The image of an American thwarting the blockade to feed hungry Germans enhanced the United States' reputation as benevolent occupier among its hosts and Hoover's ability to negotiate advanced its position as even-handed mediator among its allies.

March to the Rhineland and Settling in at Coblenz

While officials in Washington, London, and Paris worked to stave off hunger and communist threats in Germany, American soldiers went about the business of stabilizing their Rhineland zone. U.S. Commander General John J. Pershing established the Third Army on November 7, 1918. The 240,000 American troops that marched across the war zone toward their headquarters in Coblenz constituted about one-third of the Allied forces in the Rhineland.[19] Before reaching their command center, doughboys encountered female victims as they temporarily occupied territories previously held by the defeated German forces. Those women demonstrated that it was femininity in particular that needed their protection.

On November 18, after a day's march from headquarters in Ligny-en-Barrois through St. Léger, Longwy, and Briey, General Joseph T. Dickman, commander of the Third Army and his men reached Longuyon, France, near the Luxembourg border. The next morning, a group of women and young girls assembled at the municipal building to honor the victorious army and remind them of their obligations to safeguard noncombatant women and children. The festivities, according to General Dickman's memoirs, included a spirited singing of the "Marseillaise" followed by speeches replete with expressions of gratitude for the conquering Americans. The women then presented the general with a laurel wreath festooned with tricolor ribbons. A similar ritual was held two days later in the Luxembourg capital. There U.S. troops marched before the royal palace, where the Duchess, her sister, General Pershing, and other U.S. military officials reviewed them.[20]

The spectacle of women and girls thanking the U.S. military for liberating them reinforced the commonly held conviction among U.S. soldiers that the Great War was a chivalrous battle pitting evil Boche rapists against crusading protectors of womankind. The military newspaper *Stars and Stripes*, for example, had implored troops to consider themselves "Knights of the Round Table" who were "bound to hold all women as sacred." Another issue featured a C. LeRoy Baldridge illustration of a mother sitting with her children; the title proclaimed, "What We're Fighting For." After the occupation began, General Dickman visited the German Countess von Walderdorff at her château in Molsberg, where he saw a doughboy "standing as a sentinel on the rocky promontory in front of the château, where many a knight in armor had stood in feudal times, intently watching the broad expanse of territory open to his view." The Countess begged the general to keep American soldiers on her grounds, citing her need to protect her four daughters.[21] Women and children confirming the military victory and honoring American doughboys for liberating and safeguarding them from further danger encouraged the soldiers to perceive women as beings separate from their governments and in need of their protection, and would ultimately encourage romance between doughboys and *Fräuleins*.

When the Third Army crossed the German border on December 1, it occupied a territory of 2,500 square miles stretching from Cochem in the west to a radius around Coblenz to the east. The British zone lay to the immediate north of the American, with the Belgian area still farther north. The French zone extended from the Belgium border to its bridgehead around Mainz (see Figure 1.1). Only the small Belgian zone did not include a bridgehead (bridgeheads required special fortifications, as they could be used by the Germans to regain a foothold in occupied territory).

In the sparsely populated Rhineland, life still revolved around Catholic moral teachings despite the growing secularization of German society elsewhere. The region boasted agricultural products such as wheat and an abundance of renowned wine. The Neuwied basin, part of the American zone, included small steel and chemical factories.[22]

Interpretations of the Germans' receptivity of their American occupants differed dramatically. *New York Times* reporter Edwin L. James, for example, saw a "sullen, glowering mien" among the Americans' hosts. In Trier, he detected "hostility lurking beneath the smirking surface hospitality of the Hun." Others, however, described the reception using blander terms. According to General Dickman, the Germans received the conquerors with a mix of curiosity and indifference, leaving open the possibility of interaction with American soldiers.[23]

The Germans themselves reported welcoming the Americans with an eye toward reconciliation. In Trier, Rhinelanders had their greatest fear—that they would be forced to live side-by-side with French or Belgian soldiers—alleviated when the American doughboys entered triumphantly on December 18, according to a *Rheinisch-Westfälische Zeitung* reporter. So great was the relief at the sight of the American flag that the Germans felt they had actually been liberated by their enemies! Finally, the reporter assured readers, the American occupiers came not to disturb the Rhinelander but to help him.[24]

The Third Army, for the most part, concurred, displaying an attitude consistent with its missionary ideal. "We go in among [German civilians] as conquerors, there is no need to conceal that fact from them or from ourselves," the *Stars and Stripes* reminded readers. "But we must go in among them with a humble and contrite heart. For, although we enter as conquerors, we enter also as peace-makers, 'for they shall be called the children of God.'"[25] American "soldier missionaries" would teach Germans "by our every act what a democratic civilization, a republican form of government means as contrasted with that of monarchial despotism." "We are paving the way," proclaimed the *Amaroc*, the newspaper of the American occupation and successor of the *Stars and Stripes*, "for the men who will enter the European markets of the future"; therefore, "our country's reputation rests in a great measure with the officers and soldiers here." One directive instructed the Fourth Division "to help build a new government to take the place of the one we have destroyed; we must feed those whom we have overcome, and we must do all this with infinite tact and patience, and a keen appreciation of the smart that still lies in the

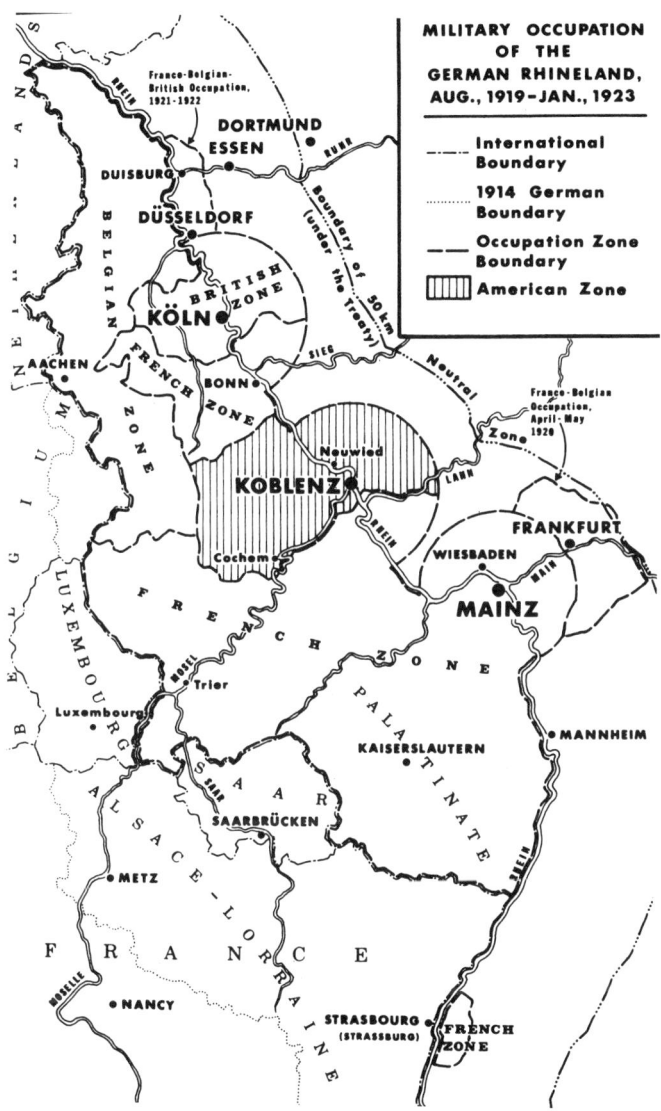

Figure 1.1 Map of the Rhineland occupation, 1918–19. Taken from Keith L. Nelson, *Victors Divided: America and the Allies in Germany, 1918–1923*, Berkeley: University of California Press, p. 147, ©1975 The Regents of the University of California

open wound of their pride." Such prose tended to overlook the fact that Germany had already created a democratic republic—albeit a weak one—because that fact interfered with doughboys' perception of themselves as conquering saviors bringing American democratic goodness and mercy to all. Despite the Fourth Division's issuance, the military claimed no desire to interfere in German politics.[26]

Field Marshal Ferdinand Foch, Commander in Chief of the Allied Armies, communicated to his British, Belgian, and American counterparts his desire that the Rhineland continue normal conditions for the population as soon as possible by leaving German civilian life largely intact. The U.S. military quickly laid a foundation for authority in its zone by appointing an Officer in Charge of Civil Affairs (OCCA), Brigadier General H. A. Smith. He served as a direct contact with the *Oberpräsident* (head of provincial government) of the Rhine Province. The American OCCA and his German civil counterparts operated in relative harmony in comparison to their French neighbors: in 1919, for example, the United States brought disciplinary actions against twenty German officials, whereas in the French zone there were more than twice as many, and for more serious infractions.[27]

Two documents facilitated the swift establishment of good relations between the occupying powers and their hosts: one was Foch's proclamation to all the inhabitants of the occupied territories, and the other was General Pershing's statement to those in the American zone. Although both documents contained many identical provisions, they differed in one important aspect: Pershing's issuance included a provision for American protection of German civilians that was absent from Foch's proclamation.

Pershing declared that local authorities would continue to exercise their functions and that measures would be limited to the health and safety of the population. "All that lawfully and peacefully abide by the regulations laid down by the military authorities," he declared, "may count on protection for their persons, homes, property, and belief."[28] On December 9, 1918, Pershing enumerated *Anordnungen*, or Ordinances, prohibiting assembly, requiring all citizens to carry identification, banning the possession of weapons, prohibiting the sale of alcoholic drinks other than wine and beer, and acknowledging the right of the American military to censor all mail.[29] Pershing also prohibited all interactions between German civilians and the U.S. military except on an official basis. The last order, the military's most controversial, became popularly known as "anti-fraternization." The commander issued the anti-fraternization rule on November 28, 1918. The order reminded American officers and soldiers that "during our occupation the civil population is under the special safeguard of the faith and honor of the American Army. . . . So long as a state of war continues, Germany remains enemy territory and there must be no intimate personal associations with its inhabitants. A dignified and reserved attitude will be maintained on your part at all times."[30] The French and British also issued bans on interactions with locals, although they reportedly enforced them with less zeal than did the Americans.[31]

From the doughboy's perspective, the ban on fraternization thwarted his ability to fulfill his perceived political mission to help democratize the Rhineland. However, for the most part, soldiers analyzed, criticized, and poked fun at the order in its romantic connotation: fraternizing became a euphemism for romancing German women, and, they lamented, the anti-fraternization order prevented them from doing it. The historian David G. Williamson recorded instances of British "Tommies" thumbing their noses at their ban, too.[32]

Patriarchal Interpretations of Women

American soldiers' responses to the fraternization directive revealed their patriarchal perceptions of women primarily as helpless victims of their male-dominated government, not as equal participants in civil society. Women, according to this view, were valuable only on the basis of their ability to reproduce (but valued nevertheless—one way in which patriarchy is perpetuated, according to Enloe).[33] Judging by their responses to fraternization, at least some German men agreed with that assessment. In addition to praising Rhineland women's attributes, some doughboys lamented the change that had transformed American women back home into independent females challenging men's prerogative as breadwinners.

Problems relating to the fraternization ban occurred soon after the occupation began. The *Stars and Stripes* reported that in Trier the *Bürgermeister* announced that "if any German girl is seen with an American soldier she would be an outcast and would not be allowed to marry on German soil" (so much for Trier's enthusiastic reception of its occupiers).[34] A report from Neuwied indicated that men in that community viewed illicit romances between Germans and Americans as shameful. The men threatened would-be *Fräulein* fraternizers with swift punishment and promised to publish lists of their names and distribute them among prospective husbands. A later issue declared that Neuwied men began blackening the illicit lovers' faces to further humiliate them and announce their transgressions.[35]

The *Amaroc* also poked fun at anti-fraternization, indicating that the ban provoked an insubordinate attitude toward the doughboy's superiors. For example, a headline appearing on May 5 asked, "Was it Really True? We Wonder." A lieutenant was billeted at a home where a "comely German *Fräulein*" served him breakfast in bed, shined his shoes, and washed his clothes. The honest young lieutenant confessed to his superiors, a major and a colonel, and asked what he should do to shun the girl and obey the anti-fraternization order. The colonel suggested that he change billets immediately and the obedient lieutenant complied. The colonel then dashed into his office, placed a quick call to determine if perhaps the billet might be available, only to find that the major had beat him to it.[36]

The discussions of the ban that appeared in the *Amaroc* indicated that soldiers primarily viewed *Rheinländerinnen* (Rhineland women) as innocent victims of their government. An unsigned editorial remarked, "Damn the military party of Germany, if you will, but why pick on these girls and good old women who never had a word to say about running the war," he wrote, confirming that women were vulnerable pawns of their government.[37] Other writers assumed that all Germans were imbued with the same unflattering, biologically determined character traits that mothers passed to their children. "For five years and more the German nation has been nourished on hatred for Britain," declared a British soldier in the *Cologne Post* and reprinted in the *Amaroc*, "and it would be an unpleasant event for an English father if the first words his offspring spoke were '*Gott strafe* [punish] *England!*'"[38] According to this view, cross-cultural hatreds were biologically induced and inevitable, and passed on through female reproduction. Another contributor, Clyde Teasdale, cautioned that bearing children with a German was risky business: "Look at the cripples and idiots there are in Germany," he warned. "You might get one." Furthermore, he accused German women of using honest but ignorant doughboys to win a free ticket to the States. Others, however, saw all German women as enemies complicit in the deceptiveness they believed inherent in German *Kultur*. One *Amaroc* poet depicted a *Fräulein* siren-temptress who tried to make American soldiers forget their loyalty to their fallen battlefield comrades.[39]

The *Amaroc* offered its readers no particular explanation as to why German women had so beguiled many American soldiers beyond the obvious fact that many "Yanks" had spent years away from their sweethearts and that feminine company had been lacking in military barracks. But American soldiers hankered after German women in part because of images of what the "girl back home" had become during his absence in Europe. Soldiers perceived Rhineland women as being more traditional, whereas in the United States, the war had bred women's liberation.[40]

Speaking of stateside girls, one punctuationally challenged writer opined, "I often wonder just where she is that good old fashioned girl You and I used to know that one with the calico dress who could sew and cook and who abhorred cigarettes and sparkling wine who has so much common sense . . . and she taught Sunday School. . . . I tell you boys I am beginning to think the time will come when the gentle sex will wear our clothes and put us in dresses I may be wrong," he warned, "but not all wrong."[41] One poetically inclined soldier, D. C. McElroy, was simply puzzled by superficial, empty-headed American girls:

> I wonder why the flappers wear
> That tired, bored, and sated air?
> Why ennui sits upon their brows
> And nothing can their spirits rouse?
> Dispassionate and blank their gaze
> And laissez-faire their weary ways . . .
> Do they bespeak the soul within—
> Sodden souls of soil and sin?
> Ah, no; these children look blasé
> 'Cause Theda Bara looks that way;
> And life evokes a weary smile
> Because just now it is the style;
> They all mean well, the little dears,
> But someone ought to pull their ears.[42]

Another soldier, discharged and already stateside, fed the doughboy's fears of the "liberated" women he may encounter when he returned. "In short I am told that through the war woman has mysteriously come into her own," he wrote. "I must prepare to acclaim emancipated women the sex-equal of men." To assuage soldiers' anxieties about modern American women, the paper printed an unsigned letter from a "Real American Girl" who acknowledged to readers that, while women working in wartime industries did wear pants to work, they nevertheless removed them when they returned home at night, just as they would relinquish those jobs when the boys returned from overseas.[43]

The possibility of women working at men's jobs did indeed worry doughboys across the Atlantic, and that fear contributed to their sense that American womanhood had somehow betrayed them. "We should worry about jobs when we get back," a *Stars and Stripes* reporter fretted, though he admitted that army life prepared men well for a variety of jobs. But positions held by young men in the prewar years were now being filled by "old men and young ladies." His final sentences betrayed additional anxieties. "We'll be able to do anything they want done back in the states," he wrote, "and then some. Why some of us can even sew on our buttons! Think of that blissful future—leaving the politics to the women while we take care of the housework!"[44] Fears of losing their privileged status upon their return troubled some of the men.

The passage of Prohibition by the U.S. Congress in 1919 confirmed those fears. Doughboys argued that the law unfairly took away their rights, and, since they linked the passage of Prohibition with femininity, they blamed women for this egregious aspect of postwar American society. One *Amaroc* writer complained, "I knew they were makin [sic] a gigantic mistake when they gave the women the vote—look at Prohibition, as their first atrocity! Next thing you know, we'll have compulsory church attendance, and matinee idols as governor."[45] Another rhymed, "I'm just a common drunken sot, mother's teachings I've forgot; if I'm not perfect that's my biz, the other guy can tend to his."[46] For another the thought of Prohibition back home made his current billet in Europe seem rather attractive by comparison. "Now if my place you'll let me choose / I'll stay where I can get some booze / When our country set us off to fight / The women clamped the lid on tight." One noted the irony, after Prohibition, of an American fighting to make the world safe for democracy:

> O give us back our old gin and whiskey.
> Before we join the Bolshevicki [sic].
> We fought to keep democracy
> Safe from the Boche across the sea
> But Liberty means naught to me
> If I can't have my straight whiskey.[47]

Negative views of American womanhood, however, were silenced in an entire issue devoted to the "American Girl." Here, *Amaroc* editors praised the stalwart young women who traversed the high seas to serve doughboys coffee and doughnuts in canteens, to entertain them at dances, to succor their wounds in hospitals: in other words, to play supporting roles to male leads. Not coincidentally, the American Girl issue, appearing on July 11, 1919, came out just as doughboys began marrying German women.[48]

Patriarchal Marriage and the Lifting of the Fraternization Ban

Marriages between soldiers and *Rheinländerinnen* supported the United States' stated reason for the occupation—safeguarding German citizens and securing stability in the occupied zone—while they signaled that German women were willing to wade through army bureaucracy and degrading medical exams to protect their offspring legally. When officials decided to end the fraternization ban on September 28, 1919, prostitution and venereal disease rates rose, which the military staunched by criminalizing the business and testing and treating prostitutes for disease (while allowing the sex workers' male partners to escape unpunished). While the army perceived soldier marriages as irksome, it recognized a greater threat to its zone's stability in illicit sex. German men perceived the rise in prostitution as a sign of moral chaos, and they, too, took steps to control it. Whether as brides, mothers, or as prostitutes, German women remained subordinate to men (albeit *valued* subordinates), as subjects under male control.

As the U.S. military's actions confirmed male privilege and female subjugation in its zone, U.S. and Allied officials in Paris brought forth a peace treaty that enabled the victors to serve just deserts to the vanquished. President Wilson and his supporters lobbied for the treaty on the basis of its inclusion of the League of Nations, which he believed would enhance American influence abroad, while his detractors at home feared that involvement in the League would reduce American power (see Chapter 3). Both American internationalists and isolationists hoped to retain their nation's strength demonstrated militarily by the Great War victory.

Back in the Rhineland, occupation troops and *Fräuleins* anticipated that the signing of a treaty would mean that Americans would be sent home. As that possibility loomed, practical-minded women and amorous men may have pressed their lovers for greater commitments, and, as the army noted, an engagement was considered the equivalent of marriage "among the lower-class Germans."⁴⁹ Thus, in the spring of 1919, several soldiers announced to their superiors—despite facing discipline for disobeying the anti-fraternization order—that they wished to marry their pregnant fiancées. Officials at military headquarters in Coblenz pondered whether they should punish the men for disobedience or protect the unwed mothers. Ultimately, the military decided to uphold the patriarchal safeguarding of German women. Authorities granted approval of the marriages that involved pregnant fiancées and did not punish the offenders, under particular circumstances. The soldiers were required to sign a written statement acknowledging their responsibility to the expecting women, while the mothers-to-be were obliged to submit to a physical examination verifying their condition. With the announcement of the military having permitted one hundred German-American marriages under this ruling, however, headquarters soon became inundated with similar requests to marry under the same circumstances: pregnant women in need of legal protection. The prospect of hundreds of married soldiers in their ranks left a bad taste in the mouths of officials who believed that an army of husband-soldiers "reduced efficiency," and posed "a constant source of trouble." The solution, accordingly, was to reduce the number of nuptials.⁵⁰

To accomplish this, headquarters enhanced the bureaucratic hoops through which a doughboy had to jump to wed his sweetheart. Marriage requests were forwarded to the General Staff at Headquarters for final approval. Such requests were investigated by staff members, who were then required to prove "the *former* good character of the girl" (implying that premarital sex had tainted the women's reputations). This, the army believed, checked the number of marriages.⁵¹

Reactions to the German-American nuptials reflected an entrenched patriarchal interpretation of women both in Germany and in the United States. One Berlin newspaper made clear its displeasure with the newlyweds. The writer linked the shame of the war guilt clause of the recently signed Treaty of Versailles with what he perceived as dishonorable female behavior. "It is not only an ignominious peace but a race shame that threatens our destruction," he declared. "The danger exists less in the marriage itself than in the fact that there live German girls capable of such an idea. One of these base women may conclude her love pact, but we will refuse to admit such a couple to our society. We will fight by all means the infusion of blood from Negroes, Frenchmen, Indians, Tonkinese, Americans and other bearers of that culture."⁵² To this writer, women served society only as wives and mothers; when *Fräuleins* married Americans, they mongrelized the German "race" with tainted blood. The U.S. commander in Coblenz responded similarly. "The numerous excess of good-looking marriageable girls in this zone over corresponding German males," wrote General Henry T. Allen to the U.S. War Department, "has accentuated the necessity of adopting [the restrictive marriage policy] cited to avoid having a partially Germanized command."[53] Like the writer of the Berlin editorial, Allen viewed nationality as a biological, racial construct passed on through female reproduction that threatened the purity, and therefore the allegiance, of his command. In the United States, the *Nation* offered its harsh condemnation of German-American marriages: soldiers marrying "Hun" women should be court-martialed.[54]

As soon as the fraternization ban was lifted, prostitutes flocked into Coblenz's brothels, raising the devilish venereal disease rate plaguing the military. Furthermore, some troops wanted to marry the sex-workers. This unwelcome prospect, added to the other reasons for limiting marriages, brought forth a new plan, instituted in July 1920. This policy announced that no marriages would be allowed if an investigation showed that the woman's character was "questionable."[55] A medical exam, performed by a German doctor, certified that the "girl" in question was free of venereal disease.[56] In addition to the requirement that the bride be "respectable," enlisted men had to prove that they had an excess of $100 to support their female dependent.[57]

By January 1921, 10 percent of the American command (or approximately 767 men), from cooks to buglers and from privates to staff sergeants, had married German women, while roughly another 10 percent had applied but had been turned down.[58] (In contrast, only 157 British soldiers had married German women by September 1921, though this figure rose to 700 by 1925.) Amorous American soldiers and German *Fräuleins* negotiated their way through language barriers, military red tape, and public repudiation of their relationships to reach the altar of wedded bliss. While "mixed" marriages appalled many on both sides of the Atlantic, they fostered mutual understanding between former enemies and therefore promoted reconciliation.[59]

No anti-German prejudices met the *Rheinländerinnen* or their soldier-husbands aboard the *St. Mihiel* as the ship docked in South Carolina in February 1923. One of the doughboys on board, *Amaroc* editor Alva L. McDonald, had married a German woman, Carma, in 1921. Donald Amaroc McDonald, the couple's one-year-old son, made the Atlantic crossing with his parents along with 280 other members of the U.S. military, including thirteen other families and twenty-one children. Following the voyage, Carma McDonald and her female compatriots became ensconced in "the homes that their husbands provided for them," as one American social worker had put it.[60] Carma McDonald wrote to her mother-in-law that she settled happily into her new abode near Fort Moultrie. Putting women back in homes signaled a return to gender "normalcy."[61]

Not all *Fräuleins* lashed themselves to American men and fled their homelands so eagerly, however. For Elisabeth Ternes the decision to marry and uproot herself from the Rhineland appeared to come slowly and with reluctance. Ternes and Alex Boyd, a U.S. army sergeant stationed in Mayen, conceived a child, but the duo did not advance to the altar right away; the couple's daughter was born in July 1921, six weeks after her parents' wedding. Since the military did not provide housing for married couples, newlyweds were encouraged to leave Germany as soon as possible, but Elisabeth Ternes Boyd and her daughter did not board a U.S.-bound ship until 1925, three years after Alex Boyd had already departed the Rhineland.[62]

While doughboys and *Rheinländerinnen* were normalizing male-female relations through marriage, the heads of state settled scores in Paris. During preliminary gatherings of the major powers, called the Council of Ten, held in February 1919, members decided to bar female representation at official treaty proceedings (see Chapter 4).[63] The signing of the Treaty of Versailles marked the highpoint of the occupying powers' enrichment of their privileged position vis-à-vis their victory over the vanquished in the Great War.[64] The document deprived Germany of around 13.5 percent of its prewar territory, approximately seven million of its citizens, and all of its overseas possessions. Alsace-Lorraine was returned to France, and Belgium received the formerly German border areas of Eupen and Malmedy. Other rearrangements included the handing over of an area of East Prussia to Lithuania and the Sudetenland to Czechoslovakia. The German military was limited to a maximum of 100,000 men, and a ban was placed upon the use of heavy artillery, gas, tanks, aircraft, and submarines. Finally, the treaty condemned Germany as the party solely responsible for the war. Compensation took the form of reparations. The Germans responded by denouncing the absence of Wilsonian self-determination as a factor in dealing with Alsace-Lorraine, East Prussia, and the Sudetenland, its exclusion from the League of

Nations, and the treaty's provision for a fifteen-year occupation of the Rhineland. The treaty had the undesired affect of temporarily eroding relations in Coblenz. "The German public," wrote Keith L. Nelson, "had begun to regard the Third Army as somewhat of a 'false friend'" from whom it had come to expect more.[65]

President Wilson hailed the League as an opportunity to exercise the United States' leadership in world affairs and to ensure normal relations between states; his opponents at home, Senators Henry Cabot Lodge and Albert J. Beveridge, saw the League as compromising American military power (especially Article 10, which called upon League members to support League actions), and, therefore, its national sovereignty. Both factions wanted a strong nation: Wilson saw the League as an opportunity to spread U.S. influence abroad, while his opponents believed that involvement would reduce the United States' ability to act unilaterally. The Senate rejected the treaty by a vote of fifty-three to thirty-eight. The isolationist Warren G. Harding won the 1920 election.

The nation that refused to sign the treaty in turn made it more palatable to the defeated enemy. To appease the German peace delegation leader Count Ulrich von Brockdorff-Rantzau's objection to the occupation, and to further curtail France's dogged determination to separate the Rhineland, the United States proposed the Rhineland Agreement as an adjunct to the treaty. The document dismantled Foch's administrative authority and gave it instead to an inter-Allied council, a civilian high commission that replaced the military governments of the four zones and was limited in power to the protection of the occupying powers. The aim of the agreement was to civilianize and normalize the occupation as much as possible, making it more amenable to the Germans but also to fulfill the British desire to rein in Foch's power. Commissioners took their seats at the American headquarters in Coblenz.[66]

Because the United States did not sign the treaty, government in its zone remained essentially in the hands of Commander General Henry T. Allen. The U.S. War Department dissolved the Third Army and created the American Forces in Germany (AFG) on July 3, 1919. Most of the troops that had marched into the Rhineland were now replaced by new recruits (of the original 240,000 troops only 15,000 remained in the U.S. zone; its geographic size was reduced in August 1920). To make its zone more compatible with those of its allies, General Allen lifted most restrictions on civilians, including the ban on fraternization (in September 1919, several weeks after the other occupying powers had lifted theirs).[67]

In 1920, the entire occupation became politicized as France marched into Frankfurt and occupied that city in retaliation for President Friedrich Ebert's dispatch of German troops to protect the Ruhr from a communist revolt. The United States continued its practice of distancing itself from radical acts and did not join the Frankfurt debacle.[68] That same year, the Germans began their calculated "Rhineland Horror" campaign, in which they claimed that France's use of colonial African troops in its zone threatened the purity of German women (see Chapter 2).[69] General Allen's views, which undercut German claims regarding African troops, were kept from the public, and by 1921, Allen and his command undertook the role of international peacemaker and mediator.[70]

Also in 1921, the U.S. government officially ended the war between the United States and Germany through the Treaty of Berlin, essentially an economic document. The treaty did not repudiate the Treaty of Versailles as the Germans had hoped it would, but Germany reluctantly signed the agreement because it still considered the United States its only hope of normalizing relations with its former belligerents and because it sought the resumption of trade. Ellis Loring Dresel, unofficial U.S. envoy to Berlin, assured Harding's Secretary of State Charles Evans Hughes that although the Germans "derive no concrete advantages from the present document itself the treaty is nevertheless to be welcomed as providing [the] basis for infinitely most important commercial negotiations to follow." Dresel offered as evidence that the Germans would accept the treaty newspapers such as the *Danziger Neueste Nachrichten*, which claimed that antagonism between Germany and America had already receded due to the fact that the United States had been the first ready to furnish "efficacious assistance towards satisfying our life needs."[71] Once again the United States was able to steer an agreeable course in its relations with Germany, while at the same time maintaining the upper hand in international relations.

"The Physical Presence of the Occupation": Prostitutes, VD, and Illegitimate Births

The lifting of the fraternization ban had liberated American doughboys in their pursuit of local women, but it spawned a variety of social problems in the American zone. Rhenish authorities interpreted prostitution, venereal disease, and illegitimate children primarily as moral problems caused by "irresponsible girls." This interpretation ultimately sparked

German men's reassertion of their control over the female population from American authorities, again stabilizing the region. Americans and Germans collaborated to harness women's illicit sexuality. (Rhineland women also monitored female sexuality in the occupied territories. Members of the *Rheinische Frauenliga*, the women's organization clamoring to rid the occupied zone of French colonial soldiers, scrutinized German women's relationships with African troops [see Chapter 2].[72])

The U.S. army already had a history of dealing with forbidden sex among its ranks before the occupation period began. The American Expeditionary Force had viewed succumbing to sexual temptation as an act of disloyalty to homeland and family.[73] But as part of its missionary zeal the occupation troops believed themselves models of righteousness for Germans to emulate, and therefore their behavior should be better. "Representing, as we do, American principles and the essentials of good soldiering," wrote an *Amaroc* reporter, "our rate should be lower than the average rate of the army."[74]

German authorities had traditionally maintained a relatively lax attitude toward prostitution by isolating sex workers to a "red light" district within towns and by examining them for disease regularly. Prior to the occupation, prostitution operated "satisfactorily" and there were no moves to change it.[75] When the fraternization ban ended, prostitution increased and venereal disease rates rose in kind. In Coblenz in 1918, for example, there were ten prostitutes, but in 1920 there were 185. The military recorded an "extremely high" annual VD rate of 422.65 per 1,000 on October 21, 1919.[76] "It is only natural," warned a German bureaucrat, "that a great number of the occupying troops will be affected by [the rise in venereal disease among prostitutes]."[77] German authorities requested the American military police to treat the business criminally.

In March 1920 authorities began arresting street walkers. Men were only asked to help authorities identify prostitutes; they were not subject to detainment, presumably because the American military also believed that visiting brothels was a "natural" activity for men.[78] The increase in rates of disease formed one reason for the crackdown, but by 1921 Germans began perceiving a decline in morality that became the basis for reasserting control over sexual activity. "It is certain that the morals in the occupied zones have declined and in particular prostitution has increased," wrote the president of the *Landkreis* (area) of Coblenz to the Rhenish provincial president.[79] Coblenz's deputy mayor became convinced that arresting prostitutes, especially young girls, could save their morals "from total corruption when arrested in due time."⁸⁰ Other Germans also registered their concern with immorality. An excerpt of the Annual Report of Municipal Administrations appeared in the *Coblenzer General-Anzeiger* under the title "Effect of Occupation on Moral Conditions in Coblenz" in April 1922. The author maintained that Germans were "filled with indignation at seeing how low thousands of German girls have sunk and how for the sake of presents of money or a modern outfit, they exceed all the bounds of both shame and official ordinances."⁸¹

The president of the Coblenz *Landkreis* agreed. "The German community is especially disgusted that such a large number of women and girls made connections [with Americans] after the demobilization of German troops." But the president conceded that economic conditions in the zone also encouraged women to seek out American men, and he pointed to American complicity in immoral behavior. "Before and also after the signing of the Treaty of Versailles the provisions of the occupation zones were insufficient, so that the ample means supplied to dependents of the occupation army created a situation that could easily be exploited and sexual conquest was an easy thing in such a situation." Most Germans reporting on rates of prostitution and venereal disease also indicated that sex workers were coming into occupied zones from France and unoccupied Germany.⁸² "One can't prevent several people from trafficking with the occupation troops," conceded the president of the *Landkreis* of Trier. *"But this must be taken seriously from the standpoint of the fatherland."* The writer blamed the "irresponsible attitude of local girls that are under the influence of American troops," though he too acknowledged that lean times contributed to the girls' recklessness.⁸³ Another writer also noted a decrease in the morals of his district's population but warned that it was not only young German girls but also married women who had succumbed to prostitution.⁸⁴

What one Trier bureaucrat called "the physical presence of the occupation"⁸⁵—the sharp rise in illegitimate births—also contributed to the German authorities' sense of moral chaos in the occupied zone. In this, too, men retained their privileged position. In Coblenz, doughboy-*Fräulein* relationships were reportedly responsible for as many as four-fifths of such births in 1921.⁸⁶ Another report indicated that in 1920, there were eighty-three *unehelich* (illegitimate) births, up from twelve in 1919. In the whole *Landkreis* of Coblenz, in half the illegal births the fathers were reportedly occupation troops.⁸⁷ According to German law, fathers of children born in Germany were required to provide support until the child reached the age of sixteen. However, as the Assessor in Coblenz admitted to the Officer in Charge of Civil Affairs (OCCA), the mother had no legal recourse to sue for aid. "The assistance which is given to the children," wrote the Assessor, " . . . depends only on the free will of the soldiers concerned."[88] While men could choose whether or not to support their progeny, mothers (short of abandoning their children) could not; German law lashed women closely to their reproductive function. The OCCA responded that the military could only assist the mother in locating the father and point out to him his *"moral* obligation" (the military also advised mothers that they could take legal action before a U.S. Court).[89] When a mother attempted to obtain child support from her sexual partner by writing to American authorities, the military responded tersely that the soldier in question had been interviewed and had either denied responsibility for the child and refused to pay child support, or that he acknowledged liability and would continue to provide for the child (sometimes with the proviso "as long as he is in Germany") but had refused to marry the mother.[90]

Local institutions sought restitution from the U.S. Army as well. The Chairman of the Infants Asylum in Coblenz, Carola Schuller, wrote to AFG Headquarters asking the American authorities for the use of building space that had been requisitioned by the U.S. Army when the occupation began. "Under the enormous increase the city as well as the charitable organization labors under great difficulties . . . knowing that an appeal to save human life will not be rejected by the American authorities," Schuller begged the Colonel "for support from the fines collection in Coblenz which have gone to the American treasury." In this case, Schuller reasoned that, since American occupying forces were responsible for the increase in illegitimate births and other adverse circumstances, they should provide funding. She did not lash out at the mothers who birthed out-of-wedlock children.[91]

When German authorities condemned *Fräuleins* for succumbing to "immoral" behavior with American soldiers, they reinscribed masculine privilege by interpreting women as mindless, uncontrollable children in need of discipline. They often overlooked the dire circumstances under which many of these women lived. Nearly 65 percent of the eleven million German men mobilized during World War I were either sent home wounded or did not come home at all.[92] The *Amaroc* heightened awareness of the devastation caused by war when it printed statistics on birth and death rates in the Rhineland town of Kreuznach. While previously births had exceeded deaths by 175 annually, in the spring of 1919 deaths exceeded births by 437 (this article noted that 30 percent of those births were illegitimate).[93] Furthermore, German men were dying at a rate greater than German women, at least in the town of Mayen. While the death rate for men reached 54.6 percent in the first six months of 1919, for women the rate was 45.4 percent. "If this relation goes back into the war years, it, in connection with war losses, indicates an existing disproportion between the sexes of considerable magnitude, and for the future, if continued, a population condition not promising for the welfare of the *Kreis*," lamented the U.S. military.[94] German women—indeed the entire Rhineland—thus faced harsh realities. Women, however, against formidable odds grew quite adept at using the resources of the state and the occupying forces to secure their own survival (see Chapter 5).

Rheinländerinnen obtained employment with the U.S. military either in official capacities (as interpreters and female prison attendants) or in unofficial capacities (as nannies or housekeepers).[95] Yet as Detlev J. K. Peukert has shown, the ratio of German women working to the total female population rose from 31.2 percent in 1907 to only 35.6 percent in 1925. In addition, throughout the Weimar period as before, women were employed in lower-paid, subordinate jobs, and even if they worked at traditionally male occupations, they were paid less than their male counterparts.[96] Furthermore, the Weimar government conspired with business and union leaders to oust women from their industrial wartime positions (though this would not have impacted the American zone as deeply, since it contained little industry).[97] Not surprisingly, un- and underemployed women, especially those with dependants, sought protection through marriage. Advertisements from women seeking husbands appeared in Rhineland newspapers, and the *Amaroc* attributed the phenomenon to the absence of German men due to the war.[98] Even Hoover's American Relief Administration received a letter from a German widow seeking relief in the form of marriage.[99] War widows demanded aid but also protectionist policies from their government, arguing that widows with orphaned children must be considered *erwerbsunfähig*, or unable to work, and therefore eligible for their husbands' full pensions (see Chapter 5).[100] In seeking protection from the state, women perpetuated the very system that kept them marginalized, in Enloe's definition of patriarchy. In any case, German women—forbidden from engaging in political behavior until 1908 and having only recently been granted the right to vote in 1918—lacked political experience in a society still steeped in patriarchal attitudes toward females, especially in the Rhineland.[101]

By 1922, the perceived moral chaos resulting from the occupation became a problem that German authorities were ready to confront. The annual report of the municipal administration in Coblenz assured citizens that despite the gloomy state of morals in the city, the administration was taking control:

> May these alarming figures [rise in prostitution, VD, and illegitimate births] awaken all those concerned to the situation of the area of Coblenz, already unhappily affected by the occupation, in order that it may receive the material and moral help it needs to gradually repair the moral and physical injuries which will continue to show their detrimental effects for decades to come, and in order to regain for the city the reputation of an honest and virtuous population. . . . Dark and sad though the future be from a political point of view, particularly with reference to conditions attendant on the occupation, yet as the municipal administration and the municipal council have not failed in their task during the past year . . . and will hold fast to the well-tried principles of true German public spirit and sacrifice.[102]

Germans and Americans had cooperated to check uncontrolled female sexuality during the occupation. When Carola Schuller requested space from occupation authorities, she received word that space would be granted. When OCCA H. S. Grier wrote to the *Regierungspräsident* (district president) in March 1920, he assured him that "all German authorities have cooperated loyally with the American authorities in an endeavor to correct and check these evils [increases in prostitution and VD rates]."[103] As late as January 1923, German Chancellor Wilhelm Cuno had asked U.S. Secretary of State Hughes to permit General Allen to remain in Coblenz after the U.S. occupation ended as "moral protection" for Germany,[104] much as German *Fräuleins* sought shelter from the severe circumstances they faced through marriage with American soldiers. Rhineland and U.S. authorities reported an improvement in rates of venereal disease and illegitimate births by 1920. Trier confirmed that *unehelich* births had peaked in January of that year and then declined, and the U.S. military reported a decline in VD rates after prostitution was criminalized.[105] A sense of social stability returned to the American zone (though economic stability remained elusive throughout Germany).

In keeping with its practice of avoiding extremes, the United States withdrew its troops from the Rhineland in January 1923 as a blow to the French invasion of the Ruhr, which it interpreted as a call to resume the European war.[106] The American occupation of the Rhineland gained the reputation of being one of the most benign in military history. As one U.S. military historian observed, "The sight of throngs of Germans gathered about the train [of departing U.S. soldiers], the sorrowful and in some cases tear-streaked countenances and shouted farewells made it difficult to realize that those leaving were soldiers of an army of occupation or that the crowds were composed of inhabitants of an occupied area."[107] The feeling was mutual. *Amaroc's* final edition showed a drawing of a Yank soldier surrounded by his two favorite German companions—a Pilsner and a *Fräulein*—sobbing loudly at the prospect of being shipped home (see Figure 1.2).[108] Unoccupied Germans, however, felt that the United States could have done much more for European peace than it did.[109]

Such tearful departing scenes probably involved people who benefited the most from the occupation: local merchants catering to soldiers, German employees of the U.S. military, and German-American couples and their families.[110] Records of the Coblenz government, however, tell a

Figure 1.2 Cartoon of U.S. occupation soldier by Swanson, Company C, *Amaroc News*, January 24, 1923

different story. While military and civilian officials on both sides proclaimed the American occupation acceptable by the local population, ordinary German civilians recorded their encounters with the American military in court. Crimes against German citizens existed, and one can imagine that not all of them were reported.[111]

Nevertheless, the relatively trouble-free nature of the occupation enabled German and American military and civilian authorities to collaborate on the reestablishment of patriarchy in the Rhineland and retention of the American advantage. Romances between occupied and occupier before the summer of 1919 signaled a lovers' conspiracy to thwart the anti-fraternization order, and after, marriages represented collaboration between Germans and Americans to protect German citizens from harm, as Pershing's proclamation had stated. From the perspective of the American soldiers, they were fulfilling their obligation and choosing brides whose Rhineland traditions more closely resembled their expectations of women's roles in marriage than did their images of liberated flappers the war had bred back home. When the immorality of prostitution and *unehelich* births was perceived as rendering Rhineland society out of control, German men reclaimed the authority to control female sexuality and bring the region back from the brink of destruction, reestablishing male privilege and female protection from the twin social evils of prostitution and illegitimate children.

German Chancellor Cuno, the mayor of Coblenz, the German press, and even the official French press in Mainz all lavished praise upon the Americans as they departed the Rhineland.[112] Victory in the Great War and success (at least by some accounts) in the occupation after enabled the United States to gain enough power and prestige to rival its allies. By 1919 the U.S. merchant fleet had ballooned to almost 60 percent over its prewar size. American exports nearly doubled in value from 1914 to 1924, and its share of world trade increased by 15 percent, barely surpassing Britain as the world's most important trading nation. The U.S. domestic economy showed even more vigor. Preferring to locate its strength at home rather than abroad, it invested its wartime profits in its homeland instead of fueling the world economy.[113] However, two Americans furthered the United States' reputation as mediator in European affairs after the U.S. withdrawal from the Rhineland; Charles G. Dawes and Owen D. Young each brokered agreements among the occupying powers to reschedule Germany's reparations payments in 1924 and 1930, respectively. Nevertheless, isolationism shored up Americans' sense of their uniqueness, while it enabled the nation to step powerfully (if tardily) into the next worldwide conflict two decades later. After that war, the same pattern of patriarchal control of occupied Germany, coupled with the Marshall Plan, allowed the United States to create a bulwark against communism and claim success in its comprehensive occupation of West Germany.[114]

Part of the United States' presumed uniqueness—if not its strength—lay in its history of immigration, a factor that resulted in a mixed ethnic population. Slavery's legacy insured a racially mixed society. Occupied Germans tried to undermine the entire Rhineland occupation and rebuild their defeated nation by launching a campaign against France's use of colonial African soldiers in its territory. Cognizant of the racial tensions inherent in the United States' diverse society, they attempted to enlist the help of Americans in their efforts. Despite the unruffled nature of the U.S. occupation, the overall humiliation of the treaty-imposed occupation produced a thorn in the side of nationalist Germans, and they fought to regain control of their society. German men's efforts at reclaiming the morality of their nation included guaranteeing the protection of German women's purity from armed African men.

2
Imperialism and Postwar Reconciliation
The International and Transnational "Rhineland Horror" Campaign

Beginning in April 1920, various German citizens' organizations, encouraged by their government, launched a campaign against France's stationing of colonial African soldiers in its zone of the German Rhineland. Far from limiting themselves to the nations directly involved in the situation, groups such as the *Volksbund Rettet die Ehre* (People's Federation to Save the Honor) and the *Rheinische Frauenliga* (Rhineland Women's League) deliberately spread their propaganda overseas in an effort to create an international furor over France's alleged transgressions. While on the face of it, the goal of the drive—known as the "Rhineland Horror" or "Black Horror" campaign—appeared to be to rid the area of African soldiers, the crusaders clearly wanted bolder outcomes. Still reeling from the cease-fire and more recently a humiliating peace settlement, the propagandists desired nothing less than the international discredit of the French, a halt to France's efforts to separate the Rhineland from the rest of Germany (see Chapter 1), an end to the entire occupation, and the restoration of German honor in the eyes of its own inhabitants and of other nations.[1] To reach these goals, the propagandists sent tentacles across the Atlantic, the North Sea, and the Baltic Sea to insure international support for their cause. In the case of the Americans, the campaigners hoped that race-baiting in the United States would draw their former enemy closer to the German side while driving a wedge between the Allied nations, a strategy that had succeeded in other issues involving the occupation (see Chapter 1).[2] As crusaders played upon racialist ideologies prevalent in Europe and in the United States (I use the term racialist to convey the idea that perceived differences among humans are inborn and located in the immutable, physical body), they hinted that the presence of African troops in Germany could foment a race war that threatened the entire world's white population, thus rendering the campaign not only international, but transnational in strategy.

Although the campaign failed to gain the allegiance of the United States or to fully discredit the French or to reestablish German honor or end the occupation, it did (though not intentionally) reveal the hypocrisy inherent in Europe's racialist justifications for overseas colonization, the continuation of previously developed assumptions of racial hierarchies and white superiority well into the supposedly "modern" twentieth century, and it foreshadowed the role of racism in events to come by providing a podium for the prognostications of demagogues such as Adolf Hitler, among others.[3] It also highlighted the extent to which the continuation of imperialism's attendant ideologies impeded postwar reconciliation between nations, since, if not for imperialism, France would have had no colonial troops to send to the Rhineland and Germany no basis for complaint; furthermore, Germans could not have persuaded others that the practice of using African troops was abusive if European and American leaders were not at least partially convinced of imperialism's racialist underpinnings. Just as colonization played a role in bringing the Great War about, so it can be blamed, in part, for keeping nations from reconciling to peace.[4]

The Rhineland Horror campaign encumbered postwar reconciliation in a more insidious, though less obvious, way as well. If the belligerent powers expected the official document that signaled the end of war, the Treaty of Versailles, to aid postwar reconciliation, then signatories to the treaty had to agree to the principle of mutual cooperation through the League of Nations that formed one of the bases of the peace (although Germany did not join the League until 1926, two other major powers involved in the campaign, France and Great Britain, were members). Instead of promoting collaboration to help end a perceived problem, the campaign, which included a prominent British political activist, relied on manufactured accusations and manipulated documents to create turmoil instead of a pathway to a solution. Indeed, historian Sally Marks could find no evidence that the German government ever officially requested that the French withdraw their colonial troops until most of them had already left the Rhineland, indicating that Weimar's real desire lay in provoking antagonism, rather than altering a troublesome policy.[5] The promise of mutual cooperation to end international strife thus remained unfulfilled, and the treaty's principles—and therefore reconciliation among its signatories—was compromised.

In another way, the Treaty of Versailles and its provisions inadvertently foreshadowed the continuation of wartime strife between nations—to which the Rhineland Horror campaign's shenanigans also contributed—instead of postwar reconciliation. In the League of Nations Covenant that formed part of the settlement, signatories agreed that only the states that elite nations deemed ready to self-govern—primarily those formerly part of the old Habsburg and Ottoman empires—would be guided by the new principle of self-determination.[6] Those states would be guided as a League of Nations mandate with little administrative oversight and would soon be allowed to determine their own futures. States considered unprepared for independence would require an intrusive administrative mandate. Those nations were located in Central and West Africa. The people living under the second type of mandate would not be allowed to form their own governments or militaries, presumably because such a move would be undertaken in order to separate from League control (see below for female internationalist activists' response to these League provisions).[7] Thus, the Treaty of Versailles left intact the notion that African people were uncivilized and incapable of governing themselves, paving the way for the bloody wars for independence that punctured the continent by mid-century. The belief that the African soldiers stationed in the Rhineland were barbarous and unable to control their physical instincts formed the centerpiece of the Rhineland Horror campaign's strategy.

Practically, the campaign did contribute to the exodus of African troops from Germany, although only indirectly.[8] While the crusade failed to garner broad support for the ousting of colonials, it left intact the notion that African males had a natural propensity toward raping white women, that females' natural vulnerability left them easy prey for such attacks, and that therefore women needed white men's protection from harm. Black men's access to white women implied a level playing field between the races that Germans perceived as a threat to their society, since the German Empire, as other European and American empires, had been built upon the notion of white supremacy. "The 'Rhineland Horror' is not only a disgrace for Germany," warned the *Grenzland Korrespondent*. "It is much more. It represents the desecration of white culture in general. At the same time, it means the beginning of the end of the predominance of the white man."[9] While Europeans such as Helena M. Swanwick and Americans such as General Henry T. Allen balked at the campaign's insistence that

African men were unable to control their sexual impulses, they remained convinced that the white race had created and represented "civilization," whereas nonwhite people epitomized barbarism.

A few women played combative roles in the battle to relieve Europe of Africans' presence, while another handful—Europeans and African Americans—exposed the racialist notions underpinning the campaign to a wide audience. One German critic, Lilli Jannasch, rendered the Rhineland Horror propaganda both racialist and sexist. Generally, however, far from providing an alternative vision of what the world should look like (or would look like, if they were in charge), as they had in the case of the peace treaty (see Chapter 4), women—as individuals and as international activists—united their rhetoric quite closely with the male policymakers and diplomats generating and responding to imperialist and racialist ideologies of the early twentieth century.[10] Women such as Ray Beveridge and Margarete Gärtner (sometimes spelled Margarethe Gartner), and women's transnational organizations such as the Women's International League for Peace and Freedom (WILPF) and sixty-six other European women's organizations,[11] acted in a manner generally consistent with the imperialist ideologies and the racial hierarchies that formed the geopolitical view of the world in which they lived; in addition, German women activists also specifically emphasized their role as upholders of middle class values in their campaign. As organizations such as the WILPF generally sided with the Germans and against the presence of Africans in the Rhineland (although some members altered their positions after listening to the African American pacifist Mary Church Terrell), members undercut their ability to offer the world a truly alternative vision—including greater freedoms for *all* women throughout the world—in the aftermath of the Great War, since in backing the Rhineland Horror campaign, they supported the racialist ideology that had rationalized the colonization of Africa (and supplied the colonial troops) before the Great War began. Those same notions of white superiority kept them from realizing their vision of a postwar world order based upon human equality rather than prejudice and discrimination (see Chapter 4).

Female and male Rhineland Horror campaign participants not only supported prevailing, imagined racial hierarchies, they also reinforced traditional gender roles, which held that imperialism represented a manly pursuit while an anti-imperialist position constituted effeminate degeneracy. A cartoon drawn by Homer Davenport for the *New York Journal*, for example, shows an apron-clad and bonneted President

McKinley pushing a broom on the eve of U.S. intervention in Cuba in 1898. The American leader feebly tries to sweep advancing waves favoring war, stirred up by the people and Congress, off the U.S. shoreline. The caption reads, "Another Old Woman Tries to Sweep Back the Sea."[12] Given Davenport's depiction of McKinley as being antiwar, the citizens and their legislators as representing a prowar position, and his implication that the peace perspective was effeminate, than presumably the warrior stance was the manly one (see Figure 2.1). Debates heard in the U.S. Congress over American intervention in the Great War in April 1917 recorded similar attitudes regarding the benefits U.S. participation in combat would bring to the nation's male youth, versus the dissoluteness of the antiwar position.[13] Theodore Roosevelt, who later vigorously supported the United States' deployment of troops "over there," must have applauded the cartoonist's interpretation of the Spanish-American War, manhood, and American imperialism. In 1899 he first uttered the words that became synonymous with his enormously influential, explicitly American life, "the strenuous life." By that phrase he meant not only the

ANOTHER OLD WOMAN TRIES TO SWEEP BACK THE SEA

Figure 2.1 Cartoon of President McKinley by Homer Davenport, *New York Journal*, 1898

dogged existence that he himself had carved out in the "wild West" frontier of the 1880s but also the national imperative of imperialism.[14]

Imperialism in U.S. History

Americans in the 1920s had inherited their views on imperialism and its relationship to race and gender from the culture of their nineteenth-century predecessors. White northern Protestants made up with their former southern foes after the Civil War by rejecting racial equality and by viewing African Americans as an alien population within the United States' geographic borders; domestic reconciliation in turn allowed the country to focus its energies abroad.[15] Darwinism, too, played a central role in how people formulated their ideas about racial vigor versus decadence, about overseas expansion, and about white manhood. In the 1910s, Clark University President G. Stanley Hall feared the slothful nature of industrialized American culture that he thought would impair the nation's ability to compete with other developed states for survival. Hall believed that the civilized races, led by highly developed, "manly" men, had to be prepared to protect the effeminate, childlike races of the uncivilized world. Like his British counterpart and Rhineland Horror campaigner, Edmund Dene Morel (see below), Hall opposed overseas adventures, and he offered his arguments as an educator. He publicly rebuked the Belgian King Leopold's brutal regime in the Congo Free State, where the dictator had enslaved nearly the entire population. To Hall, the "primitive" Congolese needed the protection, not the brutality, of their overlords, so that they too could become educated and civilized.[16]

Hall traveled to Washington, D.C. to meet with another Darwinian thinker, Theodore Roosevelt. Roosevelt, however, took the opposite view of imperialism from that of his visitor. Beginning in 1894, TR called for a renewed vigor among American men, and the challenge of imperialism represented an avenue to achieve it. Like many of his contemporary European and Anglo-American thinkers, Hall included, Roosevelt worried that white men were becoming soft and emasculated by excessive civilization. If American men no longer had Indians in the West to conquer, reasoned the Rough Rider, then they stood to lose the will and ability to fight and may relinquish the capacity to win the race for supremacy among civilized nations. The frontier had rendered pioneering men exceptionally fit to advance the blessings of civilization around the world (meanwhile, contemporary Frenchmen thought *they* offered the best hope for bringing civilization to others; see below). In an essay titled "Manhood and Statehood," Roosevelt reasoned that westward settlement had happened so rapidly and successfully that Americans had come to accept expansionism as "part of the order of Nature." Imperialists also used biological determinism to justify European and U.S. invasion of uncivilized continents, and male domination of women.[17]

Roosevelt offered imperialism as a means, not to achieve American self-aggrandizement, but to gain enlightenment for backward races, and also to extend a man's respectable domestic life into the outside world. The former constituted a "white man's burden." Kipling's poem by the same name described Filipinos as "half-devil and half-child," but not as men. Roosevelt asserted that the "essential manliness of the American character" rendered American men especially fit to bring civilization to primitive peoples. In the latter view, males served their families first by protecting their women and children from harm, and then society by providing for their collective home, the nation. In an essay called "National Duties," Roosevelt explained, "Exactly as each man, while doing first his duty to his wife and the children . . . must yet . . . strive mightily in the world outside his home, our nation, while first of all seeing to its own domestic well-being, must not shrink from playing its part among the great nations without." It would be unmanly to shrink from imperialism, or from using the "big stick," a powerful military, to achieve imperialism's ends.[18] In this interpretation, the Rough Rider co-opted the "good government is enlarged housekeeping" idea that American suffragists pushed in their campaigns for votes for women.[19] But while reformers argued that feminine influence should extend beyond domesticity into government, Roosevelt emphasized respectable men's control over both domestic *and* public spheres in the above passage, and also by referring to the frontiersmen who cleared the Western wilderness as "home-makers."[20]

Bringing civilization to backward races could get bloody, and Roosevelt acknowledged that the burden would involve violence. But, he reasoned, "it is our duty toward the people living in barbarism to see that they are freed from their chains, and we can free them only by destroying barbarism itself." As an added bonus, warfare would invigorate young boys and prepare them to take on their domestic and worldly duties as men. Besides, he assured his readers, the Tagalogs in the Philippines were infused with a "spirit of love" after the Americans had arrived, making them a happier people than they had been before.[21]

Roosevelt espoused, and advanced, all of the steps leading up the turn-of-the-twentieth-century ladder toward a fully evolved sense of nationalism and imperialism. The rungs consisted first of a strong, vibrant, white manhood to lead the nation; secondly a manhood able to protect the domestic realm and the women that reproduce and thus insure the next generation of equally hearty American men; and finally a manhood capable of extending the nation's power and authority by subduing (justified as "helping") inferior, nonwhite races to ensure continued competitiveness abroad and national security and economic growth at home. In this interpretation of national life, women could not advance up the ladder, since they were stuck on the reproductive rung. Females participated in imperialism only through their procreative function.

In any case, the untamed territories that white men conquered, it was assumed, were no place for a white lady. While that notion helps explain the lack of women in earlier histories of imperialism, more recent scholarship has revealed the complexities of Western women's experiences in European colonies and has emphasized the fact that females have been both complicit and resistant to expansionist agendas.[22] Women such as Isabelle Eberhardt, Russian émigré to French North Africa, embraced Islam and became "Algerianized," whereas British newspaperwoman and empire-builder Flora Shaw, who traveled extensively in Africa and North America, retained her presumed national character. Both women helped legitimize and perpetuate their nations' conquests in Africa. Journalist Annie Besant, on the other hand, cast a critical eye over British imperialism. While the actual activity of colonization remained primarily in the hands of men, women participated in imperialism both literally and literarily.[23]

Imperialism in European History

Germans began agitating for colonies in the 1880s, relatively late in the European scramble to subdue the African continent. Until then, German Chancellor Otto von Bismarck seemed uninterested in events beyond Europe, remarking that his "map of Africa" consisted of Germany, France, and Russia. However, the Iron Chancellor was a pragmatist, and he eventually considered colonization based upon what promised to be most advantageous for his country. Influential members of his conservative cabinet began convincing him that Germany needed new markets. Respectable publications such as the *Preussische Jahrbücher* stated alarmingly that unless additional outlets for German goods were seized, the economy and therefore domestic tranquility would be jeopardized. When a dose of healthy competitiveness aroused fears of losing out to other European powers, Bismarck began envisioning a German Empire. He plunged in vigorously to catch up with his counterparts. In a year and a half, Germany established protectorates or annexed extensive regions in Southwest Africa, Togo, Cameroon, and Tanganyika.[24] At the same time, it acquired Pacific Islands, part of New Guinea and the South Sea Islands. The government purchased other Pacific Islands from Spain, declared two large Samoan islands German protectorates, and it obtained Jiaozhou Bay and the coal fields in interior China on a ninety-nine year lease. By the end of the century the colonial German Empire consisted of over one million square miles and control over a native population numbering about twelve million people. Unlike Roosevelt's predictions, however, some of them were not happy; violent uprisings of the Hereros and Khoikhoi developed in 1904 in Southwest Africa.[25]

The French faced revolts among their African "beneficiaries," too. France's overseas ventures predated its neighbor's, but officials did not formulate an imperial doctrine until the Third Republic. The idea of a *mission civilisatrice*, a secular operation designed to civilize native populations, coincided with the return of democratic institutions to France in 1870. The French believed that they had invented civilization, and they assumed that, since Frenchmen were morally and materially superior to other people, only they were suited to impart refinement upon others. According to historian Alice L. Conklin, the French invented a set of specific limitations on what its colonial governors could and could not do, through which the contradiction between the conquest of colonies and democratic principles was blurred.

The peculiarity of the French definition of civilization lay in the term mastery, according to Conklin. Not mastery over other people (though that was what resulted from the *mission civilisatrice*) but of reason over nature, over instinct, and over despotism. Because the French had overcome tyranny before any other nation, they deemed their government, based upon rational principles, to be more refined than any other. Since the rest of the world outside Europe had failed to achieve mastery, it remained for the French to bestow civilization upon the rest of the world. By 1885, the French Empire included French West Africa, Algeria, Madagascar, and protectorates or near-protectorates in Tunisia and Morocco. Due to series of revolts in its colonies, and to increasing knowledge of African cultures, France modified its colonial policies toward the end of the Great War. In 1918, for example, recruiters in Senegal began offering French citizenship and civil rights to colonials in exchange for their military service.[26]

The British viewed the development of German and French empires as a challenge, since they had been among the first to colonize Africa. To deal with inevitable disputes regarding territorial claims among European powers, the Germans and French called all of the imperialist nations together in Berlin in 1884 and 1885. The resulting Berlin Act adjusted rival claims and recognized specific governments, including the establishment of the Congo Free State under the sovereignty of Leopold II of Belgium. In addition, the Act laid out the paternalistic views that the signatories, including Great Britain, France, Germany, Belgium, Italy, Russia, the Netherlands, the United States, and others, held toward Africa's native populations. Article VI of the document declared that

> All the Powers exercising sovereign rights or influence in the aforesaid territories bind themselves to watch over the preservation of the native tribes, and to care for the improvement of the conditions of their moral and material well-being, and to help in suppressing slavery, and especially the slave trade. They shall, without distinction of creed or nation, protect and favour all religious, scientific or charitable institutions and undertakings created and organized for the above ends, or which aim at instructing the natives and bringing home to them the blessings of civilization.[27]

Thirty-four years later, Article 22 of the League of Nations Covenant, part of the Treaty of Versailles, duplicated much of the same language. The Berlin Act, described as incorporating "vague and pious pronouncements" by one historian, proved largely ineffectual as concessionaire companies operated as they saw fit.[28] In any case, given the Europeans' stated desire to bestow upon African people "the blessings of civilization," the Rhineland Horror campaign's efforts to oust colonial troops from the presumed seat of civilization, Europe itself, seemed hypocritical.

Attitudes toward sexual relations between the conquerors and the conquered in Africa reflected a similar double standard. (The Rhineland Horror campaign resurrected this double standard, though in reversed roles, since during the occupation the Germans were the defeated and the colonial soldiers were part of the winning forces.) Due to a lack of white women, miscegenation between colonizers and colonized was accepted in the form of concubinage in the nineteenth century in many British and other European colonies, although legal marriages between whites and native women were spurned. As European women began migrating in greater numbers to the colonies in the early twentieth century, miscegenation became less acceptable. Sex between native men and European women, however, was deemed utterly offensive. In 1903, the British colony of Southern Rhodesia passed the Immorality Suppression Ordinance, penalizing illicit sex between African men and European women, while saying nothing about relations between white men and black women.[29] The sexist and racialist attitudes underpinning such laws—which held that men's sexual drives required access to native women in the absence of white women, while European women (who presumably had no sexual appetites) needed protection from African men's supposed overpowering lusts—were reflected later in the allegations of rape of German women by colonial soldiers generated by the Rhineland Horror campaign.

The perpetrators of the crusade used the racialism inherent in imperialist ideology to foment an international outrage at the presence of armed African soldiers in the Rhineland. Their publicity perpetuated the "imperialist imagination" well into the twentieth century.[30] If nineteenth-century Europeans such as Flora Shaw, and Americans like Teddy Roosevelt, upheld the "civilization versus barbarism" paradigm to legitimate their nations' conquests of "backward" peoples and lands, then the people that imperialists controlled must be barbaric. If the African males that imperialists subjugated were uncivilized and naturally oversexed, as TR believed they were, then so were the colonial troops France deployed in its Rhineland zone.[31] As such, they constituted a threat to white civilized man- and womanhood and could be used by German propagandists to undermine the entire occupation.

The Rhineland Horror Campaign

Historian Keith L. Nelson noted that race became the most perfidious weapon the French and German diplomats used against each other in postwar relations, and the diplomatic conversations that took place before the occupation began gave campaigners reason to believe that the scheme might succeed.[32] German policymakers protested the possibility of African troops in the Rhineland during armistice negotiations. Foreign Minister Wilhelm Solf had urged his representatives to prevent the Rhineland from being occupied by colonial French or African American troops when they negotiated cease-fire conditions with the United States and its allies.³³ Both British and American negotiators at the Paris peace conference sought to eliminate what they thought could be perceived as a legitimate grievance among the Germans, and German delegates to the treaty negotiations asked that "colored" troops not be part of the occupation. When Woodrow Wilson queried French Prime Minister Georges Clemenceau on the matter at Versailles, he was assured that there was only one battalion of colonial troops in the Rhineland, and that they would soon be "retired." But they were not.³⁴ The British Ambassador in Paris, Lord Derby, assumed that France chose to use colonials to humiliate the defeated enemy. In fact, however, France had little choice as it lacked other soldiers to send.

Meanwhile, in the French colony of Senegal the recruitment of soldiers produced an outrage at the enormity of sacrifice Africans were compelled to make for their French overlords. Indeed, as historian Joe Lunn has shown, the French quest for African soldiers during the Great War rivaled the confiscation of human resources during the eighteenth-century trans-Atlantic slave trade.³⁵

France's use of colonial troops dated as far back as 1779, when Senegalese units were dispatched to subdue populations in the interior of West and Equatorial Africa. In addition, over 35,000 Algerian troops had participated in the Franco-Prussian War, so Germans were not unfamiliar with the phenomenon. Indeed, Germany itself had recruited about 11,600 of its own colonial population for military and police duty before war began in 1914 (although contact between German civilians and Africans had been minimal—with the exception of German colonizers—before the Rhineland occupation).³⁶ Great Britain, too, had supplemented its army with over 100,000 colonial troops, primarily from India. In all, about 600,000 "nonwhite" soldiers from French and British colonies fought in Europe during the Great War.³⁷ Meanwhile, the U.S. Army consisted of 380,000 African American soldiers in 1918, with about 200,000 serving in Europe. After the armistice, the 369th Infantry, known as the "Harlem Hell-Fighters," reached Germany first, but the unit departed quickly on December 10, 1918.³⁸

France began its participation in the Rhineland occupation with a total of 200,000 troops, reduced to 85,000 after the treaty.³⁹ All of the powers involved debated the exact racial profile and number of colonials in the French zone. Rhineland Horror campaigners racialized the soldiers by describing them as "coal black," but few actually were, according to historian Sally Marks. Other than one brigade of men from Senegal and

Sudan (which left the Rhineland by June 1920), colonial troops were North Africans of mixed European and African descent.[40] Tussles over terms echoed in the halls of the U.S. Senate, where, in the context of arguing over the merits of the Rhineland Horror campaign, legislators debated whether a Sudanese man should be categorized as "Negro."[41]

The German Foreign Ministry claimed that the numbers of colonials reached 30–40,000, or approximately half of the French force. However, Allied observers recorded only 14,000 to 25,000 African troops. Historian Anja Schüler has stated that this was the figure claimed by the French, which she deemed more accurate.[42] In addition, the presence of colonial soldiers resulted in some 600 to 800 children born of relations between Africans and German women; they, too, also became fodder for the campaign. Crusader Ray Beveridge presented one of these offspring during her speech to a rally of protesters in Munich in February 1921, declaring the youth evidence of the "horrors" of the Rhineland occupation.[43]

In addition to presenting such live "evidence," campaigners manufactured statistics and reproduced supposed police records and witnesses' testimony to alleged atrocities, primarily against women, to signify the menace caused by colonial troops. Authors identified victims and witnesses using only initials in their reports. "We have not used the full names of our sisters who have endured the deepest of shame that a white woman can," rationalized the *Rheinische Frauenliga*, " . . . but to whomever wants to know the names we can provide the documentation."[44] Campaign output primarily took the form of pamphlets and books but also included numerous speeches heard in Germany, England, and the United States, as well as several novels and even a film. The content of each piece of propaganda remained consistent and was in many cases pornographic, evoking men's sexual anxieties and fantasies. Occasionally the pamphlets hinted at immorality among German women but more often confirmed the sexual propriety of the victims.[45]

Two historians—Schüler and Christian Koller—detected similarities between the propaganda used by the French against German soldiers who raped French women during the early months of the war and that used by the Rhineland Horror campaign, indicating a pattern among occupied populations of portraying roving, hyper-sexualized soldiers raping vulnerable women to protest military occupations.[46] In the case of the Rhineland Horror campaign, the squawkers could ratchet up the threat a notch. Since there has been a widespread belief that *all* soldiers' sexual drives are especially heightened during war and occupation (hence the tradition of constructing brothels near military barracks,[47] see Chapter 1), the Rhineland Horror campaign could play upon that notion, and then raise the stakes even higher because of whites' fears of African men's supposed overpowering lust. That occupations—and indeed, wars in general—have included soldiers' rape of women was not disputed. Rape has been a powerful weapon used to undermine social stability during and after wars, and it surely occurred in all zones of the Rhineland occupation.[48] Between June and October 1919 in the American zone, for example, the U.S. army's Officer in Charge of Civilian Affairs received seventeen accusations of rape by American soldiers against German women. Eight trials resulted; five men were convicted, with three acquittals.[49] The propaganda campaigns that have exaggerated such acts, however, served only to draw attention away from the actual atrocities committed by occupation troops by calling the veracity of all such acts into question. Instead of empowering female victims to prosecute criminal behavior, the Rhineland Horror campaign served to further reduce women's status in society by controlling women and their sexuality; firstly, by designating who women's appropriate sexual partners should be, and secondly, by provoking their fears of sexuality.

Complaints against colonial soldiers increased during times of heightened tensions between France and Germany, for example, when the Allied blockade achieved its greatest impact in March 1919, when the U.S. Senate defeated the treaty in November of that year (since Germans assumed that the Americans would no longer act as a counterweight to the French presence in the Rhineland), and again in January 1920 when the hated peace treaty came into effect.[50] But the international campaign did not begin in earnest until April 6, 1920, when French troops marched across the boundary of the occupied Rhineland and into the neutral zone in retaliation for President Friedrich Ebert's dispatch of German troops to the Ruhr to prevent a communist revolt (see Chapter 1). In Frankfurt, Moroccan forces led the French occupation of the city and, after provocation, fired fatal shots into a crowd, killing five people. The unit was withdrawn. But Germans continued to protest because the colonial troops had kept guard over two cultural bulwarks, the University of Frankfurt and the Goethe House, inflaming nationalists' sense of humiliation over the occupation. Citizens launched protests in all provinces and in all political parties, except the Independent Social Democratic Party of Germany (USPD). The National Assembly began an inquiry over the Frankfurt incident out of particular concern for German women and children.⁵¹ Lawmakers then passed a resolution backed by all political parties, again except the USPD, denouncing the use of colonial soldiers.⁵² Just prior to the Frankfurt tragedy, the French Commander Ferdinand Foch had aired his plan to install colonial troops in the British occupation headquarters in Cologne, to the chagrin of his British allies. The Germans perceived a looming breach among the Allies that they interpreted as an entrée for an international campaign.⁵³

German crusaders easily won an ally in the British writer and critic of European imperialism Edmund Morel, whose inkwell overflowed with particularly pernicious propaganda. Morel was a founding member of the British Union for Democratic Control, an organization that protested secret diplomacy, the unequal application of laws to favor the rich and well born, the arms race, militarist alliances, and, ironically, racism.⁵⁴ The propagandist authored an article about the Rhineland for the left-wing paper *The Daily Herald* on April 10, 1920, that was subsequently distributed in the form of a pamphlet entitled *The Horror on the Rhine*. The publication went through eight editions in Great Britain and was translated into German, French, Dutch, and Italian. Ultimately, Rhineland Horror pamphlets popped up in such far away places as Peru and Argentina.⁵⁵

Politicians quickly picked up the propaganda and made use of it in a variety of venues. David Lloyd George insisted at a conference in Spa in July 1920 that if Paris were to invade the Ruhr as a result of Germany defaulting on its coal deliveries to France, no black troops should be sent as part of occupation forces of the resource-rich valley; otherwise, his country would not support such a move.⁵⁶ In Germany, Morel's pamphlet found a home in a variety of political headquarters, except for the extreme left wing. Conservative pundits figuratively waved it above their heads to denounce the use of colonial troops. The National Socialist Party, for its part, created a link between the Rhineland Horror campaign and anti-Semitism by insisting that Jewish people wanted to bring non-white people to Europe in order to "bastardize" the race.⁵⁷

Liberals and leftists made similar charges. Foreign Minister Adolf Köster of the liberal Social Democratic Party (SPD) declined to engage in dishonorable race-baiting, reminding the National Assembly that hundreds and thousands of black troops had aided German soldiers in the defense of Germany's colonies. Yet he, too, called the stationing of French colonial troops in the Rhineland a crime. In fact, Köster linked the dishonor to Germany's *Volkskörper* (national body) to the French policy of using black troops, confirming that the "black shame" constituted a national problem of morality that went beyond individual criminal behavior.[58] A lobbyist for the SPD declared that the presence of colonial troops debased and demoralized German women, though he said that he was not against black people as such. The party used its organ *Vorwärts* (*Forward*) to announce their position to the reading public with the concise headline "Away with the Blacks!"[59] In agitating against the Weimar government and the Treaty of Versailles that it had signed, the *Kommunistische Partei Deutschlands* (German Communist Party) leader Hans von Hentig commented that weapons should be taken from the African soldiers and given to German workers. The communist press used the image of a colonial soldier to symbolize what it interpreted as the debasement of Germany through the Allied victory in the war.[60]

Female politicians in the Weimar government also spoke out on the "horror." Käthe Schirmacher of the German National People's Party (DNVP), and SPD members Marie Ansorge and Klara Bohm-Schuch appealed to their partisans to pass resolutions against the use of colonials. Only Luise Zietz of the Independent Socialists did not follow the consensus in the Reichstag. Zeitz claimed that the alleged atrocities were the result of militarism, not racial characteristics. Like Lilli Jannasch (see below), she compared the crimes of colonial soldiers with those committed by German soldiers in Belgium, France, China, and the German colonies.[61]

Meanwhile, the German press sent out a cavalcade of news items about atrocities involving colonial troops out onto the streets, while government agencies, such as the *Reichsheimatdienst* (National Service) and *Rheinische Volkspflege* (Rhineland Social Welfare) organized public protests.[62] German women's organizations also joined the chorus. Margarete Gärtner, founder of the Rhenish Women's League, set about mobilizing women's groups to promote the horror campaign by publishing information about alleged rapes and brothels in the French zone. The League distributed a pamphlet under the English title *Colored Frenchmen on the Rhine: An Appeal of White Women to American Womanhood* in 1920. Women also worked in mixed-gender organizations, including the *Heidelberger Vereinigung* (Heidelberg Association), whose membership included sociologist and *Bund Deutscher Frauenvereine* chairwoman Marianne Weber. The *Vereinigung* also exported publications overseas.[63]

Other groups drew up petitions for international consumption. The *Volksbund Rettet die Ehre* and the BDF, among others, sent a plea for mercy on behalf of German women signed by sixty-six female organizations from Holland, Sweden, and Austria to the League of Nations in October

1920. The document stated "that white people have worked for years to lift up the lowly races to educate them to conquer their low instincts"; but France has "legalized these abominable instincts and even makes the bearers of such instincts armed masters over her cultured neighbors. This is mockery and defiance to the missionary work of all peoples and all times." The signatories stated that they were not only protesting on behalf of the Germans, but also the "entire white race." The *Volksbund* distributed this appeal in Germany and the United States, where a copy was sent to the National Association for the Advancement of Colored People (NAACP)![64]

However, despite the appearance of unanimity created by the sheer volume of propaganda disseminated, Germans were not single-minded in the demand to oust African soldiers from the Rhine. Shortly after the Frankfurt incident, in the Rhineland itself, the *Reichskommissar* (imperial commissioner) argued that some of the claims against the troops were exaggerated, and that in reality crimes committed by African troops were no greater than those perpetrated by white French troops. At least one German newspaper editor, Georg Berhard of the *Vossische Zeitung*, wrote to the *Innenminister* (secretary of the interior), criticizing him for not retracting inflated claims about atrocities committed by African soldiers.[65]

Meanwhile, Morel—who denied he was racist—employed all of the racial and sexual stereotypes commonly used all over Europe in his written and spoken harangues.[66] Noting the "strong sex impulse" among colonial troops, he argued that Africans were unruly children that France should keep in "Eden," but instead the French military "thrust upon the Rhineland [troops whose needs] in the absence of their own women-folk *must be satisfied upon the bodies of white women.*"[67] The anti-imperialist predicted that once colonial troops were allowed to shoot and rape Europeans, they would turn against the colonizers in Africa.[68] At an April 27, 1920, protest meeting organized by the British section of the WILPF in London, Morel warned that "the militarised African, who has shot and bayoneted white men [during the war] in Europe, who has had sexual intercourse with white women in Europe," now realizes that "the white man is . . . rather a poor type, and that the key to his power is just that lethal instrument which he has obligingly taught the black man to use."[69] German propagandist Heinrich Distler parroted Morel's sentiments. "The deployment of [colonial troops] among a downtrodden, defenseless people [is] a crime on the entire culture that awakens in these half-animals the sense that white power can no longer support itself."[70] The result would be a war of extermination between the two races, in part because rapes of white women by black men were often fatal, according to Morel.[71] With the notion that the presence of African soldiers in the Rhineland would provoke race wars, the campaign took on added urgency as a threat to white people all over the world, irrespective of their particular nationality.

After the rally, the British Section of the WILPF passed resolutions against the use of colonials in the Rhineland. In doing so, members mimicked the piqued public opinion of their compatriots. One British official, alluding to continued anti-German sentiment in his homeland, noted that British citizens should not care that the victims of the Rhineland Horror were German. The simple fact that they were women meant that they needed men's protection, regardless of their nationality.[72] The British WILPF later adopted a position against occupations in general, declaring them potentially dangerous for females. Although the pacifists initially endorsed Morel's activities, they subsequently backed away from the British crusader.[73] The WILPF members did nothing publicly to discourage the racialist propaganda, however. The Harlem Renaissance poet Claude McKay, living in London in the 1920s, wrote the only openly hostile letter about Rhineland Horror propaganda to appear in a British paper.[74]

An additional threat that women back on the continent allegedly faced was the specter of numerous brothels built to service occupation forces. These structures constituted a potent reminder of one of the ways in which vanquished nations paid tribute to the winners: by providing for the presumed heightened sexual needs of the victorious military. Paul Löbe, president of the German Reichstag, counted nineteen brothels erected by colonial units within the occupied territories. The French military then charged the costs of 802,000 marks to the German realm, according to Löbe.[75] Heinrich Distler cited costs of over one million marks.[76] To accommodate its African troops, the French army built "Moorish cafes," located within barracks and staffed by Arab women brought to the Rhineland from Algeria. These, however, soon proved too expensive, and the soldiers turned to local prostitutes instead. In the towns of Landau, Diez, and Ems, French officials authorized or encouraged the creation of city bordellos by locals. In the latter two cities, local industrialists spontaneously offered to make arrangements with the city and take the profit. In other municipalities maintaining brothels, the French were not involved in either the construction or the operation, only in the patronage. Such houses were used equally by Germans,

French, and colonial troops. Each bordello hired German prostitutes, supervised through local police and medical surveillance. Homosexual brothels were also constructed. Heinrich Distler claimed that 4,900 women and girls "disappeared" in bordellos, never to be seen again. Church officials and some women's groups protested the building of such houses.[77]

Campaigners located blame for the proliferation of bordellos on France's use of colonial soldiers, once again playing upon the notion that African men were oversexed. Propagandists invented allegations that German women were forced to prostitute themselves in order to staff the houses, and they coupled such accusations with dire warnings of the spread of venereal disease.[78] German political economist Annelise Timmermann, writing her Ph.D. dissertation at Munich University in 1930, repeated the supposed public health threat that had been posed by African troops. "The high point of aggressions during the occupation came during the time when colonial regiments were in charge," claimed the scholar, "during which time also the danger of damage was highest through the transfer of disease and heredity from inferior races."[79]

French doctors certified that exaggerated stories of syphilis and sleeping sickness among African troops were fictitious as part of their nation's attempts to counteract the damage done by the campaign.[80] Additional counterpropaganda argued that the statistics produced in Rhineland Horror pamphlets regarding prostitution and disease were fabricated, that all French soldiers committing crimes were duly prosecuted, and that unions between Germans and French were consensual.[81] German women sometimes pursued colonials because money and men were scarce after the war, according to historian Sally Marks, but affluent German women also pursued them because they were perceived as exotic and novel. The colonials were preferred to Frenchmen, according to British officials, and with good reason: white French soldiers acted like conquerors, whereas Africans treated locals neutrally.[82]

The Rhineland Horror Campaign in the United States

In the American journalist Ray Beveridge the campaign found its feminine counterpart to Edmund Morel. Beveridge offered the crusade access to a U.S. audience (although her citizenship was unclear) and to a female voice that could stir up images of a cuckolded German manhood. All that is known of Beveridge's background is that she worked for a time at the German Embassy in Washington, D.C.[83] In any case, her fellow supporters made use of her ruse at rallies in Hamburg, where flyers were distributed with the words, "Americans, listen to your country woman Miss Beveridge." The orator's pretense at U.S. citizenship allowed her to cultivate the hope that American women would act on German women's behalf. She also baited the masculinity of the men in her audiences. "German men! . . . Your weapons have been taken from you, but there is always a rope and a tree! Take up the natural weapons used by our men of the South: lynch!"[84] Rhetoric insinuating that masculine honor was at stake in the alleged atrocities soon caught on elsewhere. Belgian officers stationed in the Rhineland found tangible evidence on five mark notes overprinted in gold letters: "Awake, German man of honor; lend your aid against the anguish of the Rhineland Horror."[85]

Beveridge's suggestion that the Germans resort to lynching was pointed deliberately at a U.S. audience. Lynching, a uniquely American term defined as the unlawful hanging or killing of a person at the hands of a mob, was derived from the older term *lynch law*, a concept most likely named after either Captain William Lynch or Colonel Charles Lynch. Both men were Virginians. They used vigilante procedures to punish Loyalists during the American Revolution. In the post–Civil War American South, the term connoted racial violence.[86]

Carnage against African Americans in the United States had reached its peak in 1892, when 161 victims were murdered by white mobs. Common characteristics of the murders included castration, dismemberment, and burning. Historians of the United States had commonly attributed the wave of lynchings occurring in the late nineteenth and early twentieth centuries to Reconstruction, economic depression, Populism, and Southern politics. Women's historians, however, have noted the frequency with which lynchings were coupled with accusations of rape of a white woman by a black man. The vengeful practice elevated the perceived power of white Southern manhood. At the same time, the belief that black men threatened white women rendered white womanhood delicate and in need of protection. Lynchings were necessary, perpetrators explained, because black men were uncivilized, unmanly rapists unable to control their lust. But the rhetoric was not restricted to the South. A Northern paper, the *New York Times*, while denouncing a Texarkana, Arkansas, lynching as uncivilized, nevertheless asserted that African Americans were especially prone to raping white women. The *New York Post* denounced the crimes, but still commented that Southern women were at greater risk for rape than their Northern and European sisters.[87]

The popularity of D. W. Griffith's epic film *Birth of a Nation* (1915), based upon Thomas Dixon, Jr.'s novel *The Clansman* (1905), helps explain the resonance of white supremacy in the 1910s and 1920s and the choice by the Rhineland Horror campaign to direct its propaganda across the Atlantic. Like Theodore Roosevelt's effective use of the frontier myth to denote American exceptionalism, *Birth of a Nation* portrayed an expressly American character rooted in redemption of the white race through the formation of the Ku Klux Klan, a group that lynched with abandon, in the post–Civil War era. The epic told the story of two school chums, one the son of a Northern abolitionist and the other a Southern planter's offspring. The Civil War separates the mates, but they are reunited when the Klan saves the honor of the youths' fiancés through the lynching of the black men, who, by virtue of Reconstruction, had deemed themselves worthy of white womanhood. In addition to supplying moviegoers with a renewed vision of the redemptive quality of the Civil War, *Birth of a Nation* marked Reconstruction as a period of disorder (the film portrays newly elected African American politicians as uncivilized, drunken sots whose first order of business is to give themselves access to white women), followed by the rightful return of white male political power via Klan violence. In case the audience might have missed the redemptive symbolism, the silent film's title screen spells it out: "The former enemies of North and South are united again in common defense of their Aryan birthright."[88] The Rhineland Horror campaign duplicated many of the themes of *Birth of a Nation*, such as the presumed inability of nonwhites to govern themselves (part of imperialism's paradigmatic civilized versus uncivilized supposition), the presumed natural desire on the part of black men for white women, and, of course, the myth of the black rapist. This extraordinarily popular movie (the film, which the NAACP sought to have banned, was rereleased in 1930 and 1933) reminded Americans and Europeans of what could happen if white men lost control of their society.

While familiarity with the myth of the black rapist certainly played a role in how quickly the campaign progressed in the United States, other factors dampened the enthusiasm that crusaders expected their propaganda to elicit. Although letters and publications had reached a significant readership in the United States by 1920, concern among politicians revealed misinformation in what the campaign circulated to its American audience. By June of that year, the State Department had received so many letters in response to circulating propaganda that President Wilson instructed Secretary of State Robert Lansing to determine what "facts" the

American ambassador in Paris, Bainbridge Colby, could secure about the matter. The secretary sent telegrams to the American commissioner in Berlin, Ellis Loring Dresel, and the commander of the American Forces in Germany, General Henry T. Allen, making particular inquiries about alleged mistreatments of German women by African forces.[89] Colby cautioned the President that the agitators were simply spreading the campaign to provoke an active response in the U.S. Congress.[90]

General Allen's report encouraged Americans to spurn the propaganda. The commander's survey of alleged sexual assaults by colonial troops revealed that of the presumed 25,000 colonial soldiers in the Rhineland, sixty-six cases of alleged rape, attempted rape, sodomy, or attempted sodomy had been brought to the attention of the French authorities between January 1919 and June 1920. Twenty-eight convictions resulted, with twenty-three cases still pending (Allen's study did not mention the number of crimes committed by Germans against colonial troops).[91] French military officials meted out justice in cases of legitimate crimes efficiently and thoroughly. The General also singled out newspaper stories that inflated figures of the number of French colonial troops stationed in the Rhineland and in which reports of rapes were fabricated and unsubstantiated. He confirmed beyond doubt that the Rhineland Horror was a propaganda campaign to stir animosity toward France.[92] In addition, a number of socially accepted German-colonial marriages had taken place, according to Allen. In both countries, he declared, racial segregation was not adhered to as strictly as it was in the American South.[93] Allen's comments implied that Germans' supposedly ruffled feathers in the face of colonial troops were at least partly a figment of crusaders' imaginations.

The Rhineland Horror campaign reached the peak of its hysteria as the nation inaugurated a new president, Warren G. Harding, in 1921. German-American groups heightened their activity on behalf of the cause, including distributing editorials in George S. Viereck's pro-German publication the *American Monthly* and among members of a German-American organization called the Steuben Society. Ten thousand pamphlets were distributed across the country, financed with money contributed by wealthy German- and Irish-Americans. The National Council of Catholic Women appealed to the State Department by forwarding a protest note written by the League of Catholic Women in Bohemia that gave Americans a special responsibility to the matter because of its own history of race relations. To accompany the printed page, twelve thousand people rallied for an end to the use of colonial troops in the Rhineland at Madison Square Garden in New York City on February 28, 1921.[94]

Nevertheless, despite those concerted efforts, the campaign as it appeared in the United States generally backfired, as most Americans still identified strongly with their wartime ally, and too fiercely against the enemy, to believe the propaganda. Hailing from the conservative wing of American politics, Henry Cabot Lodge, Ellis Loring Dresel, and Charles Evans Hughes rejected the campaign's claims because, as Hughes' assistant wrote in a memo, they were based on dubious charges. American Legion Commander F. W. Galbraith followed suit, physically throwing an American campaigner, Edmund von Mach, out of his office. Galbraith became so agitated by the business that he organized a counterdemonstration to the February 28 event, also at Madison Square Garden, at which double the number participated.[95]

However, it would be a grave error to assume that because the American Legion protested against the campaign it therefore rejected racial prejudice. The New York center did indeed rollick with the presence of 25,000 patriots on the eve of March 18, 1921, but the flag-wavers were there to rejuvenate war enthusiasm, not chide Germans for the offensive accusations that they had hurled toward African soldiers. Hundreds of American Legion posts marched in military regimentation into the Garden, amidst military bands and songs and the shrill battle cries that the men had shouted when they went "over the top." The hysteria reached a crescendo when General John J. Pershing, a.k.a. "Black Jack" (so named for his command of African American soldiers during the Spanish-American War), gave a speech in which he warned against those seeking to weaken the ties that bound U.S. soldiers to those with whom they had fought for American principles. He promised that "outlaw" nations would pay the full penalty for "misdeeds," though he failed to name what the offenses were. Another speaker mentioned the Rhineland Horror crusade, but only to say that "we must not dwell upon it!" The patriots rebuked their former enemy, to be sure, but not for perpetuating false claims against colonial troops. Instead, the crowd "hissed" at those who dared to undercut the wartime Allies, and cheered at the recitation of "great Americans" from George Washington to Warren G. Harding (the list did not include African Americans). There was in fact little mention at all of the Horror on the Rhine. Indeed, if the "All-American" event included any African Americans at all, that fact was kept quiet in the *New York Times* report.[96]

Historian Lucy Bland noted a similar pattern among conservative editors in England, where right-wing newspapers and journals barely touched the subject of the Rhineland Horror, instead restricting themselves to general anti-German rhetoric.[97]

Along with their conservative brethren, American liberals, too, rejected the campaign. A writer for the *Nation*, Lewis Gannett, reported from the Rhineland that a Rhenish police commissioner had assured him that colonial troops were not rabble rousers and simply obeyed orders, even though he admitted that Germans nevertheless resented the quartering of African soldiers in their midst.[98] In a March 1921 article, the magazine cited General Allen's interpretation of the German efforts as mere anti-French propaganda designed to drive a wedge between the Allies. Since the journal had earlier denounced marriages between German *Fräuleins* and U.S. soldiers as a treasonable offense (see Chapter 1), the editors may have been more interested in dismissing German claims than exonerating French policies. The journal cited Allen's assertion that the discipline of the African soldiers was "less perfect" than that of their white comrades, but confirmed that they were not the beasts the propaganda proclaimed them to be. In any case, the *Nation* declared the real culprit in postwar relations to be the occupation itself. While the journal refused to be hoodwinked by the propaganda, it nevertheless felt compelled to echo Allen's note that whites were the better disciplined soldiers.[99]

The campaign courted other Americans to gain support for its cause. German women, including the *Rheinische Frauenliga* and the Catholic Women's Association of Germany—overestimating Jane Addams' influence in society, which had been severely diminished by red-baiting after the war (see Chapter 5)—sent the reformer several pieces of campaign propaganda, asking her to act.[100] Addams received a missive from WILPF member Agnes Flehinghaus begging her to help "protect the German women from the suffering which some of them have to undergo through the occupation of the Rhineland by colored French troops." Secretary of the Nebraska League of Women Voters May Gund also wrote to Addams with a similar request.[101] In addition, a German-American organization calling itself the New York Committee Against the Horror on the Rhine invited her to speak on the topic, but she declined.[102]

Addams, co-founder of the NAACP and a critic of the film *Birth of a Nation*,[103] nevertheless vacillated when confronted with issues involving race, sex, and sexual violence. She had spoken out against lynching in an 1899 speech, commented again in an article published in the *Independent* (in which she rejected the crime as a "hideous act"), and blamed racism and whites' contempt for people that they regarded as inferior for causing the vigilantism.[104] However, she assumed that white men's charges—that the lynched African Americans had raped white women—were true (Theodore Roosevelt responded similarly to lynching).[105] In this, noted biographer Louise W. Knight, Addams "failed to do her homework" and understand the complexities of race relations in the 1890s.[106] Lucy Bland named other reformers such as Morel, Helena M. Swanwick, and George Lansbury (editor of the *Daily Herald* and women's rights supporter) as examples of progressive people who wanted African soldiers out of Europe but who denied that they were prejudiced against Africans, rationalizing that because nature had endowed Africans with heightened sexual drives, they were better off in Africa. While Swanwick appeared apprehensive about the campaign's racialist ideas, commenting that it was unfair to call men who had been kidnapped, forced to leave their homes and join a European military a "scourge" (in reference to Morel's pamphlet entitled "The Black Scourge"), she nevertheless supported the campaign.[107]

Addams' failure to question racial stereotypes stood out most starkly in her letter to Secretary of State Charles Evans Hughes dated March 5, 1921, a missive she coauthored with fellow-U.S. WILPF associate Mabel Kittredge.[108] Despite the fact that WILPF had resolved to alter customs that led to discrimination against people on the basis of race at its 1919 Zurich conference (where the reformers had also passed a resolution endorsing the League of Nations mandate system in Africa but pressed the international body to "promote the development and power of self-government of their wards [Africans]"), members' response to the Rhineland Horror campaign indicated that they were not really prepared to undertake such changes.[109] Addams and Kittredge noted that German WILPF members had contacted them, stating that their government would gladly begin to pay its reparations if not for one paralyzing circumstance. "The soul of the nation is on fire with resentment at the fact that Germany, as a great land of culture, existing for almost 1500 years, has been placed under the military despotism of colored men of the lowest standard of culture for the duration of 15 years," complained the pacifists, "and this only because the French government alone among the Entente governments has so willed it." Furthermore, Addams and Kittredge continued, "German men will not disarm while the cry of German women goes unheeded." In this the pacifists played upon men's sense of honor and women's presumed need for protection, just as Ray Beveridge had done. The reformers also remarked that black troops were committing immoral crimes against young boys. Finally, Addams and Kittredge insisted that "fine colored women" of the United States were also demanding the withdrawal of colonial troops.[110]

Mary Church Terrell was one such woman; she became a key figure in discrediting the campaign among other U.S. pacifists. Terrell had been elected to the WILPF–U.S. section as the only African American board member in 1919. When a petition requesting the removal of African troops from occupied Germany circulated among WILPF's membership, Terrell's colleagues pressed her to sign. But the reformer questioned the truthfulness of the "horrible crimes" allegedly committed by colonial troops. She refused to endorse the petition and instead pointed to a U.S. document that had circulated among the French military during the war three years earlier. That missive, dated August 7, 1918, emanated from General Pershing's headquarters and was entitled "Secret Information Concerning Black Troops." The document began with the remark that "it is important for French officers in command of black American troops to have an idea as to the position occupied by the race in the United States." African Americans were referred to as a "menace of degeneracy which had to be prevented by the gulf established between the two races . . . because of the fact that they were given to the loathsome vice of *criminally assaulting women*." The French were called upon "not to treat the Negroes with familiarity and indulgence which are matters of grievous concern to Americans and an affront to their national policy."[111] Terrell reported that President Wilson had ordered Robert R. Moton, President of Tuskegee Institute, to investigate the charges of rape outlined in the document. Moton responded that they were false. Terrell used the document to convince her fellow pacifists that the charges currently being leveled about African troops in the Rhineland were likely also bogus. She added that several German reformers had told U.S. international suffragist Carrie Chapman Catt that there was no substantial movement in Germany to remove the colonials and that most of the charges were proven untrue after investigation.[112]

Ill will among U.S. WILPF members regarding race relations continued to dog the organization, making their support for the Rhineland Horror campaign seem unsurprising. Fellow U.S. WILPF member and WILPF International Secretary Emily Greene Balch, like her colleague Jane Addams, also sympathized with the horror campaign and upheld the notion of white superiority and black inferiority. When Balch queried Terrell on a different subject, the African American woman expressed surprise that Balch would bother to request a response from her. Terrell recalled that Balch had denounced her statement at WILPF's founding conference in Zurich in 1919, in which she had declared that she and other African Americans had won their freedom through the Civil War. Balch had told Terrell that African Americans would have to wait for whites to take the lead to help them "improve their race." Terrell rebuked her colleague: "I have never seen your theory [to wait for a leader] work . . . you yourself are not following such a course. If you did you would sit quietly at home and wait for men to do for women the work you have been doing so successfully and brilliantly for years."[113]

Terrell finally succeeded in convincing Addams that the German claims were exaggerated. In a March 1921 letter to the WILPF leader, she expressed her sympathy for German women but argued that both German and U.S. soldiers were guilty of the same charges of criminal behavior that were being leveled at French colonials.[114] Addams then changed her mind, and her organization stopped discussing the debacle. The International WILPF passed a resolution against the military use of colonial populations at its conference in Vienna in July 1921, and a German delegate echoed that motion at the 1922 WILPF convention in the Netherlands.[115] However, the reformers decided to take a forceful stance against racism instead. The "Resolution on Race Prejudice" declared that because race prejudice was based on ignorance and was unreasonable, unjust, and distrustful, it sparked suspicion, antagonism, and hatred towards the people of other nations. The organization henceforth condemned racial discrimination as unworthy of civilized human beings.[116]

Other Americans, however, experienced no such epiphanies. In the U.S. Congress in August 1922, Senator Gilbert Hitchcock, Democrat of Nebraska and Senate minority leader, declared that the United States had a moral obligation to force France to withdraw its colonial troops. His colleagues listened wearily as the Senator continued to claim, as he had done several times in the past, that African troops' crimes in the Rhineland went unpunished.[117] As tensions among the Allies and Germany grew over reparations payments (see Chapter 1), even General Allen wrote to Commander Pershing that same month that African troops had become a legitimate source of grief for Germany. Allen became convinced that using colonial troops in Europe was a bad idea,[118] not so much because the campaign had convinced him of the truthfulness of its claims, but more likely because the crusaders had done damage that could not be reversed among people who needed a scapegoat to explain Germany's continued troubles. In any case, the French stopped deploying colonial troops during the Ruhr Crisis, probably because they felt that they were unnecessarily providing the Germans with fodder for propaganda that had resulted in at least some criticism of French policy among their allies.[119]

The most trenchant critique of the Rhineland Horror campaign came from a German pacifist. Lilli Jannasch, author of the 1921 pamphlet *Schwarze Schmach und schwarz-weiss-rote Schande* (*Black Dishonor and Black-White-Red Disgrace*), offered her analysis in a German magazine in November, 1920. Jannasch compared the crusade's antics to the German folktale the "Pied Piper of Hamelin," in which the piper (in this case, the Rhineland Horror campaigners) played irresistible music (of revenge, chivalric honor, and female protection) while making irresponsible claims (about the African soldiers). The German people, observed Jannasch, were being lured into a never-ending cycle of revenge by the campaign's inflated claims of dishonor at the hands of the colonial troops. Jannasch explained that in using colonials, the French were perpetuating the spirit of retribution instigated by the aggressive, baiting methods begun by the Germans during the war, particularly in their own occupation of Belgium and parts of France.

The pacifist declared that she had lived for a year in the postwar occupied Rhineland, in which more than a hundred colonial soldiers were stationed. The district administrator of the area assured her that no hostility toward women or children had occurred; the Africans were in fact quite popular with the local population, particularly when, for example, the troops had shared their provisions with hungry children. The writer noted that in many German cities, the talk of the town was that women found the colonials to be good company. Was it "white shame," Jannasch queried her readers, for these German women to admit their feelings, as appalling as the so-called "black shame"?

Jannasch interpreted aggression on the part of some colonials as an individual problem, not as a mass phenomenon, and she suggested that authorities ought to handle such situations as isolated incidences. Citizens grumbling about injustices in the occupied zone were in any case hypocritical, since as a nation Germany itself had been unfair. The pacifist reminded readers that their military had occupied Lille, the coal-rich French city near the Belgium border, and deported ten thousand women and girls in 1916 for compulsory agricultural labor elsewhere. Furthermore, most readers were aware that German colonizers had mistreated native populations. Was it not the same colonizers that were now hurling accusations of "black horror" at the French, Jannasch wondered? Furthermore, why did the *Bund Deutscher Frauenvereine*, the bourgeois women's association, not shed a tear when African women by the thousands were victimized by German colonizers? Answering her own query, Jannasch explained that "race fanatics" had argued that the inferiority of the black race excused such procedures and that the life and health of one German woman and one German child were worth one hundred African women's lives.

In this point, Jannasch extended her analysis from race to gender hierarchies in a patriarchal society. The writer questioned whether German men really valued German women's lives, and then offered evidence to the contrary; one need only to think of prostitutes, forced into the business by hunger, whose lives had been cheapened (Jannasch did not believe that only the French were to blame for the proliferation of brothels, reminding readers of the bordellos built by the German military in Belgium). So, wondered the pacifist sarcastically, where was the concern for these German women? Assistance to impoverished women, she implied, may have saved some from the sex trade, but adequate welfare was nonexistent for nearly all German women, and women (along with injured ex-soldiers) comprised the neediest group of people in the immediate postwar years. If patriarchy is maintained, in part, by valuing women's maternal and domestic functions in lieu of full equality, Jannasch denied that they were granted even that small favor. Finally, the pacifist revealed the campaign for the foreign relations problem that it had become for the German state. "As long as Germans remain under the thumb of their military," she warned, "other nations will not grant them understanding or trust."[120]

German WILPF members, including Anita Augspurg, Lida Gustava Heymann, and Gertrud Baer, agreed with Jannasch.[121] In her article for *Die Frau im Staat*, Baer dealt with the campaign's appearance in the United States and analyzed the irrational fears of African male sexuality among white women. This, opined the WILPF member, accounted for "lynch justice" and the bigotry against African Americans in the United States. The black shame campaign, she argued, needed to be reconsidered in light of the ways in which this mythology had been used to create needless suspicions between the races transnationally.[122]

Jannasch's article, appearing originally in Augspurg and Heymann's publication *Die Frau im Staat*, while not widespread, was reprinted in *Die*

Friedens-Warte (waiting for peace), a Leipzig periodical. The piece even received comment in the *New York Times*. The U.S. paper reported that Jannasch's editorial corroborated official denials by the French government of scurrilous charges voiced in the German press of wholesale abuses of women and children at the hands of colonial soldiers, thus exposing the campaign's true design: to foment discord among the Allies. Pieces such as those written by Jannasch and Baer were hard to find, but when newspapers printed opposing voices, the campaign lost credibility.[123]

From a diplomatic viewpoint, the Rhineland Horror campaign accomplished almost nothing. The French may have felt gratified by the revenge that they wreaked upon Germany with their deployment of African soldiers, and satisfied that they had achieved a small sense of security by keeping their neighbor subdued. But in return France lost the allegiance of some of its allies. The Germans, by trying to turn racial prejudices to their advantage, only managed to further alienate their former enemies, but left intact the hatreds that would in the next war destroy their own civilization. Obscured in the entire occupation ordeal were the voices of the African soldiers themselves (although the experiences of German offspring of other African men living in Germany during the occupation years have been recorded).[124] These men, uprooted from their families and livelihoods, risked their lives and well-being to serve in a military in a place far from home; their voices were finally recorded and collected by oral historian Joe Lunn.[125] As Keith Nelson summed it up, "perhaps it was also to their [Africans'] advantage that, after the experience of war and occupation, they must have found it more difficult to idealize the white man."[126]

The violence against females that did occur during the occupation, regardless of the perpetrator's race or country of origin, reduced women's chances of consolidating any gains that they won through their wartime participation in the economy and politics (see Chapter 5).[127] Instead of empowering women to become agents of their own experiences, the campaign reduced women's autonomy and individuality by outlining and publicizing how rape victims should understand the offense done to them: as one of many unjust, disgraceful aspects of the Rhineland occupation foisted upon helpless female victims and upon German society as a whole by the victorious powers. While some soldier-rapists during the occupation may have indeed felt free to violate local women because they felt that their participation in the military victory entitled them to booty,[128] the campaign did women no favors when it directed German *men* to seek revenge for those acts instead of empowering women to seek justice. In addition, as both sides of the controversy surrounding France's use of colonial soldiers during the occupation—both supporters, including the *Rheinische Frauenliga*, and detractors of the crusade, such as U.S. General Henry T. Allen—battled each other over the number and nature of alleged outrages occurring in the Rhineland, neither side questioned how rape should be understood by its victims or by society: as a shameful misdeed that women themselves were somehow also guilty of perpetrating.[129] By making women feel ashamed of their victimization, campaigners compounded the sense that women were to blame for Germany's humiliations, both during and after the war (see Chapter 5).[130]

Meanwhile, many American men and women, well trained by wartime propaganda, looked askance at presumed German character traits—such as barbaric militarism, innate chauvinism, and deviant German *Kultur*—well into the postwar period. The Rhineland Horror campaign simply confirmed their suspicion that Germans needed to be liberated from their backward culture by the victorious powers. The act of redeeming guilty Germans served two purposes: firstly, it furthered the process of reconciling with the former enemy, so that Germans could once again enter diplomatic and economic relations with the victorious powers. Secondly, the act of deliverance would solidify Americans' sense that they in fact had won the war. Americans' belief in their mythological past—especially their views of their nation as a "city on a hill"—convinced them that the job of redeeming the former enemy should belong entirely to them.

3
"What to do with the Germans?"
American Exceptionalism and German-American Reconciliation

Soon after the November 1918 armistice, U.S. politicians, writers, historians, soldiers, and others began debating the question of how the nation should end the Great War by reconciling with the former enemy. The negotiations that took place between the cease-fire and the 1921 Treaty of Berlin that ended the conflict between the United States and Germany marked the first time in history that American officials helped orchestrate treaties among several of the world's major powers. Historians' accounts and interpretations of these events are as complicated as the proceedings themselves. A noted scholar of German-American relations, Lloyd E. Ambrosius, has traced the historiography of President Woodrow Wilson's ideas and policies relating to postwar reconciliation. As the first U.S. President to engage in a post–world war settlement, Wilson shaped foreign relations for the remainder of the century, and even the events following the World Trade Center and Pentagon bombings of September 11, 2001.[1] Ambrosius argued that while historians have primarily viewed Wilson's legacies of collective security, multilateralism, and the infusion of morality into international policymaking as the globalization of American political ideology and as a crowning achievement of the presumed American mission in the world, he and a select few have proved less than enthusiastic about Wilson's bequests.[2] Ambrosius believed that historians have posed the battle between Wilson and his chief foe in the U.S. Senate, Henry Cabot Lodge, as a false dichotomy between multilateralism and unilateralism, a paradigm that has been reinforced by historians ever since. The president, according to Ambrosius, advocated *both* multi- and unilateralism in U.S. foreign policy, while Lodge and his camp were not dismissive of collective security; they favored working with the

United States' wartime allies to guarantee French borders against German aggression instead of what they perceived as subordinating the United States' sovereignty to the League of Nations. Historians, declared Ambrosius, have merely reiterated the American exceptionalism inherent in Wilson's proposals for redeeming the world through U.S. hegemony in the League by interpreting his foreign policy solely within a U.S. framework, rather than from an international perspective.[3]

Furthermore, historians' near-worshipful handling of Wilson's statecraft blinded them to his shortcomings, according to Ambrosius. The president's supposedly "new" internationalism masked old parochialisms. His ideas about national self-determination were based upon his notion of white supremacy; the League of Nations' mandates only offered democracy to the more "developed" peoples of the former Ottoman Empire (see Chapter 2), and he defeated a Japanese proposal calling for racial equality as part of the Versailles Treaty. His failure to act in the Armenian genocide of 1915 revealed the hypocrisy inherent in his apparent call for universal human rights.[4] He was a latecomer to woman suffrage (see below) and proved generally dismissive of women.[5] Wilson's visions for a truly new world order were blinkered by his prejudices.

Ambrosius argued that in refusing to create a common defense for Western Europe against possible German remilitarization (as the nation's top Republican leaders, including Lodge, Elihu Root, and Philander Knox, wanted the president to do), Wilson also sacrificed U.S. Senate approval for the treaty and the League. Had the president compromised with his Republican opponents, the United States could have remained engaged in European affairs and cooperated to preserve the peace after the First World War. Ambrosius, a historian of foreign policy adhering to the "realist" school, viewed the Republicans' desire to continue the wartime defensive alliance as a "viable alternative to the president's peace program" (it should be noted, however, that Lodge and his cohorts did not address sexual, racial, or class inequalities either), and he complained that Wilson's plan for collective security overlooked present realities in favor of future ideals.[6] One of the "present realities" in 1919, however, lay under the poppy fields of Flanders and Picardy and in military hospitals in Europe, Africa, and the Middle East; Europe's old system of alliances—an aspect of prewar Europe that Republicans wanted to maintain in order to defend France—had contributed to the Great War's "lost generation" and the additional (and unprecedented) twenty-one million battle-scarred soldiers that severely tested the welfare rolls of most belligerent nations (see Chapter 5).[7] Eight million men returned home permanently disabled; six million children lost their fathers to the war. Germany spent the highest proportion of its annual budget on war victims' pensions (20 percent); France came in next at 13.5 percent, while Great Britain spent the least at 7 percent.[8] Since realists are preoccupied with what is deemed to be in the "national interest," they must take the economic and social consequences of total war on belligerent nations into consideration in evaluating the postwar settlement.[9] Furthermore, as feminist critics have shown, "realities" are constructed by individuals, not omnipotent powers; there is no single, objective reality in the world awaiting foreign policymakers' (or historians') scrutiny.[10] Wilson's new internationalism, while dogged by his own and the world's prejudices, constituted at least a step in a different direction, rather than a step back.

The ground covered by Ambrosius, John Milton Cooper, and others over the president's rhetoric and actions from the armistice to the defeat of the treaty in the Senate, and the consequences for the United States and world, has been overturned many times.[11] Ambrosius invited historians to escape the paradigm of American exceptionalism in their histories of foreign policy by analyzing how other nations responded to Wilsonian foreign policies. Uncovering those reactions, and the ways in which public discourse over reconciliation influenced foreign relations, will help bring about the nuance in the history of the peace settlement for which Ambrosius has called.[12]

This chapter interweaves the official peacemaking between nations and the unofficial ways in which Americans sought to settle with the German enemy after the November armistice; in addition, it analyzes German middle-class women's responses to the Versailles Treaty. Ordinary people—those with sons counted among the Great War's shell shocked or shell destroyed, or who had themselves fought in the trenches—staked out a claim for grassroots influence on the peace negotiations and on foreign relations.[13] The settlement most Americans advocated reaffirmed longstanding traditions of what it meant to have fought a war: it confirmed the valor of the victors and the humiliation of the vanquished, the right of the conquerors to spiritually redeem the defeated in ways that affirmed American exceptionalism and reinforced the power that battlefield triumph had bestowed upon them, and finally it sought to restore traditional gender roles for men and women: it encouraged men to reassert their power, while it promised to protect and defend women's vulnerability. In other words, most U.S. commentators understood the

Great War as wars had always been perceived, and they expected the peace agreements to follow the same traditional paradigm of victor over vanquished.

But the Great War was not like any previous war. In the spring of 1919, all traditions and conventions, and all hopes for human progress seemed upended. The war nearly wiped out British society. One historian used the phrase "the hollow years" to describe the interwar years in France, with its low marriage and birth rates.[14] The work of some American Great War writers (discussed in Chapter 5) and the poetry and prose of British writers such as Siegfried Sassoon, Wilfred Owen, Robert Graves, and Edmund Blunden refused to romanticize or valorize what had happened in the trenches stretching from the Ypres Salient in Belgium to Beurnevisin near the Swiss border. Instead, their works employed the dominant device found in Great War literature: irony.[15] Even politicians such as British Prime Minister David Lloyd George recounted the hopelessness of modern warfare. "The thing is horrible," he said, "and beyond human nature to bear, and I feel I can't go on any longer with the bloody business." No one would print his words, he noted, since war correspondents and military censors wouldn't state the truth.[16] "There are too many guns everywhere," lamented French soldier Paul Pireaud during the Battle of Verdun in a letter to his wife Marie, "For as long as they are here both advance and retreat are impossible."[17] Wars fought prior to 1914 had featured adversaries destroyed or subdued by superior forces and victorious warriors rejoicing over enemy territory conquered. But in the Great War the only "spoils" were dead and ruined young men on both sides of the conflict. The only winner in 1918, according to British soldier-writer Edmund Blunden, was war.[18]

So when stateside writers such as George Harvey and Gerald Stanley Lee advocated reconciling with the Germans by regenerating them and making them fit American notions of the progressive betterment of humankind, Europeans could only blink in incomprehension, given the enormous political, economic, and social toll exacted by the war.[19] The American writer Paul Fussell put it most succinctly: the Great War "reversed the Idea of Progress." Fussell's work analyzed the responses of British trench fighters; historian Martha Hanna's examination of the French peasant Paul Pireaud's letters written home to his wife during the battles of Verdun and the Somme nuanced Fussell's interpretations.[20] Since American ideals of self-determination and international cooperation—Wilsonian ideals—could not convince Europeans that the massive slaughter had not been in vain, U.S. politicians retreated into isolation and pragmatic business as usual in treating with the Germans and with Europeans in general. On the other side of the Atlantic, German women, most of who were related to Great War victims, also interpreted the war in parochial terms. In addition, they viewed the conflict in gendered terms, as a war fought so brutally that it had driven German men's morals—indeed, their very humanity—underground. The German people could only be resurrected through a foreign policy infused with maternal nationalism. The women began their struggle to win back German honor by first protesting against Woodrow Wilson's policies and then the Treaty of Versailles itself (see following).[21]

The Roots of Religious American Exceptionalism and the Drive to Redeem the Enemy

U.S. serials and newspapers were peppered with comments about how the nation should make up with the German enemy well before the official negotiations began in Paris. The American occupation of the Rhineland and the United States' large German-American population, as well as enmity toward the "Hun" that had been inflamed by wartime propaganda, all ignited their passions. The predominant question capturing readers' attention became that posed by *The Public*'s editors: what to do with the Germans.[22] For while few doubted the economic benefits of recreating normal trade relations between the two warring nations, many Americans were not yet ready to bury the hatchet and kiss and make up with the hated Hun. Instead, they sought to redeem the fallen enemy by remaking it in their own image. A belief in American exceptionalism, girded with a religious zeal that had recently been invigorated by the progressive Men and Religion Forward Movement, shaped how a cross-section of Americans—from religious leaders, political commentators, and U.S. Congressmen to Woodrow Wilson himself—interpreted the defeated enemy.[23]

Some American writers reacted warily to the 1918 armistice and the political changes that had developed in Germany since the cease-fire. Given the perceived ability of German military power to resurrect itself, they believed that only an American victory march down Berlin's famed Unter-den-Linden—rather than an agreement reached in trench-scarred France—would convince the world of Germany's defeat. Furthermore, the disappearance of Kaiser Wilhelm from the throne and the institution of a Republic in Weimar did not convince them that the German people had accepted their loss or their responsibility (as perceived by the Americans and Allies) for instigating the conflagration in the first place. Teutonic civilization—in the religious language intoned by these writers—needed to be spiritually regenerated and morally redeemed by the United States. The Germans had to be convinced not only of their military defeat but also of their spiritual defeat under the morally bankrupt, militaristic Kaiserreich. After all, according to this line of reasoning, if the enemy is still spiritually buoyant, then the conquerors are unfairly robbed of the experience of a military and moral victory, and the war had been fought and lives lost in vain. Reconciliation could not commence until the parties could agree upon—or at least be seen to acknowledge—which side had won and which side had lost the war. For despite President Wilson's "peace without victory" pledge in his January 22, 1917, address to the U.S. Senate, many Americans sought exactly that: acknowledgment of military superiority that they believed their soldiers had earned at the battle of St. Mihiel and the Meuse-Argonne offensive.[24] (The Allies, it should be noted, were as intent upon a confirmed victory as the Americans; they accused the United States of depriving them of their success by trying to orchestrate the armistice without them.[25]) Combined with Americans' belief in the supremacy of their military was their sense of U.S. moral and spiritual superiority that had contributed to the overseas victory. In addition, some writers pontificating on how to reconcile with the enemy insisted on an American triumph that they thought would protect and vindicate the innocent European women whom they believed had been violated by uncivilized, immoral German barbarity.

The appetite for military conquest had been whetted even before the United States intervened in the war in April 1917. Americans and the soldiers they sent to Europe had perceived their errand in Europe as a knightly duty that promised to bestow glory and honor on the young men willing to take up the sword. Best-selling books with titles such as *The Glory of the Trenches*, *My Home in the Field of Honor*, and *Over the Top* perpetuated the notion that war ennobled young men.[26] The Allies confirmed this view of the manly honor earned by youths in battle. The French, for example, viewed doughboys as medieval knights, albeit errant ones; a Paris newspaper cartoon featured a distracted American soldier gallantly slaying a snake that had coiled itself around a comely French maid instead of battling the Teutonic enemy.[27]

Manly virtue combined with religious and moral fervor in churches and in the U.S. Congress. On Palm Sunday, 1917, prior to the vote in favor of war, Randolph McKim preached from his pulpit in Washington, D.C. on the topic "America Summoned to a Holy War."[28] Five days later, when President Wilson finally requested the war declaration from Congress, he used Biblical language to allude to the noble sacrifices that his countrymen must make in exchange for the privilege of defending the nation's principles. "There are, it may be, many months of fiery trial and sacrifice ahead of us," he warned Congress, but he assured members, "To such a task we can dedicate our lives and our fortunes, everything that we are and everything that we have, with the pride of those who know that the day has come when America is privileged to spend her blood and her might for the principles that gave her birth and happiness and the peace which she has treasured. God helping her, she can do no other."

U.S. lawmakers' muscular language in the congressional debate following the president's war declaration pointed to the power that they expected preparing for battle to bestow upon the soldiers and their country.[29] Promises of power and glory before intervention in the war made Americans' demand for the same at the close of the war entirely predictable.

The moral and spiritual self-confidence with which Americans responded to their European opponents (and their allies) had a long-standing preeminence in U.S. history rooted, in part, in the dominance of white, Protestant Christianity and its interconnected relationship to the nation. Benedict Anderson has traced the shift from the authority claimed by institutional religion to the nation in his book *Imagined Communities: Reflections on the Origin and Spread of Nationalism*. As privileged access to Latin scriptures containing existential truths lost out to widespread vernacular print in Europe, and as societies organized around divine-right monarchs and the intertwining of cosmology and history with human lives began to lose their hold over men's minds, argued Anderson, they began to develop alternative ways of linking fraternity, power, and history together in a meaningful entity that ultimately evolved into the nation. But the same quality of redemption that organized religion offered to help relieve humanity from the sorrows of daily existence—disease, death, and servitude—was retained in the nation, in which warriors dying to defend their country were redeemed of their human frailties through the building of statuary and monument and in the remembrance of fallen soldiers as heroes (see Chapter 5).[30]

From the Revolutionary period through the Civil War, Americans conceived of their nation as a "redeemer nation" sanctified by God to serve as a beacon of liberty and prosperity for the rest of the world to follow. This mythology enabled them to justify slavery and appropriate Native American lands, and it fueled the Union victory in the Civil War. Despite the sectionalism that fractured the unity of the Republic and led to that war, and notwithstanding northern radical abolitionists' attempts to disentangle the melding of whiteness with American citizenship, the end of Reconstruction and age of imperialism that followed confirmed the hegemony of white Protestant Christianity that had defined the nation since its inception and placed the power of redemption squarely in its hands.[31]

American elites' conduct of foreign policy in the 1920s (especially Woodrow Wilson's) confirmed this ideology of American exceptionalism, the mythical contortions of U.S. history, and, though to a lesser extent, the place of religion in American life.[32] As Edward J. Blum has argued, Protestantism in the late-nineteenth-century United States did not constitute a reaction to Reconstruction, industrialization, immigration, and imperialism. Instead, Protestant preachers, church leaders, and their followers drove intellectual, social, and cultural change during Reconstruction and the Gilded Age by infusing American life, including foreign relations, with Christian dogma and ideologies.[33] The late nineteenth century marked the greatest amalgamation of evangelical Protestantism with Americanism in U.S. history.[34]

Woodrow Wilson's confidence in American exceptionalism, rooted in his brand of messianic, Protestant Christianity, enabled the statesman to imagine—if not expect—the postwar world to conform to American political norms, and it helped determine the path the United States would take in reconciling with the former enemy, both officially and unofficially. American exceptionalism ensured that the United States could avoid class conflict, revolution, and the "entangling alliances" fashioned by the authoritarian regimes of Europe and present itself as a model for other nations to emulate through its hegemonic leadership of a league of nations. In his Fourteen Points speech of January 8, 1918, Wilson outlined his vision for a new world order that would enable the United States to join in world affairs on its own terms (through the League of Nations), thereby both isolating itself from the Old World's failed diplomacy of alliances and participating in (if not directing) world affairs through its new diplomacy of international cooperation based on American morals and liberal principles. The president viewed the League of Nations through the lens of his Protestant faith. He chose to call the League's founding document a "Covenant" instead of charter, and he determined to make its home Geneva, Switzerland, the birthplace of Calvinism. He identified theologian George D. Herron's aspirations for the United States—to become a shepherd leading the world's nations into the kingdom of God—as matching his own.[35]

Peace negotiations at Versailles took place eight years after the most comprehensive, gender-exclusive, evangelical religious movement in U.S. history, helping to bolster male control of this dominant aspect of American life. Churches in the United States have relied, paradoxically, on the participation of the very group that they have traditionally barred from holding authoritative positions: women.[36] Prior to the twentieth century, women had comprised about two-thirds of American church membership, a fact about U.S. religious life neither disputed nor challenged by men. In 1911, however, the Men and Religion Forward Movement (MRFM) joined a general movement to masculinize religion by harnessing the energy of men's church organizations, the International Sunday School Committee, the Gideons, and the Young Men's Christian Association, to activate greater male participation in U.S. religious life. The emergence of a corporate-driven, consumer-oriented society incited men to reject the early nineteenth-century perception that women were naturally religious and moral whereas men dominated the sphere of politics and business and that the two spheres were separate. The MRFM's discourse revealed an anxiety about female domination in the church, and the organization set out to bring religious institutions into the manly world of commerce and world affairs.[37] Its literature featured the virility of churchgoing men (along with the remasculinization of Jesus; the popular preacher Billy Sunday proclaimed Christ "the greatest scrapper who ever lived"[38]) and emphasized the logical, unsentimental character of the gospels. Its leaders ran their organization with bureaucratic efficiency coupled with aggressive advertising campaigns. Although the MRFM dealt with social issues of the day such as alcohol abuse, prostitution, and political corruption, the absence of any discussion of women's place in civic life in its pages was deafening; its silence matched the inattention paid to women by both Presidents Wilson and Harding.[39]

For his part, President Wilson continued to employ the tired rhetoric of separate spheres even as he supported woman suffrage publicly for the first time in November 1918 as a gesture of thanks for women's aid in the war.[40] The president referred to the "discipline" and the "utter self-sacrifice" women had made for the war effort, and he praised the "lustre" that they had added to the "annals of American womanhood." He applauded women's efforts on the home front during the war but noted that their stories would remain only "at our hearts," rather than acknowledged by history.[41] Finally, he honored women as men's "kinsmen," not as individuals, keeping women securely tethered to the family. The U.S. Congress owed them suffrage due to their self-sacrifice, not because women's unequal status relative to men should be corrected. By couching woman suffrage in cult-of-true-womanhood terms, the president reassured the public that feminine voters would not have much impact.[42] In any case, Wilson's speech marked one of the few instances in which the statesmen mentioned women at all; the MRFM's silence on women's rights indicated the group's dismissal of what was popularly known in the early twentieth century as "the woman question."[43]

Although the MRFM did not achieve its goal of adding 3,000,000 more men to church rolls by 1912, by 1926 the group's activism bore fruit; Protestant male church membership had risen from comprising only one-third of the total to 41.8 percent.[44] MRFM leaders credited a number of strategies for the success of the drive to increase male participation in religion, including the infusion of men's sports clubs in churches, its partnership with the Social Gospel movement, and the publication of a number of like-minded books, such as Carl Delos Case's *The Masculine in Religion* (1906), Alfred Thayer Mahan's *Harvest Within: Thoughts on the Life of the Christian* (1909), and Jason Noble Pierce's *The Masculine Power of Christ, or Christ Measured as a Man* (1912).[45] White male Protestants could justly claim a hegemonic presence in American religious life by the 1920s, and, given the predominance of religion in the United States, the question of how to reconcile with the Germans would be determined largely by Protestant men and be posed in nationalistic and religious terms.

Those advocating a harsh treaty justified punitive terms as a way to force Germans to acknowledge their sins and to prevent the nation from resurfacing militarily. They tended to oppose the League of Nations on the basis that it undercut U.S. manhood and nationhood: they interpreted the idea of international cooperation as weak and effeminate. Both those advocating a vindictive peace and those hoping for clemency argued with the self-confidence of a people victorious in battle and convinced of the righteousness of their respective positions.

American Manhood, the Cease-fire, and the Peace Treaty

American pundits first began arguing against a lenient reconciliation with the opponent by advocating a complete military routing of Germany—an indisputable demonstration of the United States' military valor and the enemy's utter defeat—that they believed would preclude the need for a negotiated settlement. The "fight to the finish" school represented the "vindication of the righteous and the punishment of the wicked," lamented Emily Greene Balch, and would only lead to renewed hostility.[46] Nevertheless, for journalist George Harvey, the notion that his government was even considering a cease-fire agreement with the Germans in October 1918 instead of an outright military victory disgraced his sense of his nation's manly honor. He claimed that those arguing for a negotiated peace were insidiously perpetuating the idea that his countrymen were tired of the war, that they disliked the "privations and inconveniences of war," and that they were therefore anxious to negotiate a peace. In Harvey's mind, a triumphant victory would counter the claim that the United States had had its fighting spirit diminished.[47] Harvey found like minds in Senator Lodge and former President Theodore Roosevelt. Both men embodied the characteristics of the "virility impulse of the progressives," according to historian James R. McGovern, and they demanded action instead of talk.[48] Lodge rejected a negotiated peace on the grounds that, as the Massachusetts Senator wrote to Roosevelt, "we shall leave Germany about where she started," that is, in an aggressive military stance. He continued, "I am sure the American people want a complete victory and an unconditional surrender." Indeed, according to historian Klaus Schwabe, large numbers of Americans from across the political spectrum urged harsh treatment of Germany.[49]

Harvey saved what he thought was his most compelling argument against peace negotiations and in favor of a military routing for last. The Germans' wartime atrocities had been so grave that they did not deserve any display of chivalrous magnanimity—in which the victor provides the beaten an opportunity to bargain rather than face certain destruction—traditionally shown to a prostrate enemy. The writer pointed particularly to German crimes against women to justify his position: "Shall we show lenience to the unrepentant murderers of Edith Cavell [the English nurse whom the Germans caught aiding escaped prisoners], to the butchers of the women and children of the *Lusitania*, to the destroyers of Louvain, to the government that ordered and carried out the deportation of the young women of Belgium and France into the 'white slavery' of enforced prostitution? . . . Toward such a foe we can show no forbearance."[50] The German military's barbarous behavior toward women—its unwillingness to gallantly protect them—signaled that it was not a civilized nation with which the Americans could or should negotiate a treaty; therefore, a military routing was necessary to establish peace.

Stanford University scientist Vernon Kellogg reinforced Harvey's point about German *Kultur* with his cryptically titled article "Unclean, Unclean" printed in the same issue of the *North American Review*. Kellogg, a specialist in evolutionary theory, likened the German people to an animal species that had evolved into highly successful predators. Germany's leaders, according to Kellogg, had perpetuated a militarism designed to "naturally select" the German race at the expense of the human race. Kellogg viewed German militarism as an infection and argued that Germans must be quarantined from the rest of the world in order to rid humanity of Germany's disease. Treating with the Germans, Kellogg implied, would lead to the spread of the malady, whereas a military routing would allow the victor to effectively isolate the defeated and cleanse the infection.[51]

But military and political officials in Washington, Berlin, London, and Paris foiled militarists' hopes for an uncompromising victory by orchestrating an armistice. On October 4, 1918, German officials directed peace feelers toward President Wilson, hoping for an arrangement based on his Fourteen Points. Wilson welcomed the opportunity to negotiate a cease-fire centered on his doctrine for world peace and stability. German political officials exchanged a series of notes with the American President and his advisors, who alerted their colleagues. When Wilson urged the German government to oust its monarch (the American president urged rather than insisted because he feared Bolshevism might fill the power vacuum) Chancellor Max von Baden forced Wilhelm's reluctant abdication on November 9, 1918. The stage was set for the cease-fire agreement.[52]

As if to assure fellow countrymen such as Harvey and Kellogg that the armistice constituted a clear military victory and not a compromise, an *Outlook* editorial trumpeted that "in everything but the name" the agreement reached between the United States, the Allies, and the Germans symbolized the "unconditional surrender" of the enemy. "Neither in Congress not out of Congress has there been any serious criticism of the armistice *under which our victory is made certain*, and the way is open for an enduring peace founded on the principles in which the Allies are united."[53] After President Wilson read the armistice terms aloud to Congress, lawmakers recorded their reactions for a *New York Times* reporter. "The terms of the armistice are in every way ample," remarked Senator Warren G. Harding as he summed up the general response, though he admitted, "It is not so spectacular as a march to Berlin." Nevertheless, "it proclaims the collapse of German autocracy, the end of the German military menace, and the dawn of a new era in the world." On the other hand, H. M. Towner seemed to regard the armistice as having the same effect as victory parade in Berlin. "I am very much pleased with the terms," he blustered, "because they are the most humiliating ever imposed upon a great nation at the close of a war." Democrats responded similarly but added high praise for President Wilson.[54] Those in and out of government agreed that the armistice marked a triumph for the United States and its military. Despite such rhetoric from lawmakers and their supportive journals, however, not everyone agreed that the U.S. military had supplied the decisive knockout punch in the war against German militarism. An anonymous letter to an *Outlook* editor from an Army officer, for example, indicated that American soldiers had done less to ensure Allied victory than the American press boasted; the United States, he counseled, would do well to "preach modesty" as it helped reconstruct Europe in the war's aftermath.[55] The Chief Executive, however, believed in the power of the American victory (despite his earlier "peace without victory" speech) as he began arranging the second phase of reconciliation: the diplomatic settlement to the Great War that would take place at the French palace.

At the same time, American pundits and policymakers began to ponder what the peace treaty should provide. Among the most commonly evoked images was that of Americans spiritually regenerating the defeated enemy and remaking him to look more like themselves. The notion that the U.S. conquest would not be complete until the victors remade the enemy in their own image echoed President Wilson's sentiment that a peace without victory would institute a new world order based upon American morals and principles and reinforced the sense among these thinkers that the military battles that Americans had won granted them the power to preside over such transformations. Furthermore, those arguing for a regenerated Germany had become convinced that the German people—and not only their leaders, many of whom had been ousted from their positions following the November Revolution—were responsible for the war and therefore the entire population needed a spiritual rebirthing. One article of faith commonly held by those ruminating over how to regenerate the Germans was that the former belligerents had mistreated women during the war and that a repentant, remade Germany would protect vulnerable females from dishonor.

At the vortex of the what-to-do-with-the-Germans debate lay the question of whether and to what extent Germans should be held accountable for the perceived wartime atrocities that their nation had perpetuated. One *San Francisco Chronicle* cartoonist, for example, visually separated the people from their militarist leader by imagining them confronting one another. A maimed Kaiser Wilhelm limps up to the front gate of a German house as a fat German matron waddles out of the domicile wielding a rolling pin. The matron, labeled "The German People," shouts threateningly at the defeated monarch, "So" while the exiled leader mutters, "Donnerwetter, now I'm in for it!"[56] Feminine figures waving rolling pins symbolized illustrators' sense of women's ridiculous pretense at political power in the political cartoons of the era, and in this case the artist emphasized the weakened position of both the citizens and their leader. Nevertheless, a depiction of the people confronting a tyrannical head of state would have resonated with a U.S. audience. Few Americans realized, however, that bourgeois members of the *Bund Deutscher Frauenvereine* (German women's associations, or BDF), far from poking kitchen implements at their Kaiser, heartily defended him in the face of his ouster (see below).[57]

Woodrow Wilson encouraged displays of faith in the German people, as opposed to their guilty leaders. As commander in chief, the president prepared Americans to accept that the war was over by rhetorically separating Germany's leaders from their people. In his speeches he stopped identifying Germany as "enemy" and "opponent" and began imbuing Germans with traits similar to those embodied by his fellow countrymen (a goal he shared with those who wanted to remake the Germans in the American image).[58] Individual freedom—a condition he believed Americans valued—had been usurped by Germany's autocrats, who had forced their people into war. Germany "has surrendered to the world," Wilson declared, "she has said 'our fate is in your hands. We are ready to do what you tell us to do.'"[59] Indeed, he had indicated in his War Message in 1917 that "the existence of autocratic governments backed by organized force . . . is controlled wholly by their will, not by the will of their people . . . we have no quarrel with the German people . . . We are . . . the sincere friends of the German people, and shall desire nothing so much as the early reestablishment of intimate relations of mutual advantage between us."[60] Wilson hoped to transition Americans from enmity toward Germans (a hostility that, admittedly, his own propaganda machine— George Creel's Committee for Public Information—had helped provoke) to at least an acceptance of reconciliation between the former foes.[61]

Unfortunately for the president, Creel did his job perhaps better than expected, and the commander in chief faced a militant attitude toward Germany among his countrymen in a midterm election year. For that reason he disguised his conciliatory tone toward German peace overtures with more bellicose language in October 1918.[62] Still, Wilson never fundamentally departed from his overall position that Germans were not responsible for the destruction of the war and ought not to be punished (though he remained convinced that Germany was guilty of instigating the war).[63] His primary motive in the armistice agreement and the treaty negotiations was to support democratic elements in German society by encouraging the enemy to join his family of nations. The statesman prepared his fellow countrymen to participate in the regeneration of the adversary by assuring Americans that the Germans were ready for their forgiveness.[64]

Historian Albert Bushnell Hart, writing in the January 1919 issue of *The Forum*, agreed that the enemy needed rebirthing, but he based his argument on his belief that all Germans were responsible for the war. Hart asserted that an "orderly world" could not be created until Germany could be made to take her place in the postwar world. "Only, that means the regeneration of Germany," he opined, "which demands, first of all, a new type of political organization, and after that a *fresh variety* of German people."[65] An *Outlook* editorial likewise jumped on the regeneration bandwagon. "When autocracy was apparently triumphant," the magazine declared, "Germans generally applauded its cruelty and brutality toward other peoples; now that it is crushed, what is needed is not only a change in the form of government but an utter reversal of that spirit of barbarism and inhumanity from which not even all German Socialists have refrained."[66]

Like that of George Harvey, Hart's primary evidence for demonstrating the depths of German barbarism involved their crimes against women. No Germans had protested against the murder of British nurse and humanitarian Edith Cavell, Hart claimed, nor against "the daily, habitual pollution of helpless women" by German soldiers.[67] A group of New York women concurred with the historian's view that the rape of women was

Germany's worst offense. They organized the Committee for the Protection of Women under International Law shortly after the armistice to insure that women in the next war would not experience what European women had endured at the hands of the "Hun." The group resolved that "whatever in the present war would or might stand as a precedent for these dangerous villainies in any future wars be met and broken by the counterprecedent [sic] of trial . . . of every officer, soldier, or civilian of either of the Central Powers . . . who shall be accused . . . of any offense against a woman."[68]

In "Leaves from a Coblenz Diary," published in the July–August 1919 issue of the *Atlantic Monthly*, American writer Louis Graves imagined a conversation overheard by a German apothecary who had been forced to house two U.S. soldiers in Coblenz. The doughboys make assumptions about the nature of the German character based on their host's mistreatment of his wife.

> "Treats his wife like a dog."
> "She's a nice sort of woman. Hard luck to be hooked up to a thing like him, eh?"
> "If we could stay here and train the children, there wouldn't be any left like him after about fifty years."
> "You're right. And Germany'll never be any good till they get rid of his kind."

Graves interpreted the American occupation as an opportunity to teach German men how to treat women properly rather than abuse them, as was their usual practice. He had rather high expectations about what the occupation could accomplish to alter what he saw as the inherently flawed character of the entire nation's population.[69] Americans viewed crimes against women as a primary sign that Germans needed to change their *Kultur*.

The drive to repair the German temperament intensified as the vanquished began soliciting economic aid from the victors. Officially, the armistice had called for the continuation of the blockade of German ports, although, in vague language, the document did require the Allies and Americans to "give consideration to the provisioning of Germany during the armistice to the extent recognized as necessary."[70] Two German women drew Americans' attention to the impoverished conditions existing in the war-weary nation. BDF president Gertrude Bäumer and member Alice Salomon wired the president's wife Edith Wilson and

Jane Addams, begging the two, "who are mothers like ourselves," to ask the U.S. government and allied governments to repeal the blockade provision of the armistice.[71] The *New York Times* published the missives. Doubting the women's veracity, the Women's National Committee of the American Defense Society charged that the telegrams were simply more German propaganda and instructed Wilson and Addams to ignore the messages.[72] In a similar vein, Dr. Wilhelm Solf, the German Foreign Secretary, pleaded with President Wilson to intervene in Germany's food shortage.[73] For some Americans, German wartime atrocities—including the alleged rape of French and Belgian women—stood in stark contrast to the former enemy's pleadings for mercy in the face of the economic blockade and proved too great a stumbling block barring the granting of food aid to the former enemy. Others used a tit-for-tat yardstick to measure the worthiness of the Germans' pleadings. "Some anxiety has been expressed by individuals and newspapers lest a sentimental desire to feed the German people would make us forget the sufferings of those peoples whom the Germans have starved," wrote one *Outlook* editorial. "We do not think Americans need to be anxious about this matter. The overwhelming desire of the people of the United States is to feed their suffering allies first and to help the Germans afterwards." One of the reasons that the United States should hesitate to feed famished Germans, argued the *Outlook*, was that the defeated nation had shown no repentance. "Since the Armistice was signed nothing has happened showing any regret for Germany's barbarism," wrote the *Outlook* editor. "The appeal to President Wilson from . . . Secretary Solf contains no word of repentance. Nor does the appeal of the German women to Mrs. Wilson and Miss Addams, which naively implores them to procure 'a change in the terms of the armistice so that the long suffering of the women and children of Germany may not end in unspeakable disaster.' The sufferings of the Germans have been brought upon themselves by themselves," proclaimed the editor in a self-righteous tone, although he warned ominously that if the former adversary goes hungry anarchy would result.[74] Whereas Harvey and Hart demanded to see a regenerated enemy, the *Outlook* editorial ratcheted the requirement up a notch by making repentance a condition for providing aid.

Alleviating suffering became equated with a sentimental, mushy-headed response to the question of what to do with the Germans, while a vengeful response represented a manly, rational answer to the dilemma among politicians and in the popular press. In November 1918, for example, the

Independent reprinted a cartoon from the *London Evening News* in which the artist personified German *Kultur* as a hypermasculine man and a forgiving sentiment as an emasculated dandy. The drawing shows an apish helmeted German carrying a club at his side (rather than in the air, indicating that German militarism had been subdued by the U.S. and Allied war effort, though not yet obliterated). The brute's devilish instincts are symbolized by the pointed tail lying at his side. Next to him stands an effeminate-looking man holding a long scroll titled "Bill Against the Huns." The man holds out his top hat, which the cartoonist labeled "Be-Kind-To-Huns-Crank." "Pity the Poor Hun!" reads the caption. "'We mustn't ask him to pay the bill,' whines the sentimentalist. 'It's such a big one.'" The cartoonist implied that the sentimentalists' reason for simply forgiving the Germans for their sins—that there were too many to enumerate—in fact justifies the demands of those insisting that Germany pay up.[75] Similarly, Senator Lodge, addressing an armistice celebration in New York City, urged the nation to show "no sentimentality to German people, who are to blame for war." Speaking again at the Capitol, the Republican advised his fellow Senators to not allow their resolve against Germany to be "weakened by sentimentality" at the peace table.[76]

The American professor and writer Gerald Stanley Lee, arguing in favor of regenerating the Germans, invoked gendered images most stridently in his *Saturday Evening Post* article "Bloodthirsty Angels: An Inquiry into How Americans Can Get On with Germans." Lee began his rumination by recounting a conversation he had on the street with an old friend.

> "What do you think we ought to do in the way of making terms with the Germans?" I said.
>
> He looked at me a little doubtfully a second. "I don't quite like to tell people just how I feel about settling up for this war with the Germans. Probably you'd call me bloodthirsty." "Got called bloodthirsty myself the other day—and by a colonel," I said.
>
> I said this a little boastfully, I am afraid.[77]

Lee indicated that although his friend felt sheepish about his vindictive attitudes toward the Germans, he equated such a position with manly strength. Lee employed the trope of "men angels" to represent Americans who insist on punitive terms for the Germans. Men angels—unlike sentimental women angels—considered the war with Germany rationally and demanded that the peace result in "spiritual satisfaction" for the victors. Such recompense could only be obtained through eliminating the fatally flawed German character. Fighting the "Hun" to a finish would have been the best way to accomplish this, wrote Lee, but since a cease-fire had been signed, the writer demanded the right to remake the enemy's character through punishing peace terms. "The only way we can make *a man's job* of ending the war is to take the eighty million Germans," he argued, ". . . [and] deal with them as the people who are responsible for this war."[78] Lee branded President Wilson's terms of reconciliation "sentimental," "muddle-headed," and "hazy," and the author drew sharp distinctions between *feelings* of magnanimity toward Germany, versus his own approach: rational and level headed. American writers like Lee used gendered language to persuade Americans that a vengeful reconciliation against the former enemy would save the world from the sentimental soppiness of an effeminate culture. Reconciliation for him meant simply reinforcing the American victory through manly strength and resolve.

Texas attorney William J. Moroney turned the tables on Gerald Stanley Lee—and others arguing for a punitive treaty—by promoting lenient treatment of Germany not as a weak response to the question of what to do with the Germans but as a strong, rational, and therefore manly response. Specifically, the Texan argued in opposition to extracting from Germany a formal admission of moral responsibility for the war, a condition that Americans demanding that Germans be regenerated insisted upon. "In both law and morale an involuntary confession is without probative effect," he explained in legalistic terms. "To force such a confession from Germany would be plausibly construed as manifesting either a purpose to impose humiliation, which would have only pernicious results, or a consciousness *of such weakness* in our own evidence as to need the support of 'third degree' methods to make out our case." Moroney perceived the demand from Americans such as George Harvey, Albert Bushnell Hart, and Lee (that Germans admit to and do penance for wartime atrocities) as signaling a "lack of confidence." The rational way to demonstrate responsibility for atrocities is to bring forth evidence against the perpetrators. Moroney, who considered the German people apart from their leaders, acknowledged that citizens did support their government in its prosecution of the war; however, he could find no proof that citizens had sanctioned atrocities that were not admitted as part of the recognized rules of war.[79]

New Yorker Heinrich Charles applied the same principles of strong, rational, and manly honor in his letter to Secretary of State Charles Evans Hughes arguing against a ruinous treaty. "I have the utmost confidence in you, Mr. Secretary, as a chivalrous, honest and straightforward gentleman," wrote Charles, "who never will consent of compelling a prostrate people, anxious to resume friendly relations with the American nation, to plead guilty under duress to an alleged crime of which they think they are innocent and in which belief practically all well-informed and fair-minded persons the world over concur."[80] Charles pointed out that guilt could not be established until and unless each of the belligerent governments opened up their archives to allow scholars to thoroughly investigate, in as detached and rational a manner as possible, the way that the war had begun in 1914. Charles, writing in 1921, noted that Berlin, Vienna, and St. Petersburg had already made their governmental papers available to scholars, but that London and Washington, D.C. had not. As an example of the inability to determine with certainty which nation was responsible for starting the war, Charles cited David Lloyd George, who, after reading memoirs and books written in the various countries of what had transpired before August 1914, concluded that no one had really meant to start a war. "'It was something into which they glided, or, rather staggered and stumbled perhaps through folly; a discussion I have no doubt, would have averted it.'" Charles lent credibility to his missive by noting that his two sons, both of whom had seen trench warfare in France, reinforced his opinion.[81]

Moroney and Charles argued that taking a rational approach to the question of what to do with the Germans—the same approach Lee claimed to be taking—would mean dismissing the question of guilt because it could not yet be ascertained due to limited evidence. Furthermore, Moroney argued that the United States should treat Germany as it had treated other nations (Spain, following the Spanish-American War) in the same condition. Charles pointed out that punishing a prostrate people did not demonstrate the manly virtue of chivalry but chivalry's opposite: barbarity. Both men equated power with justice rather than with military might. Another New Yorker, Kemper Fullerton, agreed. "We propose to compel Germany, because we have the whip-hand, to renounce the claims which we admit that she can properly make, and then leave it to the conscience of the American people to treat her fairly," he wrote. "Why do we not treat her fairly in the first place?"[82]

In addition to pointing out the futility of imposing a war guilt clause on the defeated, Americans opposing a harsh treaty cited atrocities committed by occupation troops on German women as reason to denounce the occupation and its continuation under a punitive treaty. Disavowal of the American presence in the Rhineland signaled a desire to withdraw from Germany and from European affairs. While offering the vanquished sympathy, Oswald Garrison Villard and his colleagues at *The Nation* argued that what the United States should do with the Germans is withdraw from Coblenz and simply to stay away from them (see below). A harsh peace treaty threatened to involve the United States more, not less, in European affairs.[83]

But the Treaty of Versailles proclaimed Germany's guilt in instigating the conflagration and demanded war reparations (disappointing both Moroney and Charles). It outlined the formation of a Reparations Commission that would oversee German indemnities, it called for a system for administering Germany's former colonies whereby Allied nations would act as mandates, and—to the disgust of Villard—it required a fifteen-year military occupation of the Rhineland, all of which required further U.S. involvement in Europe. The League of Nations clauses were the only survivors of Woodrow Wilson's Fourteen Points.[84] Though the treaty proved too harsh for some progressive clergy (the *Christian Century* proclaimed the terms not redemptive, and therefore un-Christian), the Federal Council of Churches endorsed the League as an application of Christian principles to international relations and as an opportunity to build the Kingdom of God on earth. Wilson's speech before the Senate as he delivered the treaty for ratification praised the document as God's doing; the negotiators were merely tools in His hands.[85] The president embarked on a speaking tour in the summer of 1919 to persuade the public of the treaty's advantages. His pontifications reflected primarily his hopes for world peace via international cooperation in the League of Nations. The tour, cut short by the president's illness, represented the greatest effort at educating public opinion on a foreign policy matter that any U.S. president had ever attempted. Most contemporary and historical assessors of the excursion regarded audience response to it as evidence of the public's enthusiasm for the treaty and the League. But as Wilson's Secretary of War, Newton Baker noted wryly, the tour's effect on the Senate was negligible.[86]

Critics in the Senate interpreted the League of Nations provisions as likely to weaken the United States' strength—proven recently in the Great War—and they romanticized and feminized the idea of international alliances to emphasize how the treaty would emasculate American power. A cartoon in the April 1919 issue of *Current History*, for example, portrays Uncle Sam being wooed by a pleading female figure. "Won't you be my mandate?" the scantily clad harem girl implores, while the leering, hapless Uncle points to his picture of Columbia and sputters, "Gosh, lady, my family wouldn't understand!" "Entangling Alliances," reads the caption: these were feminine traps to be avoided if Uncle Sam's loyalty to his true sweetheart, the United States, is to remain strong. In another cartoon, titled "The Hobble Skirt," Uncle Sam wears a long skirt made up of the flags of the League of Nations' member states (the U.S. flag hangs at the bottom of the skirt). "It may be stylish and all that," mutters Uncle Sam, "But I'd never be able to get my stride!" The artist used a female article of clothing to mock the frivolity of the perceived feminine need to be stylish, and thereby feminized and interpreted as weak, the ensnaring alliances that the League of Nations Covenant required. The entanglements, the artist feared, would hobble America's manhood and nationhood (see Figure 3.1).[87] Indeed, the U.S. Senate rejected the treaty for the second time in the fall of 1919 based primarily on the inclusion of the League of Nations and on Article X, which prescribed the use of collective security to combat territorial aggression on any member state, provisions

The Hobble Skirt

Figure 3.1 "It may be stylish and all that, but I'd never be able to get my stride!" Cartoon of Uncle Sam by C. A. Bronstrup, *San Francisco Chronicle*, reprinted in *Current History* 10 (May 1919): 373

that it believed compromised American sovereignty and power. Senator Albert J. Beveridge felt that the League threatened the nation's manhood in particular. The League was the work of "amiable old male 'grannies' who, over their afternoon tea," he harrumphed, "are planning to denationalize America and denationalize the nation's manhood."[88]

The Treaty of Berlin, U.S. Pragmatism, and the Demand for Morality in Foreign Relations

When U.S. Senators blocked passage of the treaty, the newspaper edited by soldiers of the U.S. Army of Occupation, the *Amaroc*, responded with cynicism and a sense of betrayal. German newspapers "advertise the fact that the U.S. Senate does not want to accept that which the Sons of America fought, bled, and died for," complained one editorial. American doughboys seemed ready to extend their own and their country's engagement in world affairs as a guarantee of peace. "To fight the League," admonished another writer, "just because it will place certain responsibilities upon the United States is a very poor excuse . . . responsibility is a very small price to pay for the insurance of peace." The paper further disparaged the notion that peace could be maintained via traditional balance-of-power strategies.[89]

But most Senators eschewed further involvement in Europe's business. The rejection of the peace treaty by the United States ushered in what David M. Kennedy has called the most intensely isolationist period in American history; others have argued that the term is incongruous with U.S. foreign policy.[90] Wishing to refrain from foreign affairs but eager to encourage trade, some Senators spurned the treaty and then immediately began working to facilitate an economic relationship between the two still officially hostile nations, making pragmatism a more accurate term. Senator Philander C. Knox introduced the Knox-Porter Resolution in May 1920 to achieve that goal. President Wilson vetoed the bill and an override vote failed. When President Harding delivered his first address to Congress in the spring of 1921, however, he indicated a willingness to sign the measure. He did so on July 2. The agreement claimed for America all the rights and indemnities awarded to it under the armistice and Treaty of Versailles. The Knox-Porter Resolution required Germany's acceptance before the war between the two countries would officially be over.

In order for the United States to have its cake and eat it too—to renew a trade relationship with Germany and to claim what it wanted and shun what it did not under the Treaty of Versailles, without incurring the wrath of its Allies—Harding's Secretary of State Charles Evans Hughes worked with German Minister of Foreign Affairs Friedrich Rosen, and the American Commissioner in Germany, Ellis Loring Dresel, on a peace treaty in July. Historians Sally Marks and Denis Dulude interpreted Dresel's position in Berlin as highly unusual in the history of foreign relations. Hughes insisted that the United States could not conduct official business with a belligerent nation, so all correspondence had to be routed through neutral Spain. The Secretary of State gave Dresel explicit orders to transmit the Knox-Porter Resolution to the Germans and communicate their reactions back to him, and in addition to ascertain whether the United States' allies would object to the separate peace: business normally conducted by a diplomat. The "unofficial official" way in which the Treaty of Berlin arrived at the table for signatures signaled not only the pragmatism of the Harding Administration but also its desire to maintain distance between the United States and European affairs. (The United States continued its hands-off manner until the Treaty of Versailles was largely dismantled at the end of the decade. For example, American financier Charles G. Dawes was only permitted to chair an American and Allied investigation regarding Germany's reparations payments in 1924 as a private citizen, and not as a representative of the U.S. government.) Blurring the separation between the official and the unofficial enabled Dresel to buoy American political and economic strength by retaining a hard line against an unrepentant Germany (by not dealing directly with German diplomats) and by assuring American industrialists that German markets were once again open for business. To appease its allies the United States offered Germany nothing contrary to the Versailles agreement.[91]

The Treaty of Berlin incorporated those portions of Versailles—sections I of part 4 and all of parts 5, 6, 8–12, 14, and 15—that enumerated the privileges accorded to the Allies. With at least a nod to Germany's rights, Hughes added a clause declaring that the United States would claim its rights as the victor in the late war but do so "in a manner consistent with the rights accorded to Germany under such provisions."[92] As incentive, Hughes offered the Germans immediate resumption of diplomatic relations in exchange for its signature. The official reconciliation, underscored by the words of the treaty's preamble, "Treaty between the United States and Germany Restoring Friendly Relations," was signed during a ten-minute ceremony in Berlin on August 25, 1921. It was a smashing American diplomatic victory to follow up the vaunted military one. In effect, the document drove jagged-edged nails into Wilsonian idealism. "In this business-like document is no repudiation of submarine warfare, no guaranty of neutral rights in future wars," lamented *The Nation*'s editors. "There is nothing to suggest that our part in this war is ended by the triumph of the lofty ends which those who bade us fight told us made war holy."[93] The Treaty of Berlin marked the domination and authority of business in American society and in U.S. foreign policy in the new decade, a position endorsed by Protestant churches. Church publications of the period either remained silent on issues related to money and materialism or quietly sanctioned commercial values. From the labor perspective, the Treaty of Berlin left European and American resources firmly in the hands of the capitalists and simply marked a return to the status quo ante bellum.[94] For its part, Germany reluctantly signed the agreement because it still considered the United States its only hope of normalizing relations with its former belligerents and because it sought the resumption of trade (see Chapter 1). The Germans signed the Treaty of Berlin because they needed help, and the Americans continued to be the only powerful nation capable of—and at least partially willing to—offer them anything.

For their part, Americans responding to the Treaty of Berlin interpreted it either by using traditional wartime language of victory and vengeance or as a pragmatic way to end tensions that hindered trade relations. Commentators voiced concerns over how the United States' allies might perceive the separate peace made with Germany, the likely economic benefits that Americans might enjoy as a result of reestablishing friendly relations with Germany, and finally how the settlement appeared to treat the former enemy. Herbert Hoover, supplier of bread to hungry Germans, nevertheless argued to Secretary of State Hughes against a separate peace with Germany that would heighten already strained relations among the United States and its allies.[95] Frank N. Putnam, who described himself as a lifelong Republican and loyal American, agreed: "Division and discord [among the Allies] is what the 'Hun' desires and is striving for and if gained will become an asset to that nation of treacherous and inhuman people."[96] The National Disabled Soldiers League viewed the pending treaty as a victory for the Germans and therefore a slap in the face to soldiers who had fought against German *Kultur*. Its resolution insisted that "our sacrifice shall not be in vain and that the United States senate will not disgrace us by making a separate peace with Germany, [and] be it further resolved that Germany shall receive no milder terms than those dictated by the Allied generals on armistice day at Belgium."[97]

On the other hand, Wilson Guthrie understood the treaty as vital to the health of American capitalism. "It is absolutely essential, if American industry is to recover, that peace be rapidly made with Germany, and Germany will be a great source of outlet for much of our food products and raw materials, as well as certain lines of manufactured materials, and, unless we take prompt action in this matter, Great Britain and other countries will take advantage of this tremendous market to the exclusion of our own firms." Guthrie perceived Great Britain not as a wartime ally whose needs had to be appeased but as an economic competitor to be bested.[98]

E. F. Thompson, also writing in favor of the treaty, described not the Germans but the French as the most worrisome of Europe's peoples, and he mistakenly assumed a treaty would end the American occupation of the Rhineland. "The American people want their Knox resolution adopted and our boys from Germany brought home. France will keep those beasts there," he wrote, alluding to the colonial troops employed by the French army. "It is useless for [Ferdinand] Foch to deny the awful things they do in raping women. I have been in Germany and know the German women."[99] Thompson referred to the alleged rape of women by French colonial soldiers in the occupied territories (see Chapter 2).

Oswald Garrison Villard, German-born son of railroad magnate Henry Villard, also called for the return of American doughboys. He, too, worried about French colonial soldiers' presence in the Rhine, but he advocated tearing up the Treaty of Versailles and ending the entire American and Allied military occupation as an answer to the question of what to do with the Germans. In July and August 1922, well after both treaties had been signed, Villard valiantly continued Woodrow Wilson's quest for a peace without victory that the Treaty of Versailles had clearly repudiated. Politicians, he wrote, should not be sidetracked by the need to reinforce their victory or by the desire to regenerate the Germans. "Victory would mean peace forced upon the loser, a victor's terms imposed upon the vanquished," he wrote, echoing Moroney's thoughts. "It would be accepted in humiliation, under duress, at an intolerable sacrifice, and would leave a sting, a resentment, a bitter memory upon which terms of peace would rest not permanently but only as upon quicksand." Furthermore, Allied control of Germany through the occupation was hurting the new German government and its economy.[100]

While writers such as Albert Bushnell Hart and Gerald Stanley Lee based their arguments for regenerating Germans on the belief that they were not sufficiently contrite, Villard claimed that what rankled the Germans was not their defeat in war but what had happened to them since their surrender. "It will please our vindictive Americans, I am sure, to hear it, for I meet many Americans who ask me whether the Germans know that they are beaten and are willing to admit it and if they admit that they are ground down in the dust and properly licked," he wrote sarcastically. "I should not have to answer these questions if the questioners were to visit the occupied territory."[101] Villard particularly condemned the occupied zone for what he termed its prostitution-based economy. The French, he argued, constructed brothels in every village in their territory; one *Bürgermeister* (mayor) who refused to provide a building for the business was booted from his office (Villard admitted, however, that German men partook of the women's services, too). To keep the brothels operating efficiently, a percentage of profit went back into city coffers.

Local women, according to Villard, had few economic choices left to them in occupied Germany. Either they were safely married and provided for by a husband or father or they were forced to succumb to selling their only asset. "The German women who called my attention to this particular house [of prostitution] told me . . . that they were compelled to ask themselves whether the sacrifice of those fifteen girls [who were working as prostitutes] did not save the rest of them from the possibility of attack by the colored and white soldiers who, torn away from their families, are peculiarly subject to temptation."[102] Villard's mention of the "Rhineland Horror" (see Chapter 2) indicated that he believed the occupation was to blame for the illicit sex taking place in brothels.[103] Male soldiers—regardless of race—could not be expected to behave properly under such circumstances. Villard's righteous female companions, who were not working at the bordellos, could remain untarnished by the black hand of prostitution because unattached women serviced men's perceived needs. Prostitutes thus saved "good" German girls from inevitable disaster in such conditions. For Villard, the occupation had ruined Germany's chances at creating a righteous democratic society by tainting it with an immoral economy.

Mary Lee's account of the occupation dramatized the immoral treatment of German women by soldiers and mirrored Villard's disillusionment with the peace treaties. Lee's protagonist Anne Wentworth's experiences in France and Germany—based on the author's own wartime work—enabled her to cut through the romantic view of the war that blinded the perspective of her stateside countrymen. For Wentworth, the occupation of Germany provided the final blow to any sense of the war having saved European society from autocracy. The YMCA canteen hostess visits a hospital in the U.S. zone of occupation and sees the tortured body of a young German woman writhing about on the waiting room floor. She asks the other patients what ails the suffering woman, but they only respond by mumbling the word "fraternizing." Wentworth thinks to herself, "If this treaty would only make the world safe . . . Keep the world safe from Armies of Occupation. . . . "[104] For many proponents of a lenient peace treaty, the problems Germany experienced were due not to Germany's defeat but to the postwar military occupation.

While Lee recorded the deleterious effects of the occupation, Louis Graves' "Leaves from a Coblenz Diary" viewed the "watch on the Rhine" as an opportunity to regenerate the enemy. Graves' intent was to communicate to the *Atlantic*'s readers what the German people were really like and therefore what should be done about them. The "diary" reinforced the conventional wartime wisdom regarding Germans and their *Kultur*: that Germans were unflinchingly loyal to their government and its military regardless of its obvious defeat in the war and that they were a deeply deceptive people who had superficially welcomed the American occupiers because they hoped by doing so to reduce the impact of their military loss at Versailles (even as underneath they thought American soldiers effeminate, simple-minded, and therefore easily duped). Most disturbing to the apothecary, as Graves imagines him, is that American doughboys were ruining German society by influencing German beasts-of-burden women to liberate themselves from their chauvinistic husbands. But Graves ended his diary by predicting that ultimately the American presence in Germany would not change the unalterable flaw in the German character—blind faith in the righteousness of Prussian militarism and German civilization. The occupation alone would not be enough to alter the German character.[105]

In the summer and fall of 1921, the public discourse regarding the question of what to do with the Germans began to revolve around the occupation, which, perplexingly, the Treaty of Berlin did not address at all. Congressmen, too, used pragmatic language to demand the pullout of the American Forces in Germany (AFG). Senator Hiram Johnson threatened to introduce a bill requiring the immediate troop withdrawal if President Harding would not act. Senator William Borah demanded that the secretary of war publish the size, cost, and indebtedness of the Army of Occupation. When the secretary disclosed that Germany owed the United States about $240 million for hosting doughboys on the Rhine, Johnson demanded that the troops be brought home. Senator James A. Reed feared that keeping the soldiers on the Rhine signaled that the United States would ultimately join the League of Nations. Other lawmakers countered that the United States needed to maintain troops in Germany to prevent its late enemy from resurging. Senator Frank Walsh, on the other hand, argued that the American military was needed to protect Germany from the aggressiveness of its French neighbor.[106] Nevertheless, the AFG departed the Rhineland in January 1923.

Thus in public discourses in the United States from the November armistice to the AFG withdrawal (Moroney, Charles, Villard, and Mary Lee notwithstanding), Americans signaled their willingness to treat the Germans severely in order to regenerate them. The German military's abuse of women during the Great War reinforced Americans' perceptions of Teutonic brutality and figured prominently in their reasons for demanding punitive treatment. A harsh treaty forced Germany to acknowledge its guilt and therefore accept war reparations. Both moves were designed to wash clean the sins of the former foe through confession first, followed by penance. By creating a settlement that mirrored the Treaty of Versailles the United States reinforced its military victory with a diplomatic success designed to enhance its own political and economic power, lending credence to Americans' sense of their nation's exceptionalism. For the same reason, lawmakers rejected participation in the League of Nations because they viewed the "entangling alliances" that the nation had avoided in its past as proving its exceptionalism, which in turn bolstered its power. Joining the League would undercut this sacrosanct myth. The official reconciliation thus reflected the majority of Americans' responses to the question of what to do with the Germans. Those who argued the opposite—that a democratic Germany could not be gained by exacting confession and reparations—were branded effeminate sentimentalists bent on emasculating American power and prestige instead of enhancing it.

The Versailles Treaty in International Perspective

In the end, the Versailles Treaty, as Sally Marks has noted, proved too much of a compromise between polar opposite positions. "Wilsonian idealism and French fright" made for an unworkable compromise, and a powerfully aggrieved Germany, determined to break free of treaty-imposed restrictions to its sovereignty, disrupted any tranquility that may have developed in 1919.[107] Too harsh to reconcile Germany with its foes, the peace was at the same time too lenient to weaken it and prevent it from regaining its prewar status. Negotiators left Germany surrounded by vulnerable states that (in some cases) included large minority populations of German people.[108] Representing the nationalism that existed within their own borders, Versailles negotiators missed the formidable nationalism that persisted in the enemy.

While punishing Germany politically and spiritually, the terms left open the possibility of German economic recovery, at least in the long run. Indeed, according to the Russian revolutionary Vladimir Lenin, the settlement represented a capitalist collaboration between the United States and Germany to snuff out Bolshevism (an interpretation seconded by Marxist historians subsequently).[109] Geographically, treaty makers took pains to retain Europe's economic units at the expense of ethnic homogeneity in the case of the Polish Corridor and parts of Czechoslovakia. France may have been appeased by these settlements, had they been enforced, but implementation depended upon the unity of vision of the victors, and such harmony as existed evaporated during the Ruhr Crisis. Furthermore, the German people convinced themselves that they had won the war, according to Marks; therefore, any loss of territory or reparations requirements seemed unjust (see Chapter 5).[110] In addition, they felt tricked by Wilson and his Fourteen Points into accepting the armistice. Deemed an outcast nation, Germany had been allowed no input into the settlement, so from its perspective the treaty seemed dictatorial in the extreme.[111] In the end, Wilson's hopes for integrating Germany into a peaceful family of nations had failed. The Weimar government thus gazed unreconciled (some Americans would have said, unregenerated) upon the peace settlement; nearly all Germans denounced it.[112]

For the most part, the enemy displayed little desire for the redemption offered them by U.S. politicians and intellectuals. Instead, bourgeois German women decided to direct their countrymen's spiritual rebirthing themselves. Aside from the radical wing of the women's movement (see Chapter 4) and other German pacifists, most Weimar Germans sought to regain their nation's power and prestige rather than do penance for a wrong they did not perceive to be theirs. When terms of the agreement were revealed in May 1919, German women's organizations—the BDF and women's religious organizations, and women's committees of all the major political parties from the nonsocialist left to the extreme right—quickly mobilized in dissent. The protests they launched drew attention to the spirited nationalism that continued to motivate and animate Weimar Germans after the war ended. Women's protests emphasized their concerns for their nation and specifically for the moral well-being of their country. Their rhetoric and actions staked out a space for female participation in foreign policy, and it illustrated the intersections of nationalism and maternalism and of foreign policy and morality. Like the Americans that blended morality with U.S. foreign policy, German women activists claimed to be the principled force behind reinvigorating their country's nationalism and its foreign policy.[113]

Female protesters did not wait until the peace settlement to publicize their disgust with the conduct of the United States and its allies. The BDF interpreted Wilson's peace note of December 18, 1916 as an attempt to drive a wedge between the Kaiser and his people, and they sent the American leader a letter in protest. Additionally, as treaty terms were announced, they publicized the fact that (at least in their minds) German women would support any efforts to resist a punitive treaty and a league of nations that, in their words, "would be built on trampled German honor."[114]

The variety of events that the women protested reflected the women's underlying motives. As activists insisted on their duty to deploy their femininity in service to the nation, they paradoxically continued to advocate the home as women's highest calling.[115] Arguing from the basis of women's moral superiority, sprung from their positions in the domestic sphere, the BDF demonstrated against the expatriation of the Kaiser and the other 900 men the Allies branded as war criminals because their punishment would break up the German family. Women traveled to Upper Silesia to succor German families supposedly suffering under the Polish flag, and they joined the campaign against the Rhineland Horror (see Chapter 2).[116] They protested the delivery of 810,000 German *milch* cows to France as war reparation; the measure, they argued, would amount to infanticide in their homeland. The *Frauenausschuss zur Bekämpfung der Schuldlüge* (Women's Committee to Combat the War Guilt Lie) and the *Nationaler Frauenausschuss zum Kampf gegen Versailles* (National Women's Committee for the Fight against Versailles) both claimed that the next generation of Germans should not be reared under the auspices of treaty-induced humiliation and sunken morale.[117]

Morality in foreign policy became the cornerstone of the women's activism, and they were quick to note the injustices caused by the German military (though in this they were not always united). Despite their allegiances to the German Kaiser, for example, they shunned what they saw as needless shame brought on by his warriors. The BDF resolved that the resettlement of French women during Germany's occupation of the Lille coalfields had been an error. The organization also took a stand against anti-Semitism, although prejudice against Jews pervaded the rhetoric of their partners in the right-wing *Deutschnationale Volkspartei* (German National People's Party, or DNVP).[118]

In some respects, the actions taken by the BDF and its allies served to moderate the guilt induced by the stab-in-the-back legend (which held that the German homefront, where women presided, had caused the defeat).[119] But others, such as Rosa Kempf, chair of the Bavarian Women's Committee of the German Democratic Party, refused to accept the guilty charge. She asserted that since German women had not been physically engaged in brutal battle, only they could provide the moral fortitude necessary to redeem their nation from its loss. In addition, Amélie Roth, founding member of the Women's Committee to Combat the War Guilt Lie, believed that only women could save Germany from men's inherent destructiveness. During the war, housewives had had a say in what households could bear; Roth reasoned that they now had a stake in the peace. By shaping foreign policies, she and her colleagues aimed to set standards for morality around the world.[120]

On the one hand, the German women's political activism achieved its goal: it created a rationale for women's active participation in wartime and postwar foreign policy, as opposed to women simply being passed along to the victors as "booty." On the other hand, their moralistic stance encouraged the traditional "separate spheres" notion—that women were the spiritual and moral sex, whereas men were naturally practical and businesslike—that the progressive MRFM tried to obliterate in the United States. The women's activism signaled the tenacity of nationalism, perhaps unexpected among the defeated, in a world destined to become ever more international (despite the United States' presumed isolationism) in the coming decades.

The German women's protests provided evidence for historians looking for the interplay between morality and foreign policy. Despite the shift to isolationism, U.S. theologians such as Henry Sloane Coffin, Charles D. Williams, and John Buckham looked toward a future time when Christian principles would once again drive international relations. They continued their support for Wilsonian internationalism and idealism—along with commentators such as William J. Moroney, Oswald Garrison Villard, and writers such as Mary Lee—into the 1920s. Sounding rather like Wilson himself in his 1921 Armistice Day speech at Arlington Cemetery, President Warren G. Harding—the isolationist—sounded a new call for Americans to put the world back on a higher plane.[121]

Historians of foreign relations have often dismissed efforts to find agreeable moral standards on which to base foreign policy as being "idealistic," and not "realistic." Yet, as George F. Kennan (himself a realist) has demonstrated, U.S. foreign policymakers can both act on principle and have the nation's interests—without the arrogance of American exceptionalism—in mind.[122] The ruminations on international cooperation as a guarantor of peace in the *Amaroc* and on fair treatment for the Germans in epistles written by the New Yorker Kemper Fullerton and others demonstrated the disconnect between people's sense of idealism and the absence of idealism in the Treaty of Berlin; this disconnect may help explain the postwar disillusionment expressed by Villard's colleagues at the *Nation* and by many others.

Among the disillusioned were a group of international women pacifists from the Allied and Central powers nations waiting in anxious anticipation for the travel documents that would allow them to meet in a neutral country just as negotiations were winding down at the French palace. These activists channeled their feelings of disgust and betrayal at the way scores were being settled by officials into their own document of postwar reconciliation. The principles the pacifists based their settlement on reflected their thoughts on international relations and the transnational nature of the problems of hunger, exploitation, and power politics that they thought the world could do without.

4
Women Activists in the Postwar World
Gender, Reconciliation, and Humanitarian Aid

As men representing France, Britain, Italy, the United States, and other countries each played their hands to win their nation's advantage at the Paris peace table in the spring of 1919, German and American newspaper and magazine editors depicted peacefulness nearly universally as a feminine figure in the numerous cartoons and drawings displayed between their covers. One German cartoon, for example, shows a crestfallen peace angel waving an olive branch as she sits next to an equally morose German peasant. The duo has been shut out of the conference room at Versailles; neither pacifists nor the defeated enemy would be allowed to join in the fashioning of the postwar world.[1] In the United States, readers opened their newspapers to see an ethereal washerwoman labeled "peace conference" bent over her washtub scrubbing Bolshevism, German frightfulness, and Italian claims across her washboard.[2] The League of Nations, an organization designed to help avert international conflicts in the postwar world, frequently wears a skirt in both German and American cartoons.[3] The idea that peacefulness was a feminine quality appeared to be a commonly held notion in the early twentieth century.

However, Americans often clashed with each other as to which gender could make war and which should act as the true arbiter of peace. Both Germany and the United States had conducted a total war by sending their male citizens to battle and by enticing their female members—who were not invited to take up arms—to nevertheless participate either as military auxiliaries or on the home front, a policy confirming men as combatants but acknowledging that modern warfare required women's involvement in the event.[4] German women joined the *Nationaler Frauendienst* (National Women's Service) to help their government coordinate service and employment opportunities for women during the war, while their American counterparts prodded government and civil leaders to admit women to a myriad of semimilitary organizations including the Army Nurse Corps and the Women's Department of the YMCA.[5] While women crossed perceived gender boundaries during the conflict, men did so after the war by negotiating the peace, although the verbally combative bargaining that occurred at the Versailles peace table was interpreted as hardnosed and unsentimental, and therefore manly.[6] This chapter will trace women activists' attempts at shaping international politics and peacemaking through rhetoric, and action, in an era when those touting proper gender roles for men and women—which they perceived as well-defined, immutable, and "natural"—sought to restrict women's activities to what they perceived as the private or domestic sphere.[7]

Women did not participate in peace negotiations, but it was not for lack of trying. A week after the November 1918 armistice, National American Woman Suffrage Association member Carrie Chapman Catt had asked President Wilson to invite female delegates to join him in the peacemaking process. Alice Hay Wadsworth, president of the National Association to Oppose Woman Suffrage, decried the idea that ladies should participate in the work of reconciling belligerent nations. As pacifists, Wadsworth insisted, Catt and her colleagues Jane Addams and Anna Howard Shaw would doubtlessly try to "obtain a mitigation of the terms proposed to be imposed upon the Central Powers" (in fact, Addams did not think women should accompany Wilson).[8] The Senator's wife did not protest in principle women's presence at Versailles—she would accept female Red Cross volunteers, for example—only pacifist women. The Woman Voters' Anti-Suffrage Party petitioned Wilson against the appointment of any type of woman to accompany the president's entourage to Paris. Ironically, this organization used the same sense of women's nonviolent nature to oppose their presence that Catt had used to promote it; women had not fought in the war, insisted the petitioners, therefore, they should not prepare the peace (in arguing the reverse Catt had stated that the United States could not have been victorious in the war had it not been for women's "help and support").[9] Those opposed to female peacemakers at the conference prevailed, and, despite the proliferation of dovish female figures in popular culture, President Wilson embarked on his trans-Atlantic adventure without lady negotiators present.

Since women did not engage in the give-and-take of diplomatic bargaining at Versailles, they could only hope to influence what sort of treaty officials would establish indirectly (their influence has been understated, according to women's historians).[10] U.S. pacifist Madeline Doty, for example, suggested that women would put forth a "wiser" treaty than Versailles officials, and if they did, they could shame diplomats and "[force] them into more liberal terms" for the defeated enemy.[11] Writing the history of women and reconciliation in the early twentieth century must, therefore, be done by recording the unofficial ways in which women facilitated fence-mending with the former enemy. Female members of international pacifist and humanitarian organizations influenced postwar reconciliation in a number of ways: they communicated privately with male policymakers in Paris and elsewhere before and during the fashioning of the peace treaty; they created the Women's Charter and other resolutions in which they provided a set of alternatives to the provisions outlined in the Treaty of Versailles; and finally they aided peacemaking by rebuilding the defeated enemy through their relief efforts.

But just as the presumed line separating feminine pacifists from masculine warriors blurred, women's attitudes toward precisely what their role in the reconciliation process should be remained unclear, even among activists themselves (and, as we have seen, some women rejected feminine interference out of hand). The paths that female reconcilers pursued depended on their perception of the political context in which they made their bid for power and on their understanding of women's and men's relationship to international politics and to the nation. In his influential book by the same title, Benedict Anderson has written that nations are "imagined communities" that arise from a fraternal comradeship developed among far-flung citizens, exclusive of women. Since leaders of nations were nearly all male, and because men wielded power both nationally and internationally among nations gathered at Versailles, to some extent women depended upon them to—if not invite them into the political arena—then at least to incorporate their ideas into their proceedings.[12]

At the end of the Great War, the concept of nationalism played a key role in how men and women policymakers and activists developed their rhetoric and methods for making peace. As historian Eric Hobsbawm has noted, the postwar era marked the beginning of "the apogee of nationalism," when heads of state imagined communities organized around the Wilsonian principle of linguistically and ethnically homogenous populations that would empower citizens to determine their own fate. International policymakers at Versailles offered the concept of self-determination as a replacement, in some cases, for the old system of colonial holdings (see Chapter 2).[13] Nationalism—the ideology underpinning the fraternal comradeship of the imagined community—is the individual and collective devotion of those sharing a supposedly common language, history, and culture to their nation. Elite rulers maintain loyalty in part through the dispensation of benefits, such as the opportunity to sacrifice for the nation, and to participate politically in the nation-state, to the fraternity. National unity is also maintained through the perpetuation of the mythology of a nation's common history and culture and through the control of sexuality and reproduction. As the primary administrators of nation-states, historically men have controlled sexuality legally through the creation of marriage, divorce, and custody laws, and legally and medically through the control of prostitution and sexually transmitted diseases (see Chapter 1).

Women's understanding of nationalism influenced how they attempted to make peace, but their relation to the nation-state has been less well defined. Male elites valued women as mothers for their ability to populate the nation; for example, plummeting French birthrates during the war led panicky journalists to ponder whether France would still be a nation in thirty years, tying reproduction directly to national existence.[14] But because of their historical subjugation to men, women's experience has been as people without a country, as Swedish feminist Ellen Key wrote in 1916 (U.S. feminist Katharine Anthony echoed the sentiment in the same year). But Key acknowledged that the Great War had redefined women's relationship to the nation by making her dominance in the home part of her service to the nation-state.[15]

Women's rights advocates took note of the glaring inequalities females suffered as subjects of their nations, however. They related the notion of national self-determination to women's inability to define themselves as citizens of a nation on a level equal to men, regardless of linguistic and ethnic homogeneity. Like Key, suffragists perceived women as "stateless" people who, in many countries, could not yet vote (German women received the vote in 1918, but American women had to wait until 1920 for suffrage at the national level) and who could not retain their own nationality nor, in some cases, assume their spouse's nationality when they married foreign men. After the war, for example, fifteen European nations introduced new laws that retracted a woman's nationality if she married an alien (the 1907 Expatriation Act took away the citizenship of American women marrying foreigners).[16] The United States did not automatically confer citizenship upon foreigners who married American men, and, in the case of U.S. soldiers' German brides, the newlywed became stateless since Germany *did* transfer her citizenship to her husband's country.[17] Debates over married women's status revealed the value society placed upon females but also U.S. lawmakers' possessive attitudes toward "their" women, as well as men's sense of female obligation to the nation. Arguing against the repeal of the Expatriation Act, a California representative explained, "We do not want our girls to marry foreigners" (the act was partially repealed in 1922).[18] Women who engaged in sexual intercourse outside their nationality threatened the unity of the nation, wrote the Austrian-born German nationalist Otto Bauer in 1924.[19]

Activists began looking eagerly upon international political organizations, such as the Women's International League for Peace and Freedom (WILPF) and the League of Nations, as the vehicles through which they could exercise their political views regarding women's rights and, at the same time, postwar reconciliation.[20] German pacifist Lida Gustava Heymann, for example, believed that only by opening doors for the feminine shaping of politics internationally could peace be achieved among former combatants.[21] Women internationalist reformers, like Heymann, argued from an essentialist position (in which female activists would raise the moral tone of world politics once in power) while others, notably Jane Addams, also adopted a universalist position (in which they argued that feminist pacifism encouraged universal human rights for all oppressed peoples).[22]

Historians of women have researched women's unofficial, international efforts at peacemaking and noted how reconciliation, nationalism, and humanitarian relief were themselves gendered, and as a result a clearer picture of how peacemakers of both sexes helped shape the postwar world has begun to emerge. In her book review article "Where are the Women?: The Gender Dimension in the Study of International Relations," Rosemary Foot has noted, "[It is] the extent to which governments depend on certain kinds of relations between men and women, and it is the exposure of this interconnectedness, of this nexus between the private and the public, that will help to take the study of international phenomena beyond a study of the male policy elite."[23] Altered gender roles in society in wartime and in 1919 peacetime initiated an attempted return to the status quo ante bellum. In general, male policymakers, both nationally and internationally, desired a return to gender normalcy as they spurned women's presence at the peace table, rejected their bid for self-determination (as a universal principle), and shunted women wage-workers back to their former status as protected, vulnerable domestics (see Chapter 5). Even pondering the possibility of female self-determination in the age of nationalism, according to historian Glenda Sluga, raised fears of maternal neglect and infertility; both were anathema to a robust nation. Motherhood, on the other hand, supported nationalism, since having children repopulated a society depleted from warfare and since mothers could be encouraged to rear the next generation of nationalists (or cannon fodder, from the point of view of some feminist pacifists).[24] As historian Julie Mostov has shown, the perceived well-being and status of the nation, whether strong or weak, depended upon male protection of women's reproductive ability.[25]

Despite their limited ability to obtain full citizenship rights from national governments, however, women reformers indicated their sense of female responsibility to their country by voicing concerns over falling postwar birthrates alongside their expressions of loyalty to the nation.[26] WILPF's Feminist Committee directed the organization's national sections to study population problems since women were responsible for birthrates. In its 1919 program, the *Bund Deutscher Frauenvereine* (BDF) encouraged German women to fulfill their duty to the nation by getting married and having as many children as possible.[27] BDF President Gertrud Bäumer's rhetoric lashed her organization closely to its nation: "Insofar as the women's movement is an organic institution, and wants to embody a new femininity in disposition and power . . . it will be inevitably national, built from the blood and life of its own folk."[28] In addition, WILPF supported the concept of national self-determination (for the Irish, for Germans living in the occupied Rhineland, and for people living in League of Nations mandates).[29] However, WILPF's record indicated a unanimous rejection of the overzealous nationalism that it blamed for the harsh peace treaty, a foiled reconciliation, and a perpetual state of war.

As postwar politicians reaffirmed time-honored links binding women as mothers to domesticity and to the nation, they also upheld the postwar tradition of rewarding the winners and damning the losers by extending the Allied military occupation of the Rhineland (the quartering of African soldiers there signaled further condemnation of Germany, see Chapter 2), by demanding war reparations, and by assigning Germany's former colonies to the Allied nations as mandates under the Treaty of Versailles. Male policymakers thus adhered to custom in both the private and public realms. By barring women—the presumed chiefs of domesticity—from international politics, they in effect reinforced men's primacy in policymaking, which served to reify the myth of "separate spheres."[30] To answer the question of where women have been in relation to international politics: women were excluded from diplomacy because affirming the privileges of the victors over the vanquished depended on keeping them isolated from worldwide policymaking since, as females were thought to be "naturally" pacifistic, ladies demanding access to international politics threatened to "obtain a mitigation of the terms proposed to be imposed upon the Central Powers" (as Alice Hay Wadsworth had put it) and thereby weaken the power and privilege of the conquering nations. Ironically, men (and women) denied female negotiators a role in the peace talks precisely because it was assumed that they would advocate peace and not their nations' best interests. Indeed, newspapers such as the *Washington Post* aroused such fears when they reported that women peace activists were vulnerable to German requests for a lenient peace.[31]

Women reconcilers themselves fed nationalists' fears that women's involvement in politics would weaken national potency. Not all women activists were willing to completely overturn traditional gender roles or relationships, and some eagerly vaunted women's exclusive dominion in the domestic sphere. WILPF members glued themselves to their domestic roles when they glorified their positions as housekeepers and argued that women were inherently more pacifistic than men and therefore better suited to orchestrate a peaceful, postwar world than were their male counterparts. When women made essentialist arguments for the natural peacemaking abilities of the "mothers of humanity,"[32] from the perspective of the nationalists they confirmed traditional views of femininity as the weaker sex, and weakness was anathema to the principle of nationalism just as nationalism reached its hegemonic peak.[33] When the American and German sections of WILPF laid claim to the female-as-peacemaker half of the pacifist-warrior duality, their attempts at reconciliation were easily dismissed by those desiring a strong, triumphant nation in the age of nationalism. On the other hand, when pacifists such as WILPF President Jane Addams criticized officials' methods of peacemaking, rather than the warlike nature of their gender, their arguments proved harder to deflect.

The Founding of the Women'sInternational League for Peace and Freedom

Before the gavel fell at the closing of the International Congress of Women's conference at The Hague in 1915, those in attendance established the

International Committee of Women for Permanent Peace (ICWPP) and pledged to hold a second worldwide conference of women pacifists at the conclusion of the Great War to coincide precisely with the official peace negotiations. Startled that neither women nor members from belligerent nations would be invited to the Paris conference, the pacifists quickly arranged accommodations in neutral Zurich, Switzerland, where German, Austrian, and Hungarian women would be welcomed. (Jane Addams carefully noted that the ICWPP was not the only organization to plan a meeting concurrently with the peace negotiations and also that Central Powers delegates were finally received at Versailles).[34] Several American and British delegates—Emily Greene Balch, Millicent Fawcett, and others—arrived in Paris in mid-April, where they unsuccessfully petitioned negotiators at Versailles for recognition. From there, the women boarded trains to Zurich.

In Switzerland, two hundred women coming from seventeen different nations voted to change their organization's name to the Women's International League for Peace and Freedom (WILPF) and established their philosophy and their methodology for conducting business. The Great War had reinforced their conviction that peace, which they thought required justice and equality, could not be obtained unless women participated equally in international affairs, and for many members, peace required social justice for the working class as well.[35] In Zurich in May 1919, the women established a permanent international section of the WILPF in addition to the national sections. Each national section sent two consultative members to the International Executive Committee, which was otherwise made up of individual members not representing particular countries. At all of their convocations, the women rejected any hint of nationalism from their delegates because they were convinced that the overt nationalism expressed at Versailles could never create a world reconciled to peace.

According to historian Jo Vellacott, WILPF members considered themselves as transnationals rather than as representatives of their respective nations. At the Zurich meeting, the reformers established a pattern that they pursued at subsequent colloquia: the delegate hailing from the nation that did the perceived wrong appealed to the right. The German delegates, for example, denounced Germany's invasion of Belgium and the Brest-Litovsk Treaty in 1919, while at the 1922 Hague conference the French delegates protested the use of colonial troops by their nation's military (see Chapter 2). As Vellacott has suggested, women's disfranchisement—the very circumstance keeping them isolated from politics—may in fact be interpreted as their advantage: their limited experience in national life enabled them to rise above the pettiness of nationalism that prevented men from establishing a peaceful world and allowed them to envision a new world order.[36] Theoretically, an international, gender-exclusive organization such as WILPF enabled all women to participate and hold leadership positions equally; in practice, however, WILPF succumbed to assumptions about the natural leadership capabilities of women hailing from Western Europe and the United States.[37]

Activists knew they had to engage policymakers at Versailles if they expected to influence postwar reconciliation. Secret meetings of delegates from the major powers, called the Council of Ten, had convened in early 1919, prior to the opening of the peace conference, with the purpose of determining the parameters of the forthcoming negotiations. Britain's Millicent Garrett Fawcett and other Allied women petitioned Woodrow Wilson to urge his fellow statesmen to organize a committee that would consider the conditions of children and women throughout the world and "determine whether any international regulations should be issued." The committee would invite suffrage associations to nominate some of their members to attend in an advisory capacity. The men quickly interpreted the women's request as the means by which they would make an international bid for woman suffrage. Two delegates to the Council of Ten, Indian statesman Maharaja Bikaner and Japanese Minister Baron Nobuaki Makino, replied that they thought their respective nations would not accept female voters and therefore they could not entertain the proposal. French Prime Minister Georges Clemenceau, British Foreign Secretary Arthur Balfour, and Italian Foreign Minister Baron Sidney Sonnino each remarked that while they personally favored women's voting rights, they did not think that the question should be considered by the peace negotiators. With that, Wilson withdrew his proposal.[38] Nearly a month later, a representative from the Suffrage Association of the Allied Countries again requested an audience at another Council of Ten meeting. In this instance, the council offered them the opportunity to be heard by the Commission for International Labour Legislation and the League of Nations.[39] The Council denied women's direct participation in international politics in part because members represented nations that rejected female suffrage; Clemenceau, Balfour, and Sonnino labeled women's voting rights irrelevant to world peace. Women's bid for a voice in international politics left them marginalized from the official reconciliation process, signaling that they were unlikely to make many political gains in the postwar world.[40]

While male elites barred women and the defeated enemy from helping to reconcile belligerents at Versailles, WILPF fostered postwar reconciliation unofficially. Members hailing from countries at war with one another had reached out to their counterparts even before the peace negotiations began. For example, in December 1918, shortly after the armistice, members of the British section of the International Committee of Women for Permanent Peace (WILPF's precursor organization) sent a telegram to German, Austrian, and Hungarian members, their enemy counterparts. "We the British Committee," they wrote, " . . . send warm greetings to the German and Austrian Section of the ICWPP uniting with them in the determination to continue working for just and lasting peace, promoting harmonious international relations and the peaceful development and progress of all nations." The Englishwomen assured their correspondents that they had petitioned their government to alleviate the dire food situation in Central Europe and that they would oppose vindictive terms in the treaty.[41] As she opened the Zurich convention, ICWPP president Jane Addams noted that women of diverse nations had stressed their similar wartime experiences, despite being on opposing sides of the conflict: "We have had revelations of the strength of moral scruple, of the searchings [sic] of heart of those [ICWPP members] who were absolutely separated from each other by the artificial barriers of war. Without explanation or asservation [sic] we discovered how like-minded we were when resolutions on the same thing, coming in from one country after another, were so similar in intent that the five sub-committees who sorted and combined and translated the material were often perplexed to decide which resolution most clearly expressed that which was common to them all."[42]

Such displays of international goodwill were not confined to women, although WILPF did not note that fact. As rumors of a cease-fire circulated in October 1918, for example, U.S. and German soldiers fighting in France defied orders by deliberately shooting over the heads of their opponents in an effort to save them. They later welcomed their enemies into their camps.[43] In both its method and its philosophy, WILPF cultivated a transnational sense of women's relationship to each other as fellow peace activists rather than as citizens of nations, an attitude that fostered their ability to work towards a peaceful world in which women would share political power with men.

Cracks appeared in the carefully crafted scaffolding that WILPF members erected as they tried to sustain their international community, however.[44] The ever-insightful Jane Addams struck at it preemptively. At the convocation, she acknowledged that while members felt a "sense of complicity in the common disaster of the great war," they may still need to purge themselves of "all rancorous memories of wilful misunderstanding or distrust of so-called enemies."[45] On the final morning of the Zurich meeting, German delegate Lida Gustava Heymann clasped hands with the newly arrived French delegate Jeanne Mélin. "A German woman gives her hand to a French woman," exulted Heymann, "and says in the name of the German delegation that we hope we women can build a bridge from Germany to France and from France to Germany, and that in the future we may be able to make good the wrongdoing of men."[46] Yet even in the face of such exuberance, Mary Chamberlain, correspondent for the American magazine *The Survey* and a U.S. delegate to the conference, noted dryly that "none [of the delegates] presumed to say France and Germany were united." Indeed, as Chamberlain described the Zurich conference, many members thought that the German women should have apologized for their country's belligerence toward France. In this instance, the WILPF formula of requiring delegates coming from the nation doing the wrong to appeal to the right did not hold. Chamberlain attributed the German women's neglect to their "senses [having been so] dulled by their own present suffering [that] they could not visualize the enormity of the suffering of others."[47] Nevertheless, because WILPF held its meeting in neutral Zurich, where German and Austrian women could attend, members saw the results of Allied foreign policy when they observed bodies made thin by hunger, whereas policymakers at Versailles kept themselves distant from the impact of the continued blockade. Furthermore, despite the brief animosity created by the German women's neglect, overall, the organization stood by its determination to reduce nationalist-inspired strife.

Indeed, other WILPF actions and resolutions reflected the organization's distrust of fanatical nationalism. The group's most notorious activity during the May meeting was its vociferous rejection of the Treaty of Versailles. The pacifists were the first international group to receive and discuss the treaty when it emerged from Paris. Overwhelmingly, the women condemned its terms. Members regretted that the document violated the principles outlined in Wilson's Fourteen Points; these were the principles under which the Allies had been able to secure the armistice.

WILPF had a special interest in seeing that Wilson's Fourteen Points became the basis of the treaty. At the 1915 convention at The Hague, the ICWPP had issued resolutions that it had sent to the American president. Wilson had praised the activists for creating "by far the best formulation which . . . has been put out by anybody" to insure peace and stability in the world.[48] With the exception of the League of Nations Covenant, the Treaty of Versailles contained few provisions for self-determination or for democratically controlled foreign policy, so the women inevitably rejected it.

In the treaty's League of Nations idea the women took heart, since the proposed international body represented the only hope of implementing their transnationalist vision. The League's Covenant, however, left much to be desired. Firstly, WILPF members decried the fact that not all nations desiring to be members would be invited to do so. The women interpreted the League as "a league of conquerors against the conquered" that reinforced one group of nations' power over another and simply reinstituted the old order that the war had purportedly destroyed.[49] The Covenant did not uphold the right of self-determination in territorial adjustments, and it did not provide free access to all the world's resources, nor did it require the abrogation of war-inducing policies such as the Monroe Doctrine. One provision in the Covenant hailed by the women, however, stated that women should be admitted to all positions in connection with the League (WILPF urged that the provisions should explicitly state that women were eligible for the Assembly, the Executive Council, and the Commissions proposed by the Covenant). Members then drew up the Women's Charter, which a special WILPF delegation brought to the negotiators in Paris, asking the officials to insert their document into the Treaty of Versailles.

As Jo Vellacott has noted, measuring what women produced in Zurich against what men wrote in Paris is unfair. Versailles negotiators had the resources, political support, and experience to make law, while WILPF members had little experience in international politics. Yet a crucial fact remained: Zurich organizers invited "enemy" women to join their talks, while the men kept their opponents at bay. Treaty "negotiators" therefore did not bother to hear rebuttals from the defeated (for example, when they laid the entire blame for the war at Germany's feet). WILPF members, on the other hand, purposely bothered, because they thought that women from victorious nations confronting those from rival countries should ponder *together* how best to lay plans to prevent future wars.[50]

The WILPF's Women's Charter outlined a society based upon sexual equality and justice. The document reinforced both national *and* female self-determination by requiring that in any plebiscite mandated by the Treaty of Versailles women have the same right to vote as men. Further, the document declared that "it is injurious to the community to restrict women to a position of dependence, to discourage their education or development, or to limit their opportunities" and that women's service as wage earners and "as mothers and homemakers [must be made an] essential factor in the building up of the world's peace." WILPF demanded that suffrage and equality for women (access to education, equal wages for equal work, access to professions) be granted nationally and internationally. Furthermore, upon marriage every wife should have "full personal and civil rights, including the right to use and dispose of her own earnings and property, and should not be under the tutelage of her husband." Finally, WILPF insisted that women be allowed to determine their own nationality; married women, wrote the reformers, should have the same right to retain or change their nationalities as men.[51] While male policymakers in Paris confirmed traditional relationships between men and women and between victorious and conquered nations, WILPF envisioned equality between nations and sexes rather than dominion of one country over another in the postwar world.

WILPF could count a few successes toward that goal. The League of Nations appointed a commission on behalf of Greek, Armenian, and other women and children still captive in harems. However (in contrast to the cartoon depictions of an effeminate League, see Chapter 3) it selected only one woman, Dame Rachel Crowdy, as head of the Social Questions and Opium Trafficking sections.[52] On the other hand, WILPF's advocacy of equality between sexes and nations was spreading among British thinkers. Some members of the British Union of Democratic Control—an organization advocating democratic control of foreign policy and national self-determination—agreed that women's fight for equality and justice could serve as a model for weaker countries' appeal for equality with more powerful nations.[53] Despite these successes, however, WILPF and other women's pacifist organizations limited their ability to influence reconciliation and achieve equality and self-determination for women when members argued that women were inherently better peacemakers than men. When female reformers pleaded with male lawmakers on the basis of women's natural roles as nurturers, men could dismiss those arguments as representing the perceived private sector and inappropriate for political bodies.

The U.S. Section of WILPF

As the U.S. government considered how to equip, reorganize, and train its military after the world war, U.S. section member Harriet Connor Brown deployed WILPF's gender-difference strategy in her pamphlet titled "America Menaced by Militarism: An Appeal to Women." The Californian argued that women's "special training as housekeepers" prepared them to tackle the question of appropriating the proper amount of money for defense and that "the instincts of women" would urge them to oppose a rise in military spending. Brown decried the misuse of the nation's wealth for weapons and soldiers, leaving "women next to nothing with which to do our work" of social reform. Even as she argued that women were best suited to determine the nation's budget, the reformer nevertheless retained a belief that women's prerogative was at home, away from public life.[54]

Brown's testimony during congressional hearings on disarmament and military appropriations in the House and Senate employed essentialist notions of women and their role in international politics. In January 1921, the Women's Peace Society (WPS), a U.S. organization formed in 1919 to effect complete and universal disarmament, requested a hearing before the U.S. House Committee on Military Affairs to encourage lawmakers to call for an international conference to achieve universal disarmament. In addition to Brown, WPS members invited six other women representing the American Federation of Labor and the Women's Trade Union League to join the discussion. At the time, the League of Nations and U.S. Secretary of State Charles Evans Hughes were considering ways to reduce armaments.

WPS member Jessie Hardy MacKaye spoke first and summarized the other women's reasons for testifying. She explained that newly enfranchised, pacifist women—MacKaye believed that women generally opposed war—felt it was time to make their views known. The women's purpose was to persuade lawmakers that the United States should reduce its own military and urge other nations to follow suit. MacKaye initially trumpeted women's newly won political power. But when asked if females now carried a "big stick" (Theodore Roosevelt's weapon of choice for waging the manly pursuit of American imperialism, see Chapter 2),[55] MacKaye agreed . . . to derisive laughter in the House chamber. Congressmen pressed her to say exactly how large a military the United States should have, but MacKaye deferred to male policymakers' judgment, requesting only that women be allowed to "influence" men to keep the number to a minimum. In an exchange with Rep. Charles Caldwell over why the United States should compromise any of its power for the sake of reducing arms universally, MacKaye pursued a different line of reasoning. She explained that because American women viewed their sisters overseas as cooperators instead of competitors, they perceived arms reductions as a step toward ending the suffering caused by war, not as a compromise, and therefore weapons were not an issue over which to bargain. But Caldwell did not seem to see her point. He responded, "I am afraid you want us to compromise this thing, just as we men often have to compromise with the women of our families. Without meaning any disrespect to the ladies, when we compromise with them we have to give up something. Now if the United States expects to give up its armament first, without any other country doing so . . . [w]e will have nothing to bargain with in that case, whereas if we can say to them, 'You cut your armies down and we will cut our armies down,' we will have something to bargain with."

Comparing domestic quarrels with public policy negotiations, Caldwell admitted that compromise was necessary at home, but for him public policymaking was a win-lose situation in which accepting compromise meant relinquishing power and weakening the United States' position vis-à-vis other nations.[56]

Harriet Connor Brown's testimony mirrored the transnationalism and gender difference expressed by her WPS colleague. Brown conversed with Chairman Julius Kahn about Japan's growing military threat. Brown quoted Kahn when he had warned his congressional colleagues that within seventy-five to one hundred years Japan would unite the "yellow races" against the western world and had asked rhetorically what white people were going to do about it. "I'll tell you what we white women of the Women's International League are going to do about it," declared Brown. "We are going to educate Japanese and Chinese women to cooperate with us for the peace and freedom of all nations." Kahn responded that he thought the idea a very good one. Unconvinced that he understood her point, Brown continued that because women now had the vote, "we can elect men to our Congresses and parliaments who will disarm, who are going to reflect our views. We are going to spend the next two years in an effort to enlighten the women of the world, so that when Congress convenes two years from now it will be a Congress of people pledged to disarmament." Later, Brown explained WILPF's methods for encouraging arms reduction to Rep. Charles C. Kearns.

Mr. Kearns: I judged that your idea was to educate the men and women of the world up to a point where they will hate war.
Mrs. Brown: Yes; to organize the women of the world, too, especially the voting women . . .
Mr. Kearns: So that in time you can educate the people of the world to a point where they will refuse to fight; is that it?
Mrs. Brown: Yes; I think you can educate the people to a point where they will refuse to fight, just as they refuse to go to work when they strike.

Kearns had finally conceded that governments could not make war unless they had willing combatants to fight when Rep. Harry E. Hull abruptly changed the subject to the women's desire to abolish the Chemical Warfare Service.[57] Brown and MacKaye each began their testimony with the point that women "generally" hated war. From that premise Brown reasoned that once suffrage was achieved worldwide, women would elect men favoring disarmament. But by asserting that gender determined how women voted, she implied the reverse: that men desired rearmament (although she somehow expected to find male candidates that would represent women's views). Thus, if they followed her logic, Brown's congressional adversaries could at least expect a draw at the voting booth, since women comprised only half the population.[58]

The WILPF member dramatized the distinction she saw between men and women more stridently in her testimony before the June 1923 Senate subcommittee hearing on the War Department Appropriation Bill (H.R. 10871). Brown objected to Congress' reliance on military experts to help them determine the amount of money needed to sustain the nation's military. "I wonder if you would think it would be stretching a point if I said that we women are experts?" she stated tartly. "Now you have your choice between the military expert, who is an expert in the culture of destruction, and we women, who are experts in the culture of life." As she had in her 1921 testimony, Brown threatened Congress with women's new and—she assumed—uniformly pacifistic vote. "But the [military] experts have not very many votes to give you, and we have approximately half of the electorate."[59] Overall, the Congressmen hearing the pacifists' reasons for reducing the American military and seeking disarmament around the world dismissed their arguments either by pointing out that Congress had already reduced the size of the wartime military or by noting that since other nations viewed military power as a measure of national power, the United States could not be convinced to give up the clout that it had gained through military victory. The women's strategy of contending that policymakers should include women in determining international policy issues conflicted with the Congressmen's desire to retain America's power, since the speakers confirmed that women unanimously favored peace and reduced military power. While Brown and her colleagues displayed a keen grasp of national and international affairs, they nevertheless conceded that, even with suffrage, women only influenced and did not make public policy. Indeed, during the 1921 hearing Congressmen had mocked the notion that female voters carried a "big stick."

Like Brown, U.S. WILPF officer Hannah Clothier Hull's rhetoric reinforced women's dominion in the private sphere by placing the care of children solely in female hands. She wrote to American Ambassador Frank B. Kellogg, who negotiated reparations loans to Germany as part of the Dawes Plan, asking him to address the problems that WILPF saw in Germany's inability to create a sustainable economy in the face of reparations requirements and the French occupation of the Ruhr. The welfare of children, declared Hull, could be assured only if a fund for their education be made "a first lien upon German industries, German railroads, and the German government." In addition, Hull suggested that the condition of German youth was one factor in the index of prosperity on which the estimate of its capacity to repay debts was based. Finally, Hull asked that a commission of women be assigned the task of maintaining the health and education of German young people. "Since American men had a great share in making the [Dawes] plan," she reminded Kellogg, "it is fitting that American women should take steps toward seeing that in putting it into effect, the welfare of children, *admittedly women's charge*, is in no ways jeopardized." While Hull reasonably argued that the care of Germany's youth was a political issue, she undercut the effectiveness of her claims by positioning nurturing as the responsibility of women. Men predisposed to regard childrearing as women's "natural" duty, and therefore part of the private sphere, could easily dismiss her pleadings as lying outside the purview of politics (for more on the intersection of governments and humanitarian aid, see below). Hull nevertheless claimed victory for WILPF when the Dawes Plan borrowed her organization's idea, proposed at its 1922 Hague conference, that Germany be granted a loan to pay its war reparations.[60]

The German Section of WILPF

Hull and other WILPFers understood the havoc visited upon Germans by the treaty's reparations demands and the French occupation of the Ruhr from correspondence with their overseas comrades. Pacifist feminist Germans, coming from the radical wing of the prewar women's movement, had adopted a commitment to human rights and had demanded equal political rights and opportunities for all Germans. But when war broke out in 1914, the enemy for the radical Germans became male domination, not other nations. (This was unlike their moderate colleagues in the BDF, who had adopted a nationalist position and supported the war. The BDF's goal was to expand women's activities in society, but only within the bounds of what they saw as women's proper roles, centered around motherhood and loyalty to the nation [see Chapter 3].)[61] Heymann, Augspurg, Helene Stöcker, and Auguste Kirchhoff chose a more radical position, which included rejecting the use of force—interpreted as inherent to a male-dominated society—to solve problems. Both moderates and radicals used biological determinism to make their claims. The BDF urged women to mobilize themselves as mothers to aid their nation's war effort, while the radicals argued that women, as the creators of life, must abolish the wars that destroy life. Heymann and Augspurg emphasized that their international connections with women all over the world would help make it so.[62]

The German section's rhetoric remained consistent despite the changing political context of the postwar period. Before women were granted suffrage, WILPF member Auguste Kirchhoff had noted that women, although politically powerless, did hold "a piece of the future" as mothers.[63] After the November armistice, the German section of WILPF, the only women's peace organization that survived the war, witnessed the defeated nation's struggle to establish a government. Member Gertrud Baer summed up what she called *Frauenpolitik* (female politics) during the early years of the Weimar Republic: the practice of following an untried route to "bring forth individual ethics in daily practical politics."[64] Radical women criticized Germany's male-dominated government and suggested that only by yielding to the naturally pacifistic feminine voice could their country lift the yoke of "physical power politics" that men's "base instincts" had naturally produced.[65]

For most WILPFers, German society, dominated by men, lacked a feminine sense of morality. One local branch of the German WILPF utilized the tactic of emphasizing women's moral superiority over men when it, too, called for a new *Frauenpolitik*. "We [Germans] have been known as ruffians long enough," declared German WILPF's Württemberg branch. "After the collapse of purely masculine politics it is high time that women should take part in the guidance of affairs in order to realize the new political maxim Right before Might." The German pacifists hinted that women's participation in politics would ensure that moral righteousness would prevail.[66] The Württembergers echoed Lida Gustava Heymann's remarks during the Zurich WILPF conference in which she had declared that women must "make good the wrongdoing of men." The German section of WILPF, having experienced the war and its aftermath much more directly than American members, reflected an even more blatant sense of sexual difference, which it applied to Germany's postwar political situation, than did its American counterparts (although it did not attribute that difference exclusively to biological differences).[67] Indeed, historian Amira Gelblum noted that in general the national sections of Germany, France, Hungary, and Austria—nations still suffering from the impact of war—developed more extreme responses to issues during WILPF's 1919 convention.[68]

The German section jumped at the chance to participate politically after suffrage. The reformers not only demanded female participation in public life but demanded that governing bodies should exude "the spirit of the mothers of the people."[69] However, the new government that citizens elected in January 1919 was headed by a centralized government staffed primarily by older, established politicians and values, with only a handful of women elected to the Reichstag.[70] The German WILPF warned that the new government "should also take into consideration the perspective, the way of thinking, of women, *which is by nature different from that of men*, and which must complement and broaden the latter if anything is to be created that is truly vital."[71] In contrast to the essentialist viewpoint, Jane Addams' statements reflected WILPF's universalist thinking. Like her German counterparts, Addams had also called for "a new set of motives and of habits" in governing bodies, but she did not suggest that only women could offer those qualities; indeed, she referred to the British Labour Party as a source of fresh perspective.[72]

In 1921, Heymann reiterated the same essentialist rhetoric as in previous years. "Go to work, women of good will," she directed her readers in *Die Frau im Staat*, the German WILPF's unofficial organ, "you who are not acquainted with the violent methods of men."[73] The German women's politics of good will included supporting the eight-hour day, free trade, equal employment opportunities for men and women, equal laws relating to marriage for men and women, the guarantee of basic human rights, and the abolishment of capital punishment.[74] In the realm of foreign policy, the German section condemned Britain for its policies toward Ireland, declaring that the Irish should have the right to national self-determination.[75]

Nevertheless, German members still adhered to Auguste Kirchhoff's adage that women control the future through their children when they declared that the work of the German WILPF commissions "is and remains education."[76] Gertrude Baer commented that "it goes without saying that we are aware of the need for a thoroughgoing restructuring of education at home, in school, at work, and in public life," indicating the emphasis the German WILPF placed on education in its work.[77] To that end, the German section published the *Kinder-Zeitung* (Children's Magazine) for ten- to fifteen-year-olds. The magazine included news about German youth who spent summers abroad and information about other nations, in addition to offering its readers a pen-pal program. The 1922 edition featured an article called "The Children of the World War," in which readers were reminded of the hardships that their nation had endured during the war and were encouraged to look upon the world not with hatred but with understanding.[78] The German section also urged educators to rid their classrooms of books that celebrated war and replace them with histories of other countries, and they encouraged mothers not to purchase war toys or clothes for their children.[79] The German WILPF had good reason to offer a counter to a militarized education. Nationalists bent on remilitarizing Germany's youth distributed recruiting leaflets to school children in Berlin.[80]

One of the German section's major projects was to foster peace with the French. For the German pacifists, French-German reconciliation symbolized a larger postwar project of healing and rebuilding after the carnage of war.[81] Yet here, too, the focus remained on children. "The peace of Europe depends upon German-French reconciliation," declared Gertrud Baer, "and that depends on the youth."[82] To further demonstrate its desire for fence-mending, the German section and others participating in the Youth Movement created the "Sacrifice of Reconciliation," in which they proposed to build a "House of Reconciliation" that would serve as a meeting place and library in a northern French village (Germany had occupied northern France during the war and had deported French workers from the Lille coal basins to labor in other occupied areas; see Chapter 2). However, when the German government had failed its reparations obligations, France took over German mines and railroads in the Ruhr district and attempted to establish a Rhineland Republic in a "divide and conquer" mentality, according to WILPF member Lucy Biddle Lewis. The German mark fell precipitously and the program had to be abandoned.[83] The German WILPF issued a statement acknowledging that France had a right to expect payment of debt Germany owed, but that payment depended on German rebuilding.[84] French WILPFers reciprocated their colleagues' earlier peacemaking efforts by creating the Fraternal Aid for the Children of the Ruhr as a political "protest and a gesture of reconciliation and humanity." By the time WILPF held its 1924 meeting in Washington, D.C., the French section had collected more than 12,000 francs. "I have wanted to show you German and French action that is quite independent of, and not in agreement with that of official France and official Germany," reported French section member Andrée Jouve to fellow WILPF delegates in Washington.[85] For WILPF, the Ruhr occupation and German and French responses underscored the chasm between official government foreign policies, in which fighting men invaded and the goal of national self-determination lay abandoned, and the women's work of reconciliation through international activism.

WILPF's Critics

The criticisms leveled at the United States and German sections of WILPF magnified the differences between nationalist and transnationalist viewpoints. Gertrud Baer listed a myriad of ways that German pacifist women were harassed, from censorship to expulsion.[86] Provincial authorities confiscated Lida Gustava Heymann's booklet "Eine Frage: Frauen Europas, wann erschallt Euer Ruf?" ("A Question: Women in Europe, When Will You Sound Your Call?"), and Heymann was soon expelled from Bavaria, although she remained in Munich in hiding.[87] The *Bund Deutscher Frauenvereine* publicly opposed international women's congresses and condemned the German WILPF's pacifism. Indeed, Gertrud Bäumer had refused to join the ICWPP (WILPF's precursor) at The Hague in 1915 because she had felt that during her nation's struggle for its existence, women belonged only with their own people.[88] When the Nazis came to power in 1933, Heymann and Augspurg fled to Zurich, and the German peace movement ground to a halt until after the Second World War.[89]

Meanwhile, in the United States, R. M. Whitney targeted the U.S. section of WILPF for its "friendship and sympathy for Germany" and claimed that "An outstanding feature of the WIL conference [was to] create sentiment in favor of German and against the United States and its allies." Perhaps more damning than sympathy for Germany, in Whitney's eyes, was WILPF's "lack of recognition" for "defense of country, of patriotism, *of the maintenance of nationality*, which last, in fact, is specifically deplored [by WILPF]." Finally, Whitney accused WILPF of not flying the U.S. flag at its Washington, D.C. headquarters.[90] A U.S. Senate subcommittee labeled Jane Addams and others as "dangerous, destructive, and anarchistic" and therefore a threat to the nation, and Emily Greene Balch lost her job at Wellesley College because of her pacifism.[91]

The backlash against the transnationalism of the U.S. section of WILPF continued in 1923, when the pacifists came under attack for what was derisively termed their "slacker oath." Some WILPF members (and members of WPS and the Women's Peace Union) pledged not to give the U.S. government "our children, not to encourage nor to nurse your soldiers, not to knit a sock nor roll a bandage nor drive a truck nor make a war speech nor buy a bond." The oath, written by Harriet Connor Brown, led the War Department's Chemical Warfare Bureau (which Brown and others had urged Congressmen to eliminate) to condemn several political organizations for their involvement in the "Socialist-Pacifist Movement." Lucia R. Maxwell, assistant to Brigadier General Amos A. Fries of the bureau, penned both the notorious "spider-web chart" featuring links between several leading women and men activists and alleged Bolshevik-funded organizations, and the following poem:

> Miss Bolsheviki has come to town,
> With a Russian cap and a German gown,
> In women's clubs she's sure to be found
> For she's come to disarm America.[92]

Maxwell rendered in rhyme what Brown and other women pacifists did by implication in their congressional testimony: she linked pacifism exclusively to feminism. Since Bolshevism's sources were foreign (and one a former enemy), the Brigadier's assistant perceived its goal of disarmament as designed to undermine American strength (Congressmen hearing Brown's testimony had also linked the women's pleas for disarmament with weakness). WILPF's critics demonstrated that the pacifists' visions of a future in which states transcended national competitiveness and instead cooperated to insure women's rights and peace threatened the strength of national fraternal unity.

Humanitarian Aid and the Politics of Hunger

As both the U.S. and German sections of WILPF imagined an international community of female activists reshaping world politics to include women's rights and an end to international strife, they took practical steps to alleviate the suffering caused by the late war. Their actions became a political conundrum when the emphasis they placed on women and children as victims of conflict overtook their analysis of the political causes of anguish and served only to reify women's helplessness in the face of an overwhelming loss.

For example, WILPF's German section used the drawings of German pacifist Käthe Kollwitz to illustrate several of its pamphlets and fliers. Kollwitz's *Nachdenkende Frau* (*Thoughtful Woman*), an image of a sorrowful woman holding her head in her hand, appeared on the cover of *Völkerversöhnende Frauenarbeit* (*Women's Work of Reconciliation*), while the Berlin section's *Merkblatt* (*Bulletin*) featured an untitled drawing of a mother embracing a child on its back page. Kollwitz graphically depicted the suffering of German victims, most often women and children, of the Great War.[93] On the other side of the Atlantic, when field workers seeking aid on behalf of the American Friends Service Committee (AFSC) solicited relief only for women and children, they underscored the gendered nature of the war and the peace that followed: Men nearly exclusively declared wars, directed wars, and fought wars in the early twentieth century, while females—except prostitutes—were kept isolated from barracks and battlefields. Women were real victims of wartime atrocities (of rape, U-boat disasters, and economic blockades), but they were also expected to nurse the incapacitated husbands and fathers who returned from battle and were forced to replace them as breadwinners if they did not come home at all (see Chapter 5). By viewing *only* women and children as victims (in part a conceptual consequence of arming *only* men), the American Relief Administration and the AFSC reinforced women's marginalized roles in society, emphasizing their helplessness and dependency in the face of a political crisis instead of their ability to act politically to solve problems. On the other hand, WILPF's activities and analysis of the emergency highlighted the political causes behind the hunger and the role of humanitarian efforts in postwar reconciliation that served to demonstrate fully the benefits of transnational thinking and the danger of elite rulers' habit of keeping themselves isolated from the consequences of their policies. The suffering of fellow pacifists at the Zurich meeting, as Mary Chamberlain had noted, piqued the women's sense that reconciliation could not be achieved until Europeans were properly fed, and food shortages in Central Europe had emerged as WILPF's foremost concern. Jane Addams' disappointment with political wrangling at Versailles led her to opine that relief was the only available "tonic of beneficent activity" in which women transnationals could engage.[94] The question of whether the organization should become involved directly in providing relief to war-stricken areas troubled the pacifists, however, as many feared that WILPF would lose its political potential if it became a relief organization.[95] A constant stream of aid requests appeared at WILPF's Geneva headquarters, but International WILPF Secretary Emily Greene Balch and Vice President Catherine E. Marshall of Great Britain insisted that WILPF tackle only the *political causes of the need* for aid, rather than providing the relief itself.[96] Marshall's compatriot Helena Swanwick agreed, stating that the WILPF did not want to reinforce the notion that women's only public function was to clean up the disasters made by men.[97] Some members, such as Heymann, Augspurg, and Harriet Connor Brown had refused to engage in wartime work, because they felt that it only encouraged nations to engage in battle. Nevertheless, the German WILPF's rhetoric of the "feminine principle" (mutual aid and nonviolent methods) implied an inclination towards humanitarian relief.[98] Because the Executive Committee saw the French occupation of the Ruhr as a cause of hunger there, it sent a delegation to Paris to protest France's invasion. But the Executive Committee's choice met with anger among some American members. "We are not allowed to take up work that would help starving children," complained Mabel Hyde Kittredge to WILPF President Jane Addams, "and yet we do not influence the world."[99] In fact, individual WILPF members and national sections did provide aid: Jane Addams toured hunger-stricken France and Germany with the American Friends Service Committee, Britain's Mary Sheepshanks lent her talent to the Fight the Famine Council, and the U.S. section donated $2,757 to Herbert Hoover's American Relief Committee in April 1920 (indeed, the U.S. section of WILPF made relief its primary activity in October 1919).[100] British WILPF members purchased and delivered a million rubber teats used to bottle-feed German infants whose starving mothers could not provide milk.[101]

By refusing to be pegged as a humanitarian organization, WILPF reinforced the perception that aid constituted private assistance and was therefore not a political endeavor. In both the United States and Europe there was ample precedence for that sentiment; during the war, the German government had relied on private donations to alleviate the suffering of wounded soldiers (see Chapter 5), and in the U.S. Civil War, the government had depended on the U.S. Sanitary Commission, a private charity run by women, to bind up wounds.[102] In so doing, both governments drove a wedge between the wars they prosecuted and their ruinous consequences (in the same way, peace negotiators in Paris kept themselves estranged from the damage caused by the hostilities that they were charged with healing). But when WILPF members (and their male counterparts) offered relief *and* articulated the political nature of wartime suffering at the same time, they blurred those arbitrary boundaries.

To begin with, U.S. WILPF members' relief work demonstrated to a skeptical American public that Germany's needs were genuine. Writers such as Marian Baldwin, Hamilton Holt, and W. C. Gregg, for example, interpreted Germans' requests for aid as an extension of wartime propaganda. YMCA worker Baldwin marched into Germany from France with the Third Army and described "another land; instead of desolation and ruin, a countryside untouched and unhurt by the hand of war. Nothing could look better kept and more prosperous than these well-groomed vineyards and fertile fields through which we are passing."[103] Holt and Gregg both reported seeing well-cultivated fields and very little impact from the war. Third Army officer Harry A. Franck, however, offered another view. "The only ones [in Germany] who could be said to show no signs whatever of under-nourishment," wrote Franck, "were foreigners, war profiteers, and those with a strangle-hold on the public purse."[104] U.S. Army Major Philip Haxall Bagby described the former enemy's needs most graphically: "Further evidence has come to light during the week just past showing that the national health of Germany was indeed shattered by the war," wrote the major shortly after the armistice, "its hardships and deprivations [evidenced] by its nerve-wracking, mind-destroying and body-crippling tortures."[105]

Bagby's report confirmed what most U.S. politicians believed: that the economic blockade that Britain had imposed on Germany in 1914 and that the armistice extended had pushed the defeated nation deeper into the quicksand of starvation and massive death and, more worrisome to some, onto the brink of Bolshevism, along with much of the rest of

Central Europe. In February 1919, Congress appropriated $100,000,000 for European relief, and President Wilson directed Herbert Hoover to form the American Relief Administration (ARA) to handle the allocation and distribution of assistance. In addition to the food paid for from the congressional appropriation, the ARA handled U.S. loans to governments and direct cash payments for aid.[106]

Hoover found that provisioning Germany after the armistice would not be an easy task, however. The cease-fire terms had called for the continuation of the Allied blockade, with the provision that providing for needy Germans be considered. The Allied policy of merely *contemplating* providing aid, according to historian C. Paul Vincent, was based on a complete misperception of Germany's condition. Hoover argued strenuously for relaxing the "watertight" blockade so as to allow the bare necessities that he anticipated would yield a stable German government.[107]

Hoover returned from a ten-month sojourn through Europe convinced that American prosperity, and a vital world economy, depended on European recovery. A mining engineer by profession, Hoover viewed politically engineered treaties skeptically, casting a more hopeful eye upon an economic solution—based specifically on an American model of consumerism—to heal Europe's woes.[108] The son of a Quaker, Hoover believed in a progressively managed corporate capitalist economy. Government interference in a free market system should be minimal, just enough to protect it from ruthless individual aggrandizement. The United States had to maintain foreign markets for its goods in order to keep its own workers employed. The aim of American foreign policy, according to Hoover, should be to oppose international forces and movements that tended to breed instability or economic restrictions. If the United States could convince other nations to avoid protectionist economic practices, Americans could expect a generous, if not oversized, share of the world's economic pie.

Hoover thus did not view relief as a simple matter of feeding hungry people. Instead, he viewed it as a necessary step in securing a series of political objectives that would assure Woodrow Wilson's peace settlement: restoring German productivity would yield a stable and orderly economy in Central Europe, as opposed to anarchy and Bolshevism. And he acted on this premise. In Vienna, for example, when the food czar learned of planned May Day labor demonstrations, he had placards erected warning that social unrest would result in the elimination of food distribution. The reformer admitted that he understood Europeans' frustrations that arose out of the recent war and prewar economic oppressions, but he insisted that there be no revolutionary changes to Europe's economic system. Men should take up their tools, he reasoned, and simply go back to work.[109] Hoover linked political instability to human suffering, but while he denounced the blockade, the treaty, and militarism in general, he did not condemn the war itself as the root cause of the devastation, whereas WILPF's interpretation did.[110]

The politics of revenge that WILPF blamed for so much of the postwar world's ills had worked its way into the "politics of hunger," as C. Paul Vincent titled his work. When Hoover presented his proposal to feed starving Europeans, the Allies interpreted his intentions as a desire to control Europeans' economies without consulting them, and Hoover found them disinclined to show generosity toward the Germans.[111] Furthermore, they cast Hoover's insistence that only the United States be allowed to handle American food destined for Europe as selfish economic nationalism.[112] (The Food Administrator compromised later and was declared chairman of the Supreme Council of Supply and Relief among the United States, France, Britain, and Italy.) U.S. Army Chief of Staff Tasker H. Bliss rejected Hoover's plans on the basis of the nationalism that he presumed drove the requests for aid by the recipient countries. Reporting to the American Peace Commission in February 1919, Bliss emphasized his belief that U.S. government assistance to Europe was being used by individual countries to rearm and restart the war. "Every dollar's worth of food that we give to them," he declared, "enables them to spend a dollar on military equipment." Bliss argued that the United States should refuse to give any food or supplies to any European nation and instead either sell food on a cash or "sound credit" basis or allow charitable donation. "They [European nations] are all looking for opportunities to steal each others [sic] land, to cut each others [sic] throats, with assistance that they deliberately expect to receive from the United States," warned Bliss. "All of these plans will fall, like a house of cards, if they are plainly told that no such assistance will be given."[113]

French and British officials continued to obstruct Hoover's plans. In the face of such stonewalling, the American suggested that Germany be allowed to pay for food with its gold assets. French Premier Clemenceau promptly balked, arguing that since the former enemy owed his country reparations, Germany's gold properly belonged to France. The result of the bureaucratic, diplomatic, and political impasse was, according to Hoover, an Allied policy that was starving women and children in a nation that had been defeated.¹¹⁴ A report delivered to British Prime Minister David Lloyd George and Hoover from General Herbert Plumer, Commander of the British Army of Occupation, finally broke the deadlock. Plumer's men were begging him to allow them to go home because they could no longer stand the sight of mobs of skinny, bloated children pawing over the discarded food from British cantonments. After the food czar and the Prime Minister approached the Council of Ten with a request to lift the blockade, the Council voted to allow Germany to pay for Hoover's food in gold and allowed delivery on March 8, 1919 (however, officials did not formally lift the blockade until after Germany signed the peace treaty). "Until eyewitness accounts thoroughly unmasked the reality of blockade-imposed starvation," noted Vincent, "the majority of the politicians and diplomats labored under the weight of viewing Germany too abstractly." In contrast, WILPF's method of specifically arranging to meet women from enemy lands to provide such direct observations had resulted in WILPF's immediate condemnation of the Treaty of Versailles' extension of the blockade.¹¹⁵

When Germany signed the treaty in June 1919, Hoover renamed his organization the European Children's Fund and asked the American Friends Service Committee (AFSC), a Quaker organization, to finance relief for German youths. In July, Jane Addams, Alice Hamilton, and Carolena Wood met with English Quakers in London to coordinate their journey through Germany. Addams and Hamilton visited Leipzig, Halle, Chemnitz, and Frankfurt, while Wood traveled on to Silesia. Both groups met with German physicians and social workers and toured schools, social services, hospitals and orphanages. They were able to observe firsthand the connections between hunger, compromised immune systems, disease, and reduced mental capacities. In addition, the travelers distributed twenty-five tons of clothes and $30,000 worth of food, and then reported back to the AFSC on the welfare conditions they had surveyed.¹¹⁶

Addams viewed concerns over national honor and "other abstractions dear to the heart of the diplomat" as having impaired previous attempts at solving public health problems, and she had hoped that a concrete, international response by the League of Nations would ameliorate the food crisis in postwar Europe. Had the international body bridged the gap between the private grief suffered by people and the official, detached methods used to solve an international dilemma like massive starvation, she contended, it would have been an effective organization. But because the League remained mired in old-style diplomacy and was "indifferent to the widespread misery and starvation of the world," it dashed the reformer's hopes for a new political ethic of care.[117] Addams blamed the League's failure to recognize nationalism as the culprit. "Could it [the League of Nations] have considered the multitude of starving children as its concrete problem, feeding them might have been the quickest way to restore the divided European nations to human and kindly relationship," she reasoned. "Was all this devastation the result of hyper-nationalism and might not the very recognition of a human obligation irrespective of national boundaries form the natural beginning of better international relationships?" she asked pointedly. Had the League responded to postwar food crisis, according to Addams, "it would have been recognized as indispensable."[118]

Upon her return to the United States Addams embarked on a speaking tour to secure donations to the AFSC collection for German and Austrian youth. No newspapers, she lamented, would cover her appearances, and German-American audiences offered a muted response to her calls for aid (a fact later confirmed by U.S. Department of Commerce's Christian Herter, who noted that contributions made by German Americans were "negligible.")[119] Furthermore, Addams noted that when funds were sent to AFSC in Philadelphia, they would often be earmarked for Allied countries. Several factors may explain the paucity of relief that Americans were willing to offer to Germans. Wartime hatred continued unabated in the aftermath of the conflict (see Chapter 3) and was coupled with Red Scare fears (see Chapter 5). No stranger to controversy, the blackballed Addams herself may have turned some people off from contributing to a cause she supported.

Both Addams and Hoover were careful to note that relief to Germany would be confined to food and clothes for victimized youths. Hoover's letter to the AFSC, for example, reminded potential American donors that "we have never fought with women and children." The AFSC promised contributors that "the relief work is only for children and those who have to do with the child life of Germany." While she described men who suffered horribly from want in her report to the AFSC, Addams primarily emphasized conditions relating to children and women. Hoover, and undoubtedly Addams too, understood from the outset that succoring the former enemy would not go over well with the American public (people such as R. M. Whitney, for example), and claiming that the aid would be distributed to blameless youths may have enabled them to convince more Americans to give. But by perpetuating the notion that only women and children were the innocent victims of war, the two relief workers glossed over the fact that *all* Germans (and all citizens of other belligerent countries) were equally vulnerable to food shortages and needed help (realizing, of course, that the bodies of small children and the elderly typically had less resistance to disease than those of healthy adults). By insisting that caring for children remain a female profession,[120] they rendered relief a private matter (given women's presumed dominance in the home) that could be ignored by politicians and relegated to the category of "private charity." Still, Addams' trenchant analysis of the politics of Europe's food shortage, and her conviction that the League of Nations' entrenched, old-style diplomacy had hindered it from carrying out what she believed should be its rightful duty of solving international humanitarian crises, remains a strong example of WILPF's universal, transnationalist thinking in its formative years.

On the surface, the influence WILPF had sought on postwar reconciliation had had little effect. Paris negotiators did not allow women access to their proceedings, nor did they incorporate members' Women's Charter or their ideals of gender and national equity in the Treaty of Versailles. WILPF's (and other organizations') repeated calls for a revision of the Treaty of Versailles fell on deaf ears. What the pacifists did accomplish was to form lasting relationships between women of good will that bridged the gaps left by a destructive war, perpetual strident nationalism, and damaging postwar policies such as the blockade and the French invasion of the Ruhr. WILPF's semi-annual meetings allowed like-minded female activists from around the world a forum where ideas about a political system based on gender and national equality were created and perpetuated.

Ultimately, WILPF's Janus-faced rhetoric limited its effectiveness. The pacifists' transnationalist vision called for a new era of equity between men and women and between powerful and powerless nations, and they viewed those two goals as complementary. WILPF consistently supported self-determination for nations and spurned the Treaty of Versailles' and League of Nations' provisions that empowered the victorious nations at the expense of the vanquished. But members generally adhered to what they perceived as women's primary social responsibility as "the mothers of humanity."[121] By making issues such as falling national birthrates and the care of children exclusively women's concerns, they positioned the power women held as mothers as competing with men's power in the political realm, particularly when they met face-to-face with policymakers. Thus, when Harriet Connor Brown argued before the Senate subcommittee that women and mothers were the "experts in the culture of life," she placed women in competition with men's presumed expertise in making war for the Senators' attention. While such rhetoric undoubtedly felt empowering to women, it could not compete with the real power that men granted themselves as leaders of the political sphere, and in fact, it simply reinforced the notion of "separate spheres" that kept women marginalized from full participation in politics. As Jo Vellacott noted, women's disenfranchisement allowed them to rise above nationalist sentiments and offered them a vision for a new postwar world. But too often they seemed unwilling to actually live in the ungendered world that they envisioned. Historian Susan Grayzel wrote of the Great War that "the war's lasting influence on gender was more conservative than innovative," and that women remained in essentially the same position vis-à-vis the nation at the end of the war as they were at the beginning.[122] WILPF's and AFSC's work in reconciling the war's enemy nations confirms this view. Maintaining the perceived boundaries between men's and women's domains enabled negotiators at Paris to keep pacifism out of the peace talks.

The practical work that female reconcilers did helped them recognize important differences between official and unofficial methods of peacemaking, and between nationalistic and transnational interpretations of the war, however. As Addams and the Dutch physician Aletta Jacobs traveled through the European war capitals—London, Paris, Berlin, Vienna, Budapest, and Rome—as peace envoys after the 1915 International Congress of Women at The Hague, they noticed a pattern among each set of government officials, journalists, and ordinary citizens with whom they conversed in each country. In each case, the women were solemnly assured that the particular country they were visiting fought only in self-defense to preserve its customs and values from those who would destroy them. In each nation their contacts seemed certain that their fellow-countrymen embodied similar noble qualities, while the perceived enemy suffered from lack of the same. The belligerent nations on both sides of the conflict all used identical abstractions to perpetuate myths about nations at war. The experience convinced Addams that only a comparative international and transnational perspective, derived from face-to-face interactions among ordinary people of diverse nations, could prevent future conflict. By no means did she suggest that only women had (or could have) such experiences, however. For example, one of her contacts, a man hailing from near Germany's border with Denmark, illustrated to her the absurdity of learned national hatreds and their connection to war: "I am told the men of Schleswig-Holstein are my brothers, but my grandfather before me fought them. I do not know whether they are my brothers or my grandfather's enemies; I only know I have no feeling for them different from what I have for men living farther north in Denmark itself. The truth is that neither to my grandfather nor to me do the people of Schleswig-Holstein mean anything; that he hated them and that I love them are both fictions, invented and fostered for their own purposes by the people who have an interest in war."[123]

Addams recorded similar experiences among a cadre of "new internationalist" Europeans she met during her 1915 journey; the sum total convinced her that lived experiences, rather than abstract concepts such as nationalism, would eventually make it more difficult for elite rulers to make war.[124] Having kept themselves isolated from such experiences, negotiators at Versailles upheld the old-style, nationalistic diplomacy that Addams viewed as counterproductive to a peaceful postwar world. The one instance where elite rulers had changed their minds—proving Addams' point—was in the case of supplying relief to Germany. In that instance, the British Army commander had warned diplomats that his men, so distraught by the sight of needy children, were depriving themselves of food so that they could nourish starving youths. The heads of state then agreed to allow Herbert Hoover to distribute relief.[125]

The perceived boundary between the public and the private—albeit arbitrary and ever shifting, especially during war—nevertheless proved problematic for women reconcilers in the early twentieth century. WILPF's essentialist arguments for the feminization of international politics—by which some members meant an exclusively, inherently female sense of nonviolent pacifism—was empowering for members and therefore important in assessing their strategies. But their arguments were too easily dismissed by elite rulers who discarded them as "women's issues" and therefore irrelevant to the securing of national self-interest in the postwar world (recent foreign diplomats' sense of "women's issues" is discussed in the Epilogue). When the women made use of their transnationalist perspectives (in part a consequence of women's disassociation from national politics) to determine how best to do the work of unofficial reconciliation—for example, in the case of the 1915 European peace envoy journey and the 1923 Ruhr Crisis—their work helped to mitigate the nationalistic politics of retribution and revenge inherent in the war and in the official peace treaty that followed.

Women's disconnect from policymaking on the home front came into relief as the war ended and demobilization began. Once again, the postwar world sent a double message to women. On the one hand, they were expected to heal their wounded soldiers, although they were given very few resources with which to accomplish their task. Even though both the German and U.S. governments recruited women to work in wartime industries, only male soldiers were publicly honored for wartime participation. The reconciliation of the home front to peacetime constituted a return to gender "normalcy," though not without resistance from the gentler sex.

5
Binding up "Bitter Wounds"
Gender, Nationalism, and Reconciliation on the Home Front in Germany and in the United States

Two weeks after the armistice, the American magazine the *Outlook* began helping readers reconcile themselves to peacetime by printing a public service announcement from the Committee on Public Information, the war propaganda machine created by Woodrow Wilson. "He will Come Back a Better Man!" offered the announcement; "Uncle Sam is giving him a newer and better equipment in mind and body—fitting him for a bigger, finer life." Against the backdrop of a soldier hugging and kissing his apron-clad mother, the blurb goes on to say that the future of America lies in the hands of the smiling "Victorious Crusader" who is back from winning the war. The announcement doubled as an advertisement for the American Telephone and Telegraph Company and was pitched to the mothers who had sent their "boys" off to fight; they can also shape the coming peace by writing cheery letters to keep warriors happy until they return (see Figure 5.1).[1]

The soldiering experience, according to the advertisement, had imbued American boys with all of the qualities that enabled them to return as robust male citizens. "Strong in body . . . alert and keen in mind . . . [filled with] self-control and self-reliance" were the conditions resulting from the comradeship and discipline combatants had experienced in the army, according to the announcement.[2] These became the aspects of warfare heralded in both American and German society and culture in the aftermath of the Great War. The military life, played out over and over again

---

My title comes from Robert Weldon Whalen, *Bitter Wounds: German Victims of the Great War, 1914–1939* (Ithaca, NY: Cornell University Press, 1984), who adopts the phrase from Peter Gay's *Weimar Culture: The Outsider as Insider* (New York: Harper & Row, 1968).

He Will Come Back a Better Man!

Uncle Sam is giving him a newer and better equipment, in mind and body—fitting him for a bigger, finer life

WHEN that boy of yours comes marching home a Victorious Crusader, he will be a very different person from the lad you bravely sent away with a kiss, a tear and a smile.

He will be strong in body, quick and sure in action, alert and keen in mind, firm and resolute in character, calm and even-tempered.

Self-control and self-reliance—ability to think and act in emergencies—coolness and courage in time of stress and danger —such will be the product of his training and experience.

Neatness, precision in detail without fuss and worry, promptness, reliability, scrupulous integrity, thoughtfulness and courtesy — these things come from army comradeship and discipline.

A broad-shouldered, deep-chested, square-jawed YOUNG MAN with flashing eyes and a happy smile—that's who will throw himself into your arms when "Johnny Comes Marching Home Again."

That's who is coming back to live his life in happiness with you.

And in his hands—and yours—lies the future of America.

Help him, keep him happy NOW—by cheerful, newsy letters —for your sake—and for Uncle Sam.

COMMITTEE ON PUBLIC INFORMATION
8 Jackson Place, Washington, D. C.

George Creel, Chairman The Secretary of War
The Secretary of State The Secretary of the Navy
Contributed through United States Gov't Comm.
Division of Advertising on Public Information

This space contributed for the Winning of the War by
AMERICAN TELEPHONE & TELEGRAPH COMPANY, NEW YORK

Figure 5.1 Advertisement by the American Telephone & Telegraph Company and Committee on Public Information. *Outlook* 120 (November 27, 1918): 511

in countless parades, speeches, and commemorative pageants held in the United States and Germany, reminded both the former soldiers and the rest of the nations' inhabitants that it was through war that men acquired a deeper connection to nation and citizenship ("a bigger life") and to each other. Women who participated in the total experience of the war through industrial work, through the auxiliary military, and through the loss of soldier husbands, remained marginalized in both societies as the return to peacetime also meant a return to gender "normalcy." By opposing the "front" of battle to the "home front" of supposed serene domesticity, soldiers and their governments recognized only male combatants as having made life-threatening sacrifices for the nation in the war, while their women—though contributing to the war effort—were deemed unworthy of the accolades granted to true heroes. American women YMCA workers, mindful of the distinction awarded to warriors on the front, lobbied vigorously to be stationed there.[3] Conventional European Great War histories have also tended to contrast the home front with the Western front; Martha Hanna's recent work on French peasants' wartime correspondence counters this opposition.[4]

This chapter examines the gendered nature of how nations reconciled themselves internally to peacetime after the Great War. As U.S. historians Susan Zeiger and David M. Kennedy and German historians Ute Daniel, Susanne Rouette, and Karin Hausen have ably demonstrated, in both nations women gained little from their wartime experience (with the exception of the vote), as German and American female wartime laborers were shunted back to their former positions in what were generally considered female occupations, such as domestic service and the needle trades, in favor of returning soldiers.[5] Most histories of the postwar era, however, focus on the economic aspects of postwar society within the single national experience. Earlier studies underestimated women's contributions to wartime economies, and therefore women remain hidden in postconflict analyses.[6] By examining diverse postwar phenomena in both societies (such as work, welfare, and war commemoration, as well as art and literature), a comparative picture illustrates that despite women's active patriotism during the war, men continued to dominate in both the victorious and defeated nations as they returned to peacetime. For example, as women were excused from munitions factories, American and German men and women began the work of commemorating the soldier experience through myriad groups of "memory activists," as Jay Winter calls them.[7] While women's contributions to the national economy and war effort were loudly praised in both countries during the conflict, that applause became muted as organizations such as the American Legion Women's Auxiliary and the People's Alliance for the Care of German War Graves began valorizing the male soldier. Advertisements, such as the one appearing in the *Outlook*, as well as speeches, art, songs, and poetry produced in both nations, assured inhabitants that peacetime would also help usher in a return to gender normalcy.

As men retook their dominant positions in society, nationalism renewed its strength in both the victorious and defeated nations after the conflict, despite widespread disillusionment with war. In the United States, the welfare of the nation dominated the social and political climate of the 1920s, ideologically through isolationism and the first Red Scare (many of its victims were female reformers) and politically through anti-immigration legislation. Meanwhile, ceremonies and speeches commemorating anniversaries in 1924 and 1928 assured Germans that neither militarist ideology nor even the war itself had truly ended, offering national regeneration through the "cult of the fallen soldier."[8] Despite the efforts of women's transnational organizations to mitigate overzealousness, renewed nationalism proved to be the dominant thrust in both nations, regardless of whether victorious or defeated in the war, and it accompanied the return to gender normalcy. Perhaps the difference between the two nations' postwar experiences lies in the degree of bitterness expressed by those binding up the wounds.

As a nation, Germany experienced much more devastation from the war than did the United States. Around 1.7 million German soldiers died in the conflict, while the American figure stood at approximately 116,000. Some 600,000 German women were widowed, while comparatively only about 33,000 American wives dressed in black.[9] There is no U.S. counterpart to Helene Hurwitz-Stranz's *Kriegerwitwen gestalten ihr Schicksal: Lebenskämpfe deutscher Kriegerwitwen nach eigenen Darstellung* (*War Widows Create Their Fate: Life Struggles of German War Widows in Their Own Words*), an anthology of eighteen autobiographical accounts of women who lost their soldier husbands. Hurwitz-Stranz's collection highlights the impact of loss on survivors, but also the ways in which widows rebuilt their lives and the life of the nation. "*Aus der Kriegszeit schon daran gewöhnt, verantwortlich und frei zu handeln, hatte die Frau . . . die Möglichkeit am Wiederaufbau unseres Vaterlandes mitzuarbeiten* [Being accustomed to war time, woman had the chance to responsibly and freely partake together in the rebuilding of the fatherland]," as activist Martha Harnoss wrote in the epilogue of the book.[10] Women's attempts at rebuilding the homeland formed a nexus between women and the nation that politicized the lives of many German women. The reformers faced seemingly impenetrable barriers erected by the patriarchal society and culture into which they were born; harsh postwar conditions including hunger, unemployment, and inflation brought in part by the continuing blockade and a punishing peace treaty; and Weimar Germany's resistance to any alteration of gender roles in postwar society.[11] While the widows anthologized in Hurwitz-Stranz's book heeded Harnoss' call to design their own fate and of the future of their nation, the political and economic instability that followed defeat in war, along with the inevitable bitterness, exacted a grave toll from feminists and other Germans courting change in the postwar years.

For German war widows, returning to some state of "normalcy" may also have seemed futile. Leonhard Frank's fictional account of the World War dramatizes a widow's realization that for her, the end of the war will mean exclusion, rather than integration into a "normal," peacetime society: *"Der Krieg ist aus, alle Menschen freuen sich grenzenlos . . . , und mein Mann ist tot, kommt nicht zurück. Kommt nie mehr!* [The war is over, everyone engages in unbridled rejoicing . . . and my husband is dead, isn't coming back. Won't come anymore!]"[12] For Germans, defeat meant that the return to peacetime would be punctuated by reminders of national and individual loss. While U.S. reformers encountered similar resistance to change, as a whole Americans did not face the prospect of fundamental social, political, and economic reconstruction as did their German counterparts.[13]

Loss of nearly a generation of young German men meant that responsibility for rebuilding the family income and for nursing ex-soldiers and facilitating their reentry into the family and work, and for binding up the nation's wounds, fell disproportionately upon the widows and the wives of the severely injured.[14] Women working politically to improve their lot did so in the face of resentment toward them by returning soldiers (especially those touting the "stab-in-the-back" theory) and by the bourgeois women's movement's own disavowal of the possibility of change.[15] The Weimar Constitution had granted women equality "in principle," and German women activists such as Harnoss took that document as their starting point for political activism,[16] but political equality remained elusive in both countries. Women exercised their voting rights, but German political parties kept women "well away from high-level politics," according to Ute

Frevert, and after a majority the states ratified woman suffrage in 1920 in the United States, women did not vote as a bloc, voted in smaller numbers than men, and marked ballots the same way as their male relatives, leaving much of the political power in both countries safely in the hands of men.[17]

Susan R. Grayzel has written that for the French and British the end of the Great War fostered a return to gender normalcy rather than opening new opportunities for women as was previously supposed.[18] Despite some political and economic gains, when women reinforced traditional gender roles for men and women—by commemorating male war heroes and by relegating childrearing exclusively to the female sphere through their support of protective legislation—they contributed to the reinscription of gender normalcy in Germany and in the United States as well. Female reformers sought to construct connections between what they perceived as women's duties to their country and the nation itself, but they were often unwilling to untie the knot that they believed bound women inextricably to home, motherhood, and family—to traditional gender roles.[19] The question of what a woman's proper place was in society, whether as a wife and mother, a working member of society, or as a full and equal citizen, or all three, remained unclear when the war ended. In Germany and in the United States, activists touted their ability to contribute to society in ways other than in having and raising children, and reformers in both nations demanded recognition for women as having been equally victimized by the war. But women's voices were muted in both countries by the amplified clarion calls for renewed nationalism and militarism in the postwar era.

Postwar Germany: Work and Welfare

The rebuilding of German society had begun already during the war. Less than a year after the conflict began, it was clear that extraordinary measures would be required to heal the devastation inflicted by total war, as 2.7 million men were sent home permanently wounded just one year into belligerency.[20] The process began in April 1915, when the German League for Private Charity gathered representatives from all organizations involved in the care of injured soldiers and survivors in Berlin to discuss strategies for action. Reconvening in the Reichstag buildings again in November 1915, delegates called themselves the Administrative Committee for War Widows and Orphan Care. Several reformers, including

Ernest Francke, Helene Simon, Lina Roepp, Alice Solomon, and Josephine Levy-Rathenau, presented speeches on various topics. Participants later filed reports, published in 1916 as "Working Women's Skills and War Widows." The pamphlet provided overviews of leading German reformers' wartime attitudes and expectations with regard to female wageworkers and survivors and their ability to help rebuild families and German society as a whole.[21]

About 800,000 additional women and girls went to work in German industries from 1913 through 1918. As they moved into what were traditionally men's jobs, no more conjecture about their weak constitutions, their lesser capabilities, or the inappropriateness of women working for wages could be heard from those in business or government.[22] Josephine Levy-Rathenau asserted that working women would be a permanent fixture in German society by the end of belligerency and would therefore play a major role in the peacetime economy, despite the fact that women recruited to work during the war expected to relinquish their positions to returning soldiers.[23] But Levy-Rathenau expected continuity between the wartime and postwar years: she knew that in laboring women's places would step wives in need of work, whose breadwinner husbands had lost their limbs or their lives during the war. Furthermore, widows expecting to remarry faced a very somber situation, given the already-vast number of battlefield casualties by November 1915. Loss of husbands became an important factor determining the fate of the female worker, as the enormous toll of Germany's war-induced fatalities helped ensure that women remained marginalized but still valued for their reproductive abilities in the postwar society. As a conquered force, Germans looked for ways to regenerate their nation through a reinvigorated manhood and renewed fertility.

Levy-Rathenau reminded readers that Germany as a nation had an interest in cultivating quality workers, and women wartime workers had proven their worth. A highly trained female work force had made (and should continue to make) Germany a competitive nation in world markets. Given women's important contributions, female laborers could not afford to be burdened with domestic duties or with fears that their housework and family life would deteriorate while they toiled. Levy-Rathenau referred to an ongoing debate in German society: should women be protected from work for wages that may interfere with their function as housewives and mothers?[24] These arguments led, in contradictory fashion, to demands for greater political rights for women but also to discrimination against females. Historian Susanne Rouette argued that protective legislation during the Weimar Republic marked the first steps taken by the government to reinstitute gender normalcy; women were, as they'd been before the war, barred from some workplaces due to dangers posed, and female blue-collar workers were banned from night work. Government officials considered the reintroduction of protective legislation as a means of reducing the female workforce.[25] Levy-Rathenau conceded that women's bodily and spiritual abilities should be tested, but argued that wartime work had proved that women performed just as well and occasionally better than their male counterparts. The reformer seemed to regard women's inferior positions in Germany's workforce as a matter of ignorance: female employees, she claimed, would only be accepted in German society (including among women themselves) once people actually saw women working.

Levy-Rathenau detected prejudice in other aspects of wartime Germany as well. For example, those involved in survivors' care often assumed that when a fallen soldier had maintained a business in his civilian life, his widow or daughter could not continue the enterprise and would depend on either a new husband or other male relative to keep it solvent. (By contrast, Hurwitz-Stranz's anthology applauds a farmer's wife who not only kept her family's business by working the fields and raising four sons during her soldier-husband's absence, but even added to her family's holdings.[26]) Here again, Levy-Rathenau believed that an increase in the number of businesswomen would help reduce bigoted attitudes toward females. Concurring with the reformer's enlightened view of female workers, a workplace inspector predicted that at war's end a high estimation of women workers would develop because females had ably filled men's positions (U.S. physician John Rich McDill, who performed relief work in Germany before the United States entered the war, agreed).[27] Furthermore, employers would want to keep women workers because they paid them less than men.[28]

The positive determination among wartime conferees conveyed their sense that German society could smoothly transition to peace. But by the February 1918 convention—which took place after the terrible "turnip winter" of 1916–1917 and another famine in the winter of 1917–1918—participants' buoyant spirit had turned dour. Proceedings of the meeting were recorded in *The State and Future Developments of War Widows and Orphans' Welfare*, and they indicated a grim outlook for continued financing of the welfare system. While the goal remained training childless widows for work, missing was the implication that working women benefited

German society. Instead, the conference chairman considered employing widows to be *"Dankespflicht für die Gefallenen an deren Hinterbliebenen, an deren Witwen und Waisen auszuüben* [dutiful thanks to the dead soldier, whose survivors, widows, and orphans must carry on]," shifting the strategy from heralding women's skills and abilities to honoring the dead warrior instead.[29] In addition, welfare offices reminded clients that women's real contributions took place in the home, according to the Secretary of the *Reichsarbeitsministerium* (minister of labor) Hermann Geib. "[Welfare workers] never lost sight of the higher goal," Geib insisted, "to preserve the mother's care for her home and her children."[30] At the same time, the government began taking further steps to dismiss women from their jobs. Business, government, unions, and the women themselves considered female labor as substitute labor, and women were ousted from their positions with "relatively little difficulty."[31] Job placement services were made available only to people deemed "dependent on their own earnings," and after February 1919 manufacturers wishing to hire more than five workers had to go through the job placement office, enabling bureaucrats to channel female work into "suitable" jobs. Female officials in trade unions, along with their sisters in the Social Democratic Party and the bourgeois women's movement, agreed that women should take their place behind men for available work.[32] As historian Ute Daniel has shown, female employment in Germany rose by only 5.1 percent from 1907 to 1925, making women workers seem only a marginal part of the workforce despite their aid to their country in wartime and in contrast to Levy-Rathenau's rosy predictions.[33]

Meanwhile, females' positions in welfare offices were co-opted by men working in the field and also by the government, as historian Young-Sun Hong has shown. Reformers argued that feminine nature suited women best for social work, so activists had lobbied the government for greater status. The director of an infant welfare and healthcare organization, Leo Langstein, responded that women were too emotional to run bureaucracies, and, with government approval, he squashed reformers' efforts. An entire female-staffed welfare office in Guben, Germany, resigned in protest. At nearly all levels of German society into which women had asserted themselves during the war, resistance to their inroads had succeeded by the mid-1920s.[34]

In the area of war survivors' organizations, however, war widows gained valuable political and organizational skills, although they remained secondary in status to veterans. Welfare for needy survivors teetered amid chaos by November 1918. As Richard Bessel has pointed out, no nation plans for its own defeat during war, and Germany was no exception. After the nation collapsed militarily, it faced political revolution and economic dislocation as millions of soldiers poured across the Rhine all at once, as per the armistice agreement.[35] In the aftermaths of wars, nations typically establish worker-training programs or offer government loans to veterans, since former combatants were more likely to threaten the peace.[36] The Weimar government followed this pattern, but its offerings were deemed inadequate. During the war, the care of injured soldiers had been the responsibility of numerous volunteer groups from trade unions to bourgeois women's and church organizations.[37] But soldiers and their caretakers felt that the government that had sent them to war owed them more than "the thanks of the Fatherland."[38] After demobilization veterans began banding together with war widows to promote survivors' welfare. On December 22, 1918, in a grisly parody of the patriotic off-to-war parades of August 1914, ten thousand maimed and blinded ex-soldiers bundled in tattered uniforms marched to the War Ministry in Berlin, and—accompanied by widows—demanded something more substantial from their government for their service.[39] By 1921 there were seven war victims' groups, representing 1.4 million members. But survivors' groups also fought for men's privileged positions in society. The leader of the Rhineland branch of the war survivors' group *Zentralverband* argued that women's primary concern should be ensuring the education of their sons and daughters, which furthered the power of the family in the nation.[40] The Ludwigshafen branch of the *Reichsbund der Kriegsbeschädigten, Kriegsteilnehmer und Kriegshinterbliebenen* (Association of War Damaged, War Participants, and War Survivors), the largest of the seven survivors' organizations, in September 1919 passed a resolution to protest against the continued employment of females. "Many young men and women dissipate in an irresponsible manner," members reasoned, "the money which they steal from the war victims in so shameless a manner."[41] A resolution passed at a meeting of more than 700 regional *Reichsbund* members demanded welfare reform and discharge of all females not dependent on gainful employment to be replaced by those injured in the war and by veterans. In the wake of their release, female laborers should rely on pensions to compensate for their income loss.[42] Thus, rather than earning their own bread, women should become dependants of the state in the minds of some veterans and survivors. The government took a step in that direction in October 1919 when it approved one hundred million marks for war victims.[43]

By 1920, the Weimar government revolutionized Germany's social welfare policies through the *Reichsversorgungsgesetz* (RVG). The law shifted the welfare burden from province to nation and abolished the previous practice of doling out survivor benefits based on military rank. Instead, the amount a wounded soldier received was calculated as a percentage of total disability; for example, men deemed 50 percent or higher disabled received a severe disability allowance. There were also additional allowances depending on what position the soldier would have held had he not been immobilized (called the "equalization allowance") and whether he needed at-home care or unemployment allowance until he could find work. Widows' pensions were calculated by assuming that their husbands were 100 percent disabled; however, they received only 30 percent of that amount. A widow over the age of fifty, or who was herself disabled, or who had children to care for, received 50 percent. Orphans were also paid pensions, as were dependent parents. The crucial new feature of the law was the provision requiring pensioners to apply for benefits; determination of amount received depended on the evaluation of a local pension office.[44]

Widows received paltry sums, particularly in the inflation years of 1921 and 1922. A study conducted in Darmstadt in 1930 demonstrated that widows living alone or with growing children were likely worse off than if their husbands had still been living.[45] Welfare-dependant war widows who did not remarry generally constituted those living in the direst circumstances in the early 1920s.[46] One war widow in Hurwitz-Stranz's anthology recalled that her pension payment for two weeks purchased only four pounds of bread. "*Ein jämmerlicher Trost*" (of little comfort), explained a captain's widow sarcastically in the *Reichsbund* journal, "[is the new RVG law] for a mother, who sees her children standing in front of the sweet-smelling bakeshop with hungry eyes . . . [and who has] to say to them: come, it won't work, we lost the war, we are poor!"[47] In addition, women had less access to welfare and were subjected to more degrading controls and tests than men.[48]

The government set up pension courts that heard demands for larger payments or for other special allowances. These courts operated extremely inefficiently: five years after the war's end millions of people still did not know what their pension would be.[49] One widow recounted that, ten weeks pregnant at the time, she had to rely on "poor relief" for six months while authorities investigated her husband's war-related injury that had resulted in his death.[50] In addition, the government began cutting back on benefits and eliminated some altogether. It also sharply reduced its staff, meaning that veterans and widows had to wait longer to get their cases heard. By 1923, many of the gains won in the fight to obtain benefits had been lost. Tumultuous events of those years, including the 1920 Kapp *Putsch* and the Ruhr Crisis three years later, hampered the Weimar government's effectiveness in dealing with domestic crises.[51]

Widows confronting the pension bureaucracy certainly did not gain much from their experience other than meager benefits and, in at least one case, a cynical view of the lingering class system in postwar Germany. "*Ein jämmerlicher Trost*," repeated the captain's widow, "[is the new RVG law] in the face of those whom I have observed sitting in their automobiles and carriages, [and] who . . . spend thousands on wine and champagne while at the spa." Her experiences as a war widow left her stripped of all but her dignity. "I'd rather be a horse thief, rather be a prostitute," she explained, "than go begging to the welfare office." Interviews with widows at welfare offices were coupled with visitations at the beneficiaries' homes, where circumstances were checked against the widows' applications for discrepancies.[52] Forcing supplicants to grovel for their pensions and then surveilling their homes served to reinforce the "stab-in-the-back" mentality, making it seem as though women were guilty of causing the defeat and now were getting their just deserts.[53]

Uniformed women fared no better. The German military began hiring *Etappenhelferinnen* (rear-echelon assistants) in 1917; a total of about twenty thousand served in this capacity (alongside another twenty-eight thousand army nurses). But garrisoned females gained little for their efforts; nurses, for example, received 70 *Pfennig* per day, while the average wageworker in Germany earned 5.5 marks daily (the average female wageworker earned 2.28 marks during the war). Paltry offerings to military auxiliaries reinforced the sense that women's work carried little value in the larger society.[54]

Still, those that fought for their rights, either through the pages of the *Reichsbund* journal or on the streets, or before the *Reichspräsident* (president of the Reich) himself, learned to take control of their own lives and tried, in their organizations, to determine the fate of their nation.[55] In the larger groups, such as the *Internationaler Bund*, the *Reichsbund*, the *Reichsverband*, and the *Zentralverband*, women served on executive committees locally (though seldom in regional organizations).⁵⁶ In 1921, however, a group of *Kriegsopfer* (war victim) representatives met with government officials, including the *Reichspräsident*. Half of those in attendance were women. The authorities heard arguments for raising pensions but responded that, due in part to reparations demands, there was no money available. In addition, widows demanded equal rights to job training programs as orphans received under the *Reichsversorgungsgesetz* (Ute Daniel noted that the vocational training and qualification of women workers in Germany during the war actually declined).⁵⁷ Women's involvement in the war victims' movement did serve to introduce them into organized activism.

Nevertheless, the government continued to insist that women's primary concern remained the home, and they were warned that work for wages interfered with that priority. "*Die Dankbarkeit gegen unsere gefallenen Krieger legt uns die Pflicht auf, ihre Häuslichkeit in ihren Sinne zu erhalten. Nichts beeinträchtigt diese aber mehr, als die mütterliche Erwerbsarbeit* [We are obligated by a sense of duty to preserve domesticity for the fallen soldiers as our thankfulness to them. Nothing impairs this more than working mothers.]."⁵⁸ These opening words of the July 1915 meeting of the Permanent Committee for the Promotion of Female Workers' Interests confirmed that women's roles in the family constituted their contribution to the war effort. To preserve women's ties to their children, war widows demanded legal protection from having to work for wages. Widows with one or more children, they argued, were *erwerbsunfähig* (unemployable) and should be excluded from the workplace.⁵⁹ Some widows reinforced this plea by suggesting that the morality of the children would falter if mothers were obliged to work outside the home.⁶⁰ This served to undercut glowing reputation of the woman worker that Levy-Rathenau had hailed and kept women confined, at least rhetorically, to the perceived "private" sphere.

Yet several of the *Kriegerwitwen* anthologized in Hurwitz-Stranz's book affirmed work for wages as a therapeutic balm on their war-induced sorrows. For another, however, work alone did not suffice. Born into an impoverished family, this particular widow complained that she toiled half the night after she had tended to her housework and put her children to bed. But she could not bear a life of only work and sleep. "My life should not be without substance, or ideals," she wrote. Thanks to her mother, who cared for her offspring during the day, the widow went on to join the Social Democratic Party (to fulfill her duties as an equal citizen, she explained), and became the recording clerk of her local Work

Council. Her constituency then elected her to the City Council, and she took a seat on the Board of Directors of the regional Welfare Office as well. In the latter position, she concluded proudly, she was able to fulfill her ideal of fighting for the rights of war victims.[61]

Others suggested that widows remarry, both as an alternative to work for wages and as a means of repopulating and regenerating the Fatherland. The Weimar Constitution acknowledged marriage as the bedrock of family life and of the life of the nation. In her study of the postwar unions in the province of Saxony, Ida Rost warned that "if marriage is disturbed, family life is thereby endangered, and if marriage difficulties become particularly numerous, the *preservation* and propagation of the nation will also be impaired," tying nuptials to the survival of Germany itself.[62] Karl Kuetti's comparison of birthrates among German women and war widows demonstrated that widows had far fewer children than the female population in general. "We have here in one special snippet the hardest result of the war," he lamented, "the strengthening of the low birthrate through the raised death rate [due to lost husbands]."[63] More marriages equaled more children and therefore a more robust Germany. Employing alarmist language, sociologist Hans Harmsen warned that the Fatherland might become sterile if war widows do not remarry.[64] Illustrating a perceived lack of morality in postwar culture, the scholar noted that growing numbers of widows were living with men rather than forfeiting their widows' benefits by marrying (Harmsen referred to cohabiting women as *konkubine*).

As a solution, he cited developments in the welfare office in the town of Magdeburg, where war widows were paired romantically with war-damaged soldiers. About 120 unions resulted from the effort. In addition to (at least theoretically) boosting birthrates, economics played a key role in the matchmaking effort. Harmsen noted that the town's economy benefited from the reduction in the number of husbandless women. In addition, Harmsen reported that a Magdeburg baker's widow could not operate her dead husband's business (contrary to Levy-Rathenau's contention that widows could do so), and she soon profited from the marriage-broker's assistance.[65]

Chaotic economic, political, and social conditions in Germany during and after the war account for the bitter edge prevalent in Weimar war survivors' interpretations of the war. The misery from hunger and resulting disease that women fought as individuals doubled and tripled if they had children's mouths to feed as well. While underweight, fatigued women and children queued up for long hours in cities to receive inadequate, poor-quality, high-priced food during the war and indeed until the blockade was officially lifted with passage of the 1919 treaty, their American counterparts generally escaped such dehumanizing wretchedness.[66] While German women labored, both for wages and for government survivors' benefits, their positions relative to men remained subordinate, as men regained their privileged positions in business, industry, and politics after the war.

Despite the limitation of being female, Helene Hurwitz-Stranz found a way to shape postwar German society. She recorded her experiences as an observer on the National Pension Court, a position that enabled her to influence decisions regarding whether and how much money widows would receive. Active involvement in the state empowered her, and she co-opted the government's own language to suggest that women, too, deserved their nation's esteem. "[By being court observers] women can make a significant contribution in the administration of justice and can substantiate the offer made to war victims: the thanks of the Fatherland."[67]

The Postwar United States: Work and Welfare

In 1918, the Sweet-Orr Company of New York sent copies of a pamphlet to manufacturers all over the United States, heralding its invention of the "Womanall," a supposedly more feminine—but actually barely distinguishable—version of a conventional pair of overalls. This article of clothing, the manufacturers claimed, was "designed by wearing apparel experts to present an attractive skin-like appearance without sacrificing any practical qualities that are essential." Alerting personnel managers to the dangers of accidents that could occur among their female, skirt-wearing workers, Sweet-Orr advised, "Think how impossible men would find working at lathes or around machinery if they had to wear a skirt!" The information to be passed along to the workers themselves was that "womanalls are actually MORE modest than the usual short skirt and open neck waist."[68] In this way, American industries prepared for the onslaught of women working in munitions plants and other war-related industries after April 1917. The message was clear: women workers and their bosses needed to become more pragmatic in their approach to females at the workplace. The women themselves needed assurances that they could be practical, but feminine, as they transferred from the traditional female trades to occupations usually considered appropriate only for men.

U.S. historians David M. Kennedy and Maurine Weiner Greenwald have characterized the typical American female wartime worker as single women moving up from low-paying positions in service or domestic work to highly skilled wartime industries. The federal censuses of 1910 and 1920 revealed that the Great War did not result in a massive shift of non–wage earning women into the paid labor market. Between 1910 and 1920 there was a modest 6.3 percent increase in the female labor force (as compared to Germany's 5.1 percent, see above). Kennedy argues that established trade unions such as the American Federation of Labor and the Central Federated Union of New York were largely to blame for the animosity shown towards the woman worker and for her resulting inability to take advantage of her wartime experiences and become a permanent fixture in the American workplace. Eric Foner's study agrees.[69]

The picture appears to be more complicated than mere union ill will, however. In her study of the Pennsylvania Rail Road (PRR), Janet F. Davidson shows that railroad officials and the federal government that operated the PRR during the war reinstituted a culture of masculinity in the business after the armistice. While Washington had created a bureaucracy, the Women's Service Section (WSS), to encourage the recruitment and training of women during the war, the PRR collaborated with government officials to reduce the number of female workers after 1918 by accusing them of lacking respectability, by misapplying seniority rules, and by instituting new classification systems. Both the WSS and individual workers resisted railroad officials' moves to reduce its female staff. The policy of ousting women was part of a general move to gain over control of labor in the postwar years. However, wartime experiences did prove that men could no longer assume that only they had "an inalienable right to railroad work."[70]

Activists also took heart when Congress created the Department of Labor's U.S. Women's Bureau (WB) in 1920, lending credence to the idea that women were now an indispensable part of the labor force. As the WB's first director, Mary Anderson compiled a nationwide survey of industries that employed female workers called *The New Position of Women in American Industry* in 1920. As the title suggests, Anderson expected that women's accomplishments during the war would guarantee their positions in industry. The WB's rhetoric harmonized closely with that expressed by the German reformer Josephine Levy-Rathenau.

"While women in industry were serving the Nation in war," wrote the Bureau, "they were demonstrating to themselves, to industry, and to the public to what extent . . . they were capable of serving in wider fields of industrial responsibility in times of peace." Like her German counterpart, Anderson expected that the demands weighing in upon industries to develop foreign markets would require manufacturers to continue utilizing women, despite union resistance to female employees (the molders' union, for example, did not admit females and fined members caught teaching them skills!). Anderson argued that now was the time to end the prejudices already washed away by the nation's need for female labor during the war and by the formidable ways that women had proven their worth to industrial employers.[71] Yet American industry chose not to take advantage of female potential, and, indeed, "women's contributions were quickly erased from sight and memory," according to Davidson.[72] Evidence of this forgetfulness can be found in Paul Anthony Samuelson's and Everett Einar Hagen's 1943 study *After the War: Military and Economic Demobilization of the United States*, in which the two economists analyze post–World War I conditions. The authors devote only one page in their forty-five-page study to the female worker, whom they contend was satisfied to retire to her kitchen stove.[73]

The WB's praise for the female worker was echoed by the Women's Auxiliary of the American Legion (WAAL). This entity, created in 1919 by amendment to the American Legion Constitution and limited in membership to female relatives of servicemen and women, did not list the championing of women's rights as part of its program. Nevertheless, its leader trumpeted the wartime accomplishments of females and even called for revisionist history of the war that would include women. WAAL leader Vye Smeigh Thompson proclaimed that the average American man appreciated the sterling worth of the nation's womanhood as it marched into the ranks of industry during the war. Furthermore, announced Thompson, "when the impartial history of the World War is written the women of America and of the Allied Nations will have large mention, for they helped to make that history" (compare Woodrow Wilson's summation of women's wartime work, in which the commander-in-chief declined to view their contributions as historically significant; see Chapter 3). Women's *dismissal* from service after the war, however, barely merited mention in Thompson's view. "Many of the causes for which the women of America gave their best are no longer needing their services," she explained, and left it at that.[74]

Like the Women's Bureau and the WAAL, the Women's Trade Union League (WTUL) also assessed women's place in the American labor force after the war, but its rhetoric differed from the other two organizations. Founded in 1903, the WTUL fostered women's union activities, studied working conditions in factories (particularly in the needle trades), and advocated protective legislation. After the war, members Margaret Dreier Robins, Emma Steghagen, and others, reported on the organization's December 1918 convention. Rather than trumpeting women's abilities in wartime industries, Robins and Steghagen's prose made women's participation in all aspects of society (except military combat) seem obvious, as though females *were already* inherently equal to their male counterparts and therefore needed no special treatment: "Yesterday, Democracy called to the nations to train their men to fight; today Democracy calls to the nations to train their citizens to think. . . . The citizens of today are not a group of men and women set apart for a specific service; the citizens of today are the men and women in the factories and workshops and counting houses, in the mills and the mines, in the fields and the forests, tillers of the soil, workers of hand and brain, hewers and thinkers."[75]

Rather than singling women out as contributors to the nation's war effort, the WTUL set out the standards for a democratic society in which men and women workers could not be distinguished from one another. To achieve those standards, the organization asked that their Labor Standards be included in the Treaty of Versailles. These included compulsory education up to sixteen years of age, the abolition of child labor, an eight-hour day, equal pay for equal work and equal training for men and women, old age pensions and—the exception to its rhetoric of sexual equality—maternity benefits and the abolishment of night work for women.

Striking similar notes to the Women's International League for Peace and Freedom's response to the Versailles Treaty, the Women's Charter (see Chapter 4), the WTUL offered a list of reconstruction policies as guidelines for the rest of the world. These included free speech, press, and assemblage and the removal of all wartime restrictions on the interchange of ideas and movements of people, and amnesty for political prisoners. They urged woman suffrage and complete political, legal, and industrial equality. To ensure the smooth return to a peacetime economy in all belligerent nations, the WTUL advocated a Commission on Demobilization, where both sexes would represent labor's interests, to formulate plans to ensure employment for all workers at standard rates, and it advocated that soldiers not be demobilized in a greater ratio that industry can absorb. Finally, the women demanded that wartime workers be considered equally with servicemen in the plans for a peacetime economy. Members also demanded that motherhood be protected.[76]

The one way, of course, in which the WTUL argued that women did require special treatment was in the area of protective legislation. Here, Robins and Steghagen adopted an ideology of motherhood that blended with their sense that there was an inherently beneficent quality to the feminine nature to rationalize their support for protective legislation. In response to feminists' complaints that such rhetoric served only to keep women marginalized in the work force, Robins shot back that "individualistic," elite reformers like Alice Paul and Suzanne La Follette lacked compassion and had not witnessed the brutal aspects of industry.[77] The WTUL, by demanding economic, political, and social equality for women, offered a more progressive outlook than other organizations but still retained traditional views of motherhood in its rhetoric.

Although German and American women experienced similar attitudes toward female workers, in matters relating to welfare the two countries differed, making clear the advantages of residing in the victorious nation. Even so, both the defeated and conquering nations confirmed the economic dependency of their female populations. In the United States, lawmakers revamped the federal military pensions system with the nation's entry in the World War. President Wilson signed the War Insurance Law on October 6, 1917. Economist William H. Glasson heralded the new law as a "radical departure" from the existing pension system, citing the provision's support for dependents of enlisted men during the war through a "family allowance" system (made up of equal contributions by the soldier and the government; German and French families with husbands or fathers serving in the armed forces also received such allowances[78]), and a compensation system provided to both enlisted men and officers in the case of death or disability of servicemen and women incurred during his or her military service that was no longer tied to rank. The law provided for compensation based on the degree of impairment of his earning capacity and the size of the family of dependents (widows' benefits were based on family size). So while not tied to rank, compensation was linked to economic class. The law charged a new bureaucracy, the Division of Military and Naval Insurance, with determining the reduction of earning capacity. The injured servicemen and women were required to submit "reasonable" medical exams, at the discretion of the bureau. Under the family allowance provision of the law, female enlistees' families only received money if the dependents were children, grandchildren, parents, or siblings; husbands of servicewomen were not compensated, presumably because a man would not have been dependent upon his wife for income.[79] So while both nations' governments offered veterans and survivors similar benefits, the Weimar government had an increasingly difficult time meeting its survivors' needs (the U.S. government's difficulties were not made clear until the Great Depression hit its peak in 1932, when Bonus Army Marchers demanded early payments).[80]

Female veterans in the United States were not altogether pleased with their benefits or with their status within the military itself. In arguing in favor of greater female presence, however, activists employed rhetoric that served to validate the masculine soldier hero instead of the work that women actually performed. The Women's Overseas Service League (WOSL) formed the most significant female veterans' organization in the United States, and its members worked the hardest at defending women's achievements in the military against an assault coming from within the bureaucracy itself. After U.S. intervention, the Commission on Training Camp Activities, a military entity made up of male and female reformers, took on responsibility for the morals and the morale of servicemen. But after demobilization, the army absorbed that responsibility itself. In 1923 the War Department held a conference to discuss methods for ensuring the moral uplift of troops, but it did not invite a single female reformer. In 1925 the U.S. Navy proclaimed that enlistment could only come from "male citizens of the United States" instead of from the population at large, as had been the case during the war.

In a nationally broadcast speech, WOSL President Mildred Taubles pledged to lobby Congress to have *all* women involved in overseas military service eligible to receive the benefits awarded to servicemen. She complained that of the 22,000 women who had served Uncle Sam in the war, only half that number received government payments as nurses in either the Army or the Navy. As historian Susan Zeiger has shown, however, the WOSL president adopted a masculine view of citizenship in her speech, arguing that only by risking death through combat could women expect citizenship. The Weimar government in Germany advanced the same argument, except that its parliament explicitly ruled out females serving as combatants (see below).[81]

Women and War Remembrance in Germany

In explaining the differences between war memorials in the victorious and vanquished nations, historian George L. Mosse wrote, "Germany had no antiwar monuments and no enraged mothers. Neither could have helped to regenerate the nation, infusing it with new youth, energy, and vigor so that it might overcome defeat."[82] Instead, Germans relied on the "cult of the fallen hero" to compensate for their wartime losses. Germans and Americans each hoped that by uniting to commemorate their soldier heroes they could reinvigorate their war-weary societies. In these rituals, too, women played only a secondary role, which reinforced their marginal status in society. In any case, participating in war remembrance ceremonies served to privilege men's wartime experiences and discount women's. Glorifying fallen soldiers reminded inhabitants of the sacrifices men had made to keep the nation strong and the culture pure. Women's contributions to the war effort, either as nurses or in munitions factories or in caring for soldiers' families, were seldom recalled.

In Germany, the cease-fire did not mark the end of militarism or the war. Military and political leaders attempted to skirt a threatening sense of disillusionment about the defeat in ceremonial speeches and memorials. A *Reichstag* Commission investigating the responsibility for both the 1914 outbreak of war and the 1918 defeat called Field Marshal von Hindenburg in for questioning. In a prepared speech, the general blamed the enemy and traitorous home front for the loss. In December 1918 Social Democrat President Friedrich Ebert welcomed soldiers back in Berlin with the remark that they were returning undefeated;[83] six years later, on the ten-year anniversary of the outbreak of the war, he delivered a speech in which he proclaimed that his country had only fought the war in self-defense and that warriors' sacrifice had enabled the nation to live.[84] Women who served the military as nurses or *Etappenhelferinnen* (rear-echelon assistants) were imagined as sacrificial mothers or as official camp-followers, respectively, to undercut their possible claims to heroism; they were not celebrated in public memory after the war.[85] Images of females as prostitutes and helpmeets could be seen in a variety of venues in postwar Germany. The artist Otto Dix, for example, painted a syphilitic prostitute corrupting a disfigured soldier in *Whore with War Cripple* (1923). Editors of *Der Stahlhelm* (steel helmet), a magazine published by a nationalist veterans' organization, announced births in their "*Familie Nachrichten*" (family news) section in the back pages of their journal. Male births were heralded as *Kräftigen Stahlhelmjungen* (husky steel-helmeted boy); if female, a *Kräftigen Stahlhelm Marketenderin* (strong camp-follower).[86] Meanwhile, secret military units called the *Freikorps* arose and a new rearmament program began, in violation of the Treaty of Versailles.[87]

German nationalism intensified in the early 1920s. Nationalist rhetoric brought honor to the nation by perpetuating the idea that, since the war had been defensive, the heroes' actions and motives were pure (best illustrated by the frequently invoked metaphor of the *Stahlbad* (steel bath), which emphasized the therapeutic, rejuvenating nature of war[88]) and that their deaths had not been in vain, since they served the higher purpose of assuring the nation's survival. Robert Weldon Whalen listed a myriad of commonly used German words describing *Heldentum* (heroism), including *Heldenzone* (heroes' zone), *Heldentaten* (heroic deeds), *Heldenblut* (heroes' blood), *Heldentod* (heroic death), *Heldengrab* (heroes' graves), *Heldenhain* (heroes' grove), *Heldenbücher* (heroic books), and even *Heldenbibliothek* (heroes' library) in his book.[89] All of the qualities embodied in the war hero—courage, self-sacrifice, and virility, or "warfare as welfare, violence as regeneration, virility as virtue," as Michael Geyer put it—were mirrored in nationalist ideology. Historians such as Hermann Rex, Franz Schauwecker, Georg Soldan, and Ernst Junger supported these interpretations.[90] Indeed, no other nation, according to U.S. historian Kurt Piehler, rivaled Germany in presenting the war as a "cult of the fallen" and as a positive good in its war memorials, infusing the defeated nation with a sense of hopeful renewal.[91] At the same time, Germans (both men and women) looked to women as mothers to aid in the project of postwar renewal, making women feel valued, though still subordinated to men.[92]

This nationalist-militarist rhetoric did not go unchallenged, however. Pacifism in Germany reached its high point in 1924, just as patriots and nationalists began honoring the fallen soldiers in cultish proportions. Artists Ernst Friedrich, Käthe Kollwitz, and Otto Dix exhibited their antiwar imagery together in Friedrich's Antiwar Museum in Berlin in August 1924. Yet as art historian Dora Apel has shown, even pacifists' interpretations of German wartime women upheld conventional gender stereotypes (although they contested traditional, romanticized images of soldiers). Artists' depictions cast warriors as innocent sacrificial lambs while women were shown as either corrupting camp-followers or as victimized mothers. Friedrich's book *War Against War!* (1924) implored mothers to keep war toys away from their children and war service away from their husbands, implicating women for their failure to do so prior to the war, thereby making them responsible for the continued militarization of Weimar culture. In addition to art critics, antiwar images were fiercely countered by right-wing journals such as the *Deutsche Rundschau*, where suggestions that the war was not yet over were also made.[93] But, given the popular challenge of antiwar imagery and literature of the time to nationalist, militarist rhetoric (Friedrich's work had gone through ten editions by 1930), what accounts for the ultimate triumph of nationalism and militarist ideology in Germany?

Historian Michael Geyer points to the ability of nationalists to disconnect themselves from Weimar political institutions and instead mobilize the masses. At the same time, the Social Democratic Party and the Center Party worked to hobble the antiwar movement (though it took them until 1924 to do so).[94] In addition, the cult of the fallen soldier and the trope of war as regeneration had already sunk deep historical roots in German soil in part through the poetry of Theodor Körner and the canvasses of Caspar David Friedrich in the early nineteenth century.[95] Against such traditions, pacifists' foothold foundered during the Weimar Republic, and the stage was set for nationalist-militarist mobilization beginning in the mid-1920s.

In addition to veterans' organizations, the *Volksbund Deutsche Kriegsgräberfürsorge* (VDK), a private association, formed in 1919 to maintain soldiers' graves in foreign countries in the face of the government's inability to afford the upkeep. The group also became a driving force behind commemorative activities, including the institution of a *Volkstrauertag* (memorial day) for fallen war heroes and celebration of the ten-year anniversary of the beginning of the war in 1924 (an American Legion celebration held at Madison Square Garden in 1921 sounded similar themes; see Chapter 2). The commemoration program indicated that the purpose of the event was to honor the fallen victims and their sacrifices. Catholic and Evangelical army chaplains delivered speeches to inaugurate the festivities, followed by the singing of *Trauermusik* (mourning music) that included the nationalist hymn *"Vaterland,"* the worshipful *"Heldenfeier"* ("Heroes' Celebration"), *"Wir treten zum Beten"* ("We Step In to Pray"), and *"Ich hatt' einen Kameraden"* ("I Had a Comrade"). The lyrics to the latter glorified the sacrifices soldiers made for their country, forsaking even their ties to each other:

Will mir die Hand noch reichen
Derweil ich eben lad'
Kann dir die Hand nicht geben,
Bleib du im ew'gen Leben
Mein guter Kamerad![96]

(His hand is still reaching for
The clasp I cannot give
For duty calls me onward
Good-bye my good comrade,
Our love shall live on.)

Just over a year later, in November 1925, the return of the remains of Manfred von Richtofen, better known as the Red Baron, to his homeland became a national event. The VDK also had a hand in staging the occasion. Thousands of people turned out to witness the train carrying Richtofen's body as it chugged across the Rhine River and made its way toward Potsdam Station in central Berlin. Choruses of *"Ich hatt' einen Kameraden"* could be heard as military bands played and an airplane circled overhead. The Baron's brother recalled later that the event enabled Germans to mourn all of their soldier heroes, most of whom were buried in France and whose families could not afford to bring the body home.[97]

Several bourgeois women's organizations were signatories to the consortium of VDK's umbrella, including the *Bund Deutscher Frauenvereine* and numerous religious women's groups. Women signed on to the VDK's plans for war heroes' tribute on the *Volkstrauertag* but did not appear to be active in any official commemoration activities.[98] Ann-Marie Claire Hughes has written that in the aftermath of the war in Britain, women were seen primarily as mourners of men but never as casualties themselves.[99] Karin Hausen argued that distinctions made by Germans between *Kriegsopfer* (war victims) and *Kriegshinterbliebenen* (war survivors) helped to reify the sense that survivors were not also victims, obscuring women's experiences in the conflict.[100] To counter this notion, the war survivors' biweekly supplement in the *Reichsbund* journal argued that survivors were heroes, too. A writer identifying herself as Frau Bahersdorff called upon the *Reichsbund's* female members to become *Kameradin*, an act she hoped would confirm that widows had sacrificed their husbands to the Fatherland in the same way that the *Kamerad* of the famous song had given his life.[101] Finally, books such as *Kriegerwitwen gestalten ihr Schicksal* also tried to mitigate the image that only men could be victims of war.[102]

Women and War Remembrance in the United States

In the United States, as in Germany, warriors were remembered and honored while the contributions of women were largely ignored; American writers typically relied on stalwart soldiers contrasted with a flabby, effeminate domestic culture to weave their wartime stories. But the Germanic "cult of the fallen soldier" rituals did not appear in the United States, where the civilian population remained largely oblivious to the horror of European trenches. The majority of American doughboys, giddy with anticipation as they arrived in France in 1917, were too late to experience the kind of butchery intimately—and achingly—recalled by most Europeans. The rawness of military barracks life staged by playwrights Laurence Stallings and Maxwell Anderson in their 1924 play *What Price Glory?* was likely *imagined* as war's grim reality by American audiences, but seldom compared to actual lived experiences in the way that Europeans read the prose of Erich Maria Remarque in *All Quiet on the Western Front* (1929) or the poetry of Robert Graves in "A Dead Boche" (1916). Indeed, the three American writers best known for their Great War narratives—John Dos Passos, Ernest Hemingway, and E.E. Cummings—had all fought with foreign units. As David M. Kennedy has written, doughboys viewed themselves as part fighter, part tourist, and the military did nothing to dissuade them of this notion, offering special pink passes to "gay Paree" in addition to scheduling R and R in a variety of places on a rotating basis so that as many troops got to see as much of France as possible.[103]

Arriving U.S. soldiers generally recorded their exhilaration at the adventure that lay in front of them. Even after their combat experiences ended in November 1918, one doughboy reflected, "what a glorious adventure it has all been to me."[104] Others expressed their dismay at the banality of American culture when they returned stateside. Willa Cather's Pulitzer Prize winning novel *One of Ours* (1923), in which farm boy Claude Wheeler's frontier spirit is juxtaposed with the predictability of his life in Nebraska, finds new purpose and meaning in the war. The American literature that emerged from the carnage of war tended to "cackle with positive excitement,"[105] unlike the British Great War literature, where the hero typically understood his experiences as ironic (see Chapter 3). Like some of the German antiwar imagery, even the American Great War literature deemed "disillusioned" by critics uses the cliché of comparing dull civilization with the adrenaline rush of combat.[106]

By the mid-1920s the high-tide of inspirational war literature had receded (in Germany, the trend moved in the opposite direction: by 1924 war remembrance activities began to eclipse antiwar imagery). One Harvard literary reviewer skewered John Dos Passos' *Three Soldiers* (1921) for its dishonor to American soldiers. But the novel struck a chord, and a long list of works typically considered to represent "disillusionment" with the war quickly followed. Yet some critics have noted that unlike the German writer Erich Maria Remarque's brooding sense of hopelessness in *All Quiet on the Western Front*, these narratives were driven by too high a level of energy to be described as "disillusioned." While William March's *Company K* (1931) and Dos Passos' *USA: 1919* (1932) disabused readers of their illusions of the nobility of warfare, their cynicism did not seem to be directed at violence or carnage: rather, it was aimed either at military authority figures, or at the insipidity of what they interpreted as a feminized American culture. John Dos Passos, for example, mocked traditional U.S. literature and civilization as mimicking "a well brought up and intelligent woman, tolerant, versed in the things of the world, quietly humorous, but bound tightly in the fetters of 'niceness,' of the middle-class outlook."[107] Willa Cather's character Claude Wheeler feels stifled by the predictability of the domestic life his young wife Enid has made for him in rural Nebraska. When Claude's mother visits her son and his bride at their home, she marvels at "how well their little establishment was conducted, how cheerful and attractive Enid looked when one happened to drop in there, [and] she wondered that Claude was not happy. And Claude himself wondered." Claude eagerly rushes off to training camp when the United States enters the war.[108]

One antiwar writer, Mary Lee, expressed disillusionment with the conflict because of its violence against women in her novel *It's a Great War!* (1929).[109] Lee based her story on her own experiences as a YMCA volunteer with a hospital unit in Bordeaux, in Paris, and near the front. Reviewers remarked that the book brought home the indecencies, the obscenities, and the incongruities that are a part of war. One noted that Lee ranked above John Dos Passos in offering the American public superlative war literature.[110] And yet today Lee's name is forgotten. A better-known writer, Katherine Anne Porter, described the pressured nature of U.S. war bond drives and the guilt experienced by medically impaired men when they could not do their duty in her antiwar novel, *Pale Horse, Pale Rider* (1939).[111] But the tradition of remembering combat as a romantic adventure instead of meaningless butchery remained strong. Indeed, American Legion halls rang out with the lyrics of Legionnaires' favorite wartime hymn, "Mademoiselle from Armentières,"

'Twas a hell of a war, as I recall,
But a damned sight better than no war at all.[112]

In the aftermath of the war, U.S. politicians and political commentators seemed determined to capitalize on the sense of victory that the war had engendered. Since the eve of U.S. intervention and continuing through the military occupation, Americans commemorated the victorious combat that imbued soldiering men with the manly virtues of strength and chivalry. Soldiers credited warfare for their heightened sense of manhood and for their nation's good fortune. As the advertisement that opened this chapter suggested, the doughboy—and the nation that armed him and sent him to battle—should use the newfound power to build a better future for himself and for his country. Lawmakers had reacted to the armistice as a sign of U.S. military and political power (see Chapter 1) and the Treaty of Berlin as an indication of American economic might. Hoping to sustain its political and economic advantage, the United States endeavored to isolate itself from outside influences that could threaten its well-being relative to Europe. The United States' rhetorical isolationism intensified Americans' sense of their exceptionalism (see Chapter 3).

Isolationism divided Americans in the aftermath of the war, leaving women's pacifist organizations and other international or transnational groups ostracized from mainstream American culture. The roots of the Red Scare lay in the Bureau of Investigation's suppression of German-Americans, socialists, and Industrial Workers of the World through intimidation, raids, and persecution during the war. The U.S. Congress passed the Espionage and Sedition Acts (1917 and 1918), making it a crime to compromise U.S. military actions and use scurrilous language against the U.S. government. Industrialists and politicians sensed an opportunity during the war to pass legislation intended to squash labor radicalism.[113] Wartime repression provoked a swift and dangerous reaction. Retaliation began shortly after the war in June 1919 when three government officials—the mayor of Seattle, a U.S. Senator, and U.S. Attorney General A. Mitchell Palmer—each received homemade bombs at their homes. Anarchists blew up the Wall Street office of J. P. Morgan in September 1920. Antiwar activists Emma Goldman, Alexander Berkman, and hundreds of other foreign-born radicals were deported in December 1919. President Coolidge signed the Immigration Act of 1924, freezing immigration from Southern and Eastern Europe and Asia. The infamous Joint Legislative Committee of the State of New York Investigating Seditious Activities (better known as the Lusk Committee) branded two American leaders of the Women's International League for Peace and Freedom

(WILPF), Jane Addams and Emily Greene Balch, as subversives who threatened to abolish the "patriotic, war-like spirit" of the nation.[114]

Both the American Legion and the Women's Overseas Service League condemned the WILPF, too.[115] The American Legion is surely the organization most closely identified with patriotic war remembrance in the United States, and the group also struck at perceived anti-Americanism. Colonel Theodore Roosevelt, Jr., had organized the American Legion in Paris in part to preserve soldiers' combat and camaraderie but also to prevent vulnerable, demobilized soldiers from linking arms with Bolshevik elements back home.[116] In an effort to counteract the WILPF's perceived dissidence, the WAAL's Americanism Committee pledged to promote proper observance of patriotic holidays and a higher standard of citizenship in the nation, and to provide a deeper sense of the obligation of the citizen to his country and its institutions.[117]

The WAAL also emphasized war remembrance, following the example set by its parent organization, but it offered at least written evidence of the potential of women workers to revolutionize the way Americans remembered wars. Vye Smeigh Thompson, WAAL president, juxtaposed two contradictory views of women during and after war in her history. First, she enumerated and proclaimed the contributions of women in America's wartime industries and their successes (see above). But Thompson's summation of the war indicated that in the act of war remembrance, women would only be honored as auxiliaries of soldiering men, and that, as in Germany, aiding war widows is *"Dankespflicht für die Gefallenen* [dutiful thanks to the fallen soldier]": "These former service men are combining in one great organization [the American Legion] for the preservation of those principles for which they offered their lives and for which so many thousands of their comrades made the supreme sacrifice. Along with this is the determination to honor the memory of those who died for their country by seeing that their widows and orphans are not forgotten, but shall receive all that is possible for a nation to give to make up their great loss."[118]

In this case, the author mentions women's sacrifices only in relation to their male relatives. While the American Legion Constitution did acknowledge servicewomen by allowing their relatives to be members of the organization, Thompson obscured that possibility in her history, instead describing the relationship between the American Legion and the WAAL this way: "The American Legion is an organization of the men who, when their country's honor was assailed, united to punish the assailant. The American Legion Auxiliary is an organization composed of the wives, mothers, sisters and daughters of those men." Using the same pattern of subordinating women's patriotism to their male counterparts, while at the same time reviving the warrior spirit, she continues,

> The patriotic devotion that expressed itself in millions of men assembling in camps to prepare, and when prepared crossing an enemy-infested ocean to the battlefields of Europe, evidenced the spirit of America, *a spirit too fine to be allowed to depart when the days of fighting were past*. A similar spirit, less in evidence, perhaps, but not in the fineness of its devotion, was that of the women of America. The speedy and conclusive decision of the War was due to the heroic faithfulness of America's soldiers and the faithful heroism of America's women . . . A reading of the pages of this book will reveal the character of that work and the immensity of it. The work is that which woman is by nature qualified to do; the extent of it is such that without her it could not be done.[119]

Thompson reasoned that women's "natural" work is in caring for ex-servicemen in hospitals and in aiding their families. While the WAAL worked to keep the United States' involvement in the war alive in the public imagination, it tied that objective specifically to men's service instead of women's. In so doing, the auxiliary served to obscure the female laborers that, in the first part of her book, Thompson claimed had done no less than rewrite history. Unlike the German prose that confined bravery to fallen warriors, Thompson's narrative did take note of women's heroism. Once the war ended, however, women's industrial work vanished from sight and from the history of the war itself.

U.S. women who volunteered during the war asserted their right to be publicly recognized for their service. Like the WAAL, the American War Mothers (AWM) also promoted women's work as helpmeets and war spirit revivalists. The AWM was formed in September 1917 by "blood mothers" who had sacrificed their sons to the war. The group's leaders petitioned Congress in 1924 to be granted a charter that would serve as public recognition of the women's service to their country during the war as mothers. Specifically, the proposed bill stated that the objective of the organization was to "*keep alive and develop the spirit that prompted world service*; to maintain the ties of fellowship born of that service, and . . . to assist in any way in their power men and women who served and were wounded . . . in the World War." Margaret N. McCluer, legislative chairman of the AWM, testified at a joint hearing before the Senate and House Committees on the Judiciary to argue in favor of the incorporation of the organization. McCluer asked that congressional recognition take the form of a monument to mothers during the war, an act that she felt would "let our allied countries see that our America realized what its women did and has made this recognition of their sacrifices."

McCluer and her congressional opponents sparred over whether such a charter was necessary. Congressmen Leonidas C. Dyer hinted that the AWM simply duplicated work already performed by the American Legion and Veterans of Foreign Wars and pestered McCluer to explain what necessitated the granting of a charter, noting that the public already honored American mothers (presumably, Dyer meant the 1914 establishment of Mothers' Day). McCluer responded that congressional recognition would add distinction to their organization and enable them to do their work "more efficiently." When later testimony revealed some Congressmen's contempt for "a woman who stayed at home and took care of the knitting" during the conflict, McCluer responded defensively that "many mothers tried to go overseas and do service there, but they were exempt for two reasons, that they were too old and that they had a son in service," she explained, "But we served in the Army camps as housemothers, and we walked the streets to sell Liberty bonds and did everything that was asked of us." Yet the Congressmen did not seem to place the high value upon women's contributions as McCluer had hoped. When Earl C. Michener asked McCluer whether the American War Mothers expected their group to continue even after her generation of war mothers had died, the AWM representative responded that the members intended for the AWM to last in perpetuity, patterned after the Daughters of the American Revolution. "*It would perpetuate this World War*," insisted McCluer, "and all pertaining to it just as the D.A.R. did of the Revolutionary War." Finally accepting this, Congressmen then voiced the concern that the AWM's real intention was to become a political interest group if Congress granted its request. To counter this claim, AWM member Mrs. George Gordon Seibold simply repeated the group's definitive patriotism. "What we are asking you to give is small, indeed, in comparison with the last full measure of devotion laid on *the altar of country* by the American soldier, and as the mother of one who made the supreme sacrifice and who lies among the 'unknown,' I urge speedy adoption of this bill." Congress granted the charter in February 1925.[120]

In employing the phrase "altar of country" Seibold duplicated a trope heard repeatedly in German songs and poems about Great War soldiers, *Opfer auf den Altar des Vaterlandes* (sacrifice on the altar of the Fatherland). Use of this phrase subtly implicated women in the losses sustained in the war. In 1916, soldier and writer Karl Jünger published a series of essays written by German women in response to the outbreak of war. In his preface, Jünger noted that women were expected to send their men to battle, to "lay her husband and son and father, her fiancé and brother as a sacrifice on the altar of the Fatherland."[121] When soldiers died during the war, army officers wrote to their wives or mothers, repeating the familiar phrase. This ritual prompted the sarcastic voice heard in Leonhard Frank's antiwar novel *Der Mensch ist Gut* (*Humanity is Good*). When a young wife hears the news that her husband sacrificed his life on the altar of the Fatherland, she repeats the term dully: "Sacrificed on the altar of the Fatherland. Al-tar of the Father-land. She tasted the words with her tongue, gazed into the distance, tried to imagine the Altar of the Fatherland. She couldn't do it."[122] In a similar vein, playwright William March had the commanding officer in his work *Company K* erase the flowery language of sacrifice he had been taught to use when reporting a casualty to a warrior's mother in favor of brutal honesty. "Dear Madam: Your son, Francis, died needlessly in Belleau Wood. You will be interested to hear that at the time of his death, he was crawling with vermin and weak from diarrhea." Then the officer implicated the boy's mother for her son's presence in the war, as Karl Jünger had done in his work. "He had learned long ago that what he had been taught to believe by you, his mother, who loved him, under the meaningless names of honor, courage, patriotism, were all lies."[123] The ways in which German and American writers related women to the idea of soldiers' sacrifice to the nation, whether to honor the fallen or to disabuse readers of its sanctity, implicated women in the losses that war perpetrated, thus marking them responsible for (not merely victims of) the conflict.

In both countries, members of nearly all sectors of society (welfare, work, government, industry, art, and literature) encouraged traditional gender roles for men and women. Deviation from the norm was accompanied by backlash, such as the case of the German women welfare officers that demanded greater status from their government, and the condemnation of WILPF members Addams and Balch. Militarists and nationalists alike supported traditional gender roles by valorizing male warriors but keeping servicewomen separated from military honors.

Women, however, were still valued for their ability to repopulate the nation. As Susanne Rouette has pointed out, the first German *Reichstag* to be elected with the help of women voters determined that citizenship required military duty, and as such could not be fully transferred to females. As an alternative, the legislative body resolved that women's duty as mothers was equal in value to military service (adding the caveat that only "fundamental," and not absolute, equality could be offered), thereby helping to keep women subordinate in society, but still feel esteemed in their reduced status.[124]

Americans also privileged motherhood as the feminine quality that contributed the most significantly to society. The American War Mothers and the Women's Auxiliary of the American Legion both paired womanhood consistently with children in their rhetoric, and both emphasized the special relationship mothers felt toward their boy soldiers. An additional organization, the Gold Star Mothers Association (GSMA), lobbied the military and Congress for pilgrimages for mothers of men killed in the war so that they could visit their sons' overseas graves. Although the Congressional Act sponsoring the voyages also invited widows to join the mothers, in their testimony before Congress the GSMA placed special emphasis on the mother-son bond, indicating that it surpassed marital ties. Several songs, such as "The Heavens Are a Mother's Service Flag" (1919), were written to commend mothers' and wives' wartime sacrifices, but over time song lyrics placed greater emphasis on maternity.

> Each little mother who gave up a boy
> Is a "hero" as brave as can be
> Though she never fought with sword or gun
> Her deeds are greater when the battle is done
> The stars above shine for heroes so brave
> Unrewarded their burdens they drag
> But God up on high, keeps a mark in the sky
> For the Heavens are a mother's service flag.[125]

In Germany, mothers' sacrifices were honored in this song called "Eine Heldenmutter!" (a hero's mother):

> Ich segne Dich, Du Priesterin
> An dem Altar des Vaterlands.
> Für Deinen opferstillen Sinn
> Reich' Dir der Herr den Lebenskranz.[126]

(I bless you, priestess
On the altar of the Fatherland
For your quiet sacrificial spirit
May God extend the crown of life to you.)

   The song goes on to praise the son's bold heroics in battle. Both lyrics, while taking note of the man's gallantry in war, underscored the spiritual aspects of a mother's sacrifice, connecting motherhood to the "bigger life" that awaited the returning American crusader noted in the advertisement analyzed in the beginning of this chapter—except that in the case of the wartime mother, the expanded life could only be achieved through loss, and then could only be spiritual, as opposed to the concrete benefits of public life that the ex-soldier could expect to enjoy, and in contrast to the literally concrete war monuments dedicated to fallen soldiers. In any case, it was primarily as mothers, or as prostitutes, that women appeared in the cultural expressions that both nations produced as they shifted from war to peace.

Epilogue

It is difficult to imagine how women, either individually or collectively, could have made many political gains in the twentieth century without having first won the right to vote in several European nations and in North America shortly after the Great War. Suffragists honed their political skills while campaigning for their rights, and the franchise gave women access to ballot boxes and an opportunity to shape electoral politics at the local and national level. Participating in representative democracy through voting, organizing campaigns, and garnering support for initiatives and referenda must have made women (at least those who did participate) feel more connected to citizenship within their nations than ever before.[1]

Aside from the significant increase in nations granting women voting rights after the First World War, women living in countries without suffrage laws had to wait—several more decades in some African, Asian, and Latin American nations—for the right to fill in a ballot sheet.[2] In any case, a look at conditions for women across time and space reveals that the ability of suffrage to empower women has had clear limitations. According to United Nations statistics collected in 2000, two-thirds of the world's 876 million illiterate people were female; women unable to read or write lacked the ability to participate fully in democratic institutions.[3] In addition, voting rights alone have not proven to be a guarantor of female reproductive rights or women's ability to live without abuse in their own homes. In Chile, for example, women had gained full voting rights by 1949, but it was not until 1994 that Chile's legislature passed a Domestic Violence Law, revolutionizing the way its courts responded to domestic abuse; in addition, although all abortions were illegal in Chile,

35 percent of pregnancies were terminated by women seeking the right to do so.[4] Fertility rates were declining throughout the world in 2000, but the number of women raising children on their own went up, and female heads of households were often deprived economically. Indeed, women were at an economic disadvantage throughout the world, since they remained at the lower end of segregated labor markets, were concentrated in only a few occupations, and held positions that offered less compensation than men. Women were severely underrepresented in the world's parliaments, and there were few female executives heading national governments despite women's ability to vote in nearly all the world's nations by 2000.[5]

An initial glance at women's involvement in *international* politics after the Second World War may seem disheartening. While female reformers had confidently approached Versailles negotiators to gain access to peace talks in 1919 (but were rejected, see Chapter 4), there were few opportunities, or people, to even ask in 1945. The history of the end of the Second World War demonstrated that women activists had little chance to cut their international policymaking teeth. U.S. Secretary of State Cordell Hull had outlined several principles pertaining to postwar treatment of Germany in 1943, including the creation of a United Nations–orchestrated decentralized government in Germany, and the mandating of German war reparations payments and total German disarmament. Most importantly, Hull called for the unconditional surrender of Germany to Allied forces.[6] Not wishing to repeat another Versailles disaster, U.S. President Franklin D. Roosevelt and his advisors agreed to these plans and left it to the European Advisory Commission, a body composed of the Allied military commanders, to sort out the procedures of Germany's postwar governance. Hitler's successor Admiral Karl Dönitz and other German military leaders signed unconditional surrenders piecemeal at various front lines during May 1945.[7] Military domination of the process of producing the cease-fire and the governance of the defeated nearly guaranteed that no women would participate directly in the official postwar reconciliation, since females were excluded from the upper echelons of the military in belligerent nations during the Second World War.

As had been the case in 1919, female international and transnational activists quickly found other avenues to facilitate peacemaking and the prevention of further butchery after 1945, however. Deaths resulting from the Second World War had proven to be much higher than in the

Great War: over fifty million people lost their lives during World War II, while roughly 9.4 million had died in the earlier conflict. The Holocaust, among other ghastly atrocities committed during the two world wars, helped make the twentieth century the most murderous in human history.[8] The empowerment of nongovernmental organizations (NGOs) in the interwar years, including many female-only or predominantly female groups such as the Women's International League for Peace and Freedom (WILPF) and the American Association of University Women, had resulted in the granting of consultative status within the United Nations (UN) to transnational NGOs through Article 71 of the UN Charter (historian Dorothy B. Robins speculated that U.S. delegates were eager for participation by NGOs because they recalled the U.S. Senate's rejection of the League of Nations and hoped that citizens' groups would have a positive influence on U.S. lawmakers).[9] Perhaps more encouragingly for the future of women's involvement in foreign policy, Eleanor Roosevelt chaired the UN Commission on Human Rights. This body was tasked with writing the world's first human rights declaration, and Roosevelt also headed the drafting committee.

The fifty-eight member states that signed the United Nations Universal Declaration of Human Rights (UNDHR) represented governments from a broad spectrum of political systems, ideologies, economies, and cultures. The document served as the first international recognition that freedoms and rights were to be applied universally, across national boundaries, and provided a template for subsequent human rights documents such as the 1955 South African Freedom Charter. The UN declaration stressed the "inherent dignity" of all people; it emphasized rights to liberty, life, security, and equality before the law and the right to vote, to an adequate standard of living, and to sufficient health care (the WILPF had passed resolutions similar to those found in the UNDHR in 1919, with the exception of the last two provisions).[10] The document acknowledged that citizens' duties to their societies limited their rights, and it also accepted the ability of nations to limit human rights, but only for the purposes of national security. Significantly, the drafters specifically included women in their manifesto, and they replaced the noun "men" used in similar, preceding documents such as the U.S. Declaration of Independence and the French Declaration of Rights of Man, with the word "humans." In addition, while writers initially called the document the International Declaration of Human Rights, they later changed it to "universal," indicating that they recognized that human rights belonged to all people, regardless of nationality, rather than only to signatory governments representing specific nations.[11]

Eleanor Roosevelt's achievements in the United Nations represented an important symbolic first for the intersection of women with international policymaking; but as the wife of a former U.S. president, Roosevelt, like her predecessors Jane Addams and Dame Rachel Crowdy, represented elite women who had relatively easy access to national and international politics (Addams was the daughter of John Addams, an Illinois state legislator and good friend of Abraham Lincoln, and King George V granted Crowdy her Order of the British Empire title in 1918).[12] Interactions between ordinary women and international politics, foreign policy, and international relations remain more difficult for historians to detect. Women Studies Professor Cynthia Enloe's work has made important connections between international relations and women's lives. In her book *Bananas, Beaches, and Bases: Making Feminist Sense of International Politics*, for example, Enloe forefronts the impact of such presumably male-dominated international actions—such as governments promoting tourism, militaries installing overseas bases, and multinational companies opening factories overseas—on the women living in those areas and demonstrates how dependent governments, militaries, and corporate entities are on certain prescribed notions of femininity to conduct their businesses.[13]

During the 1994 Bosnian War, over seventy years after women activists had first lobbied for access to Versailles peace negotiations and after U.S. reformer Carrie Chapman Catt and others had pressed President Wilson to invite them on his overseas venture, U.S. Ambassador to Austria Swanee Hunt noticed that official peace negotiators still approach the peace table directly from the war room.[14] In that year, despite the work of forty women's organizations on the ground in Bosnia to stop the war, none of them had been invited to the Dayton Peace Accords held in Dayton, Ohio. With Yugoslavian women being the most highly educated in central and eastern Europe, Hunt wondered why they had been excluded. Just as the Woman Voters' Anti-Suffrage Party had denied women the opportunity to shape the peace in 1919 because they had not made the war (see Chapter 4), Hunt attributed women's absence at the peace table in Dayton to the sense among official peace negotiators that women were not war-makers.[15]

At the start of the twenty-first century, Hunt had greater cause for optimism. In 2000, the U.N. Security Council passed Resolution 1325. This document mandated female participation in the protection of women during armed conflict and in implementing peace settlements, in peacekeeping tactics, and in UN reporting systems and programs related to conflict and peacekeeping.[16] Furthermore, U.S. Ambassador to Angola Donald K. Steinberg remarked in a speech made in 2003 that women's participation in wars and in postwar reconciliation must be elevated within foreign policy establishments, indicating that others besides Hunt in the upper echelons of the U.S. State Department were beginning to take notice of the benefits of female participation.[17] Until then, women had been considered the "soft side" of foreign policy.[18] When the invasion of Iraq ended Saddam Hussein's regime in March 2003, the Coalition Provisional Authority (the transitional government made up of primarily U.S. and British authorities with executive, legislative, and judicial powers over Iraq from April 2003 to its dissolution in June 2004) formally recognized the benefits of female participation in restoring postwar Iraq. The results in Iraq have been mixed: women were absent from the writing of the new Iraqi Constitution and have been excluded from leadership positions in political parties and in ministerial positions, but they did make up more than 25 percent of the National Assembly (Iraq's parliament). Despite the inclusive rhetoric favoring women's participation in postwar reconciliation, practical implementation of such rhetoric has been incremental at best.[19]

In 1919 the Versailles negotiators had determined that women suffrage was irrelevant to world peace (see Chapter 4). More recently, however, diplomats have begun to recognize that female political empowerment may provide the key to maintaining peace and stability in postwar reconciliation. Both Ambassadors Hunt and Steinberg emphasized that the purpose of instituting gender parity in international policymaking bodies is not merely to provide equal access to women but instead to demonstrate that problems previously demoted as "women's issues" are really issues of national importance (such as hunger, poor education systems, lack of employment opportunities for women, lack of childcare) and to insure that crimes against women are brought to justice. Without such assurances, the rule of law—the reestablishment of which is often the primary goal of reconstruction efforts (and of military occupations) in postwar societies—cannot be sustained.[20] Campaigns to elevate the concerns of women to the national level, to place women at all levels of international policymaking organizations, and to eliminate crimes against women in postwar societies, however, must begin during times of peace, as the postwar period has too often resulted in the reinstitution of patriarchy. During the transition from war to peace, according to Sheila Meintjes, Anu Pillay, and Meredeth Turshen, the rhetoric of equality and rights tends to obscure the reconstruction of patriarchal power in formerly belligerent nations.[21] Certainly, that was the case after the Great War.

Notes

Introduction

1. Ernest Hemingway, *A Farewell to Arms* (New York: Charles Scribner's Sons, 1929; repr. 1993), 49–50.
2. Paul Fussell, *The Great War and Modern Memory* (New York: Oxford University Press, 1975), 21–22, provides a list of feudal words and phrases in use by the British during the war; Stefan Goebel, *The Great War and Medieval Memory: War, Remembrance and Medievalism in Britain and Germany, 1914–1940* (Cambridge: Cambridge University Press, 2007), compares medievalism in Great Britain and Germany.
3. Kenneth S. Zagacki, "Rhetoric, Redemption, and Reconciliation: a Study of Twentieth Century Postwar Rhetoric," PhD diss. (University of Texas at Austin, 1986), 5.
4. I am using Cynthia Enloe's definition of patriarchy in her book *The Curious Feminist: Searching for Women in a New Age of Empire* (Berkeley: University of California Press, 2004), 4–6.
5. "AHR Conversation: On Transnational History," *American Historical Review* 111, no. 5 (December 2006): 1441–64; Vera Mackie, "Review of Rumi Yasutake *Transnational Women's Activism: The United States, Japan, and Japanese Immigrant Communities in California, 1859–1920*," in *Women and Social Movements in the United States, 1600–2000* 9, no. 3 (September 2005), http://www.binghamton.edu/womhist/reviewmackie.htm (accessed July 18, 2007).
6. David M. Kennedy, *Over Here: The First World War and American Society* (New York: Oxford University Press, 1980), 229; Susanne Rouette, *Sozialpolitik als Geschlechterpolitik: Die Regulierung der Frauenarbeit nach dem Ersten Weltkrieg* (Frankfurt: Campus, 1993), 7–8; Jeffrey S. Reznick offers the same argument about Britain in *Healing the Nation: Soldiers and the Culture of Care-giving in*

Britain During the Great War (Manchester: Manchester University Press, 2004), 9; Henry F. May, *The End of American Innocence: A Study of the First Years of Our Own Time, 1912–1917* (New York: Alfred A. Knopf. 1959), 393–97.
7. Sheila Meintjes, Anu Pillay, and Meredeth Turshen, "There is No Aftermath for Women," in *The Aftermath: Women in Post-Conflict Transformation*, ed. Meintjes, Pillay, and Turshen (London: Zed Books, 2002), 4.
8. Keith L. Nelson, *Victors Divided: America and the Allies in Germany, 1918–1923* (Berkeley: University of California Press, 1975).
9. Sally Marks, *The Illusion of Peace: International Relations in Europe, 1918–1933* (New York: St. Martin's, 1976; repr. Basingstoke: Palgrave Macmillan, 2003); Klaus Schwabe, *Woodrow Wilson, Revolutionary Germany, and Peacemaking, 1918–1919: Missionary Diplomacy and the Realities of Power*, trans. Rita Kimber and Robert Kimber (Chapel Hill: University of North Carolina Press, 1985).
10. Norman Rich, *The Age of Nationalism and Reform, 1850–1890*, 2nd ed. (New York: W. W. Norton, 1977), xiv, 101–44.
11. Shelley Anderson, "Women's Many Roles in Reconciliation," in *People Building Peace: 35 Inspiring Stories from Around the World*, ed. European Centre for Conflict Prevention (Maastricht: European Centre for Conflict Prevention, 1999), 230–36.
12. Aristophanes, *Lysistrata/The Acharnians the Clouds*, trans. Alan H. Sommerstein (New York: Penguin Classics, 1974), 227–29.
13. Maurice Rickards, *Posters of the First World War* (New York: Walker, 1968), 114–35.
14. Rafael Scheck, "Women against Versailles: Maternalism and Nationalism of Female Bourgeois Politicians in the Early Weimar Republic," *German Studies Review* 22, no. 1 (February 1999): 21–22.
15. Jane Addams, *Peace and Bread in Time of War*, ed. Blance Wiesen Cook (New York: Garland, 1972). 208; Alice Hamilton and Jane Addams, "After the Lean Years: Impressions of Food Conditions in Germany When Peace was Signed," *Survey* (September 6, 1919): 793–97.
16. Karen Hagemann, "Home/Front: The Military, Violence and Gender Relations in the Age of the World Wars," in *Home/Front: The Military, War and Gender in Twentieth-Century Germany*, ed. Hagemann and Stefanie Schüler-Springorum (London: Berg, 2002), 2, analyzes the ways in which the traditional categories of "home" and "front" perpetuated the privileging of male soldiers and the marginalization of women; chapter 1 of the present volume addresses the categories of "victor" and "vanquished," and specifically the U.S.'s placement within those categories (Germany's placement is discussed in chapters 3 and 5); for histories that do not question the victor-vanquished binary, see Arno J. Mayer, *Politics and Diplomacy of Peacemaking: Containment and Counterrevolution at Versailles, 1918–1919* (New York: Knopf, 1967), in which the author discusses the victors and the armistice (53–89), and the vanquished and the

armistice (90–116); and Paul Kecskemeti, *Strategic Surrender: The Politics of Victory and Defeat* (New York: Atheneum, 1964).
17. Eric J. Hobsbawm, *Nations and Nationalism Since 1780: Programme, Myth, Reality* (New York: Cambridge University Press, 1992), 131.
18. Jay Winter, *Remembering War: The Great War Between Memory and History in the Twentieth Century* (New Haven, CT: Yale University Press, 2006), 136; Winter himself borrows the term from Carol Gluck.

Chapter 1

1. This pattern can be traced in the only monograph written of the American occupation after the First World War, Keith L. Nelson's *Victors Divided: America and the Allies in Germany, 1918–1923* (Berkeley: University of California Press, 1975). There are numerous primary sources including Philip H. Bagby, *The American Representation in Germany, 1920–1921*, vols. 1 and 2 (Coblenz: United States Army, American Forces in Germany, 1922); Henry T. Allen, *My Rhineland Journal* (Boston: Houghton Mifflin, 1923); Joseph T. Dickman, *The Great Crusade: a Narrative of the World War* (New York, London: D. Appleton, 1927); Center for Military History, *United States Army in the World War, 1917–1919: American Occupation of Germany*, vol. 11 (Washington: G.P.O., 1948); Truman Smith, *The American Military Government of Occupied Germany, 1918–1920: Report of the Officer in Charge of Civil Affairs, Third Army and American Forces in Germany* (Washington: G.P.O., 1943); Otto Peters, ed., *Kampf um den Rhein: Beiträge zur Geschichte des Rheinlandes und seiner Fremdherrschaft, 1918–1930* (Mainz: Mainzer Verlagsanstalt, 1930). Other book-length studies include C. Paul Vincent, *The Politics of Hunger: the Allied Blockade of Germany, 1915–1919* (Athens: Ohio University Press, 1985); Alfred E. Cornebise, *The Amaroc News: the Daily Newspaper of the American Forces in Occupied German 1919–1923* (Carbondale: Southern Illinois University Press, 1981). Although we know little about the sexual behavior of U.S. troops in occupied Iraq beginning in 2003, at least parts of the same patriarchal pattern were repeated when two Florida National Guard soldiers disobeyed an anti-fraternization order and married Iraqi women; Iraqi men threatened the women—but not their American grooms—for their disloyalty to their people, according to reports; Larry Kaplow, "2 Soldiers Defy Order, Marry Baghdad Women," *Chicago Tribune*, August 28, 2003, 8; more than 1,500 American soldiers have asked to bring home Iraqi fiancées or spouses since the war began, according to Julie Sullivan, "Joined by Love and War," *Sunday Oregonian*, July 23, 2006, A1.
2. Akira Iriye, "The United States as an Occupier," *Reviews in American History* 16, no. 1 (1988): 72; John Willoughby, "The Sexual Behavior of American GIs During the Early Years of the Occupation of Germany," *Journal of Military History* 62, no. 1 (1998): 174; a revised version of Willoughby's article appears

in his book *Remaking the Conquering Heroes: The Social and Geopolitical Impact of the Post-War American Occupation of Germany* (New York: Palgrave, 2001), 29–47; little information exists on soldiers' homosexual activity during or after the First World War, except accusations of the rape of German boys by French colonial soldiers by Germans during the "black horror on the Rhine." See Keith L. Nelson, *Victors Divided*, 177–78, and Chapter 2 of this volume; *Under the Yoke of Foreign Rule: Sufferings of the Rhineland Population* (Leipzig: K. F. Koehler, 1923), 1:4.

3. J. Ann Tickner, *Gender in International Relations: Feminist Perspectives on Achieving Global Security* (New York: Columbia University Press), 19.
4. Nelson, *Victors Divided*, 4.
5. Center for Military History, *United States Army in the World War*, 204.
6. Cynthia Enloe, *The Curious Feminist: Searching for Women in a New Age of Empire* (Berkeley: University of California Press, 2004), 4, 5–6; Gerda Lerner, *The Creation of Patriarchy* (Oxford: Oxford University Press, 1986), 31.
7. David M. Edelstein, "Occupational Hazards: Why Military Occupations Succeed or Fail," *International Security* 29 (2004): 53–54.
8. Susanne Rouette, *Sozialpoltik als Geschlechterpolitik: Die Regulierung der Frauenarbeit nach dem Ersten Weltkrieg* (Frankfurt: Campus, 1993), 33–36; Susan R. Grayzel, *Women's Identities at War: Gender, Motherhood, and Politics in Britain and France During the First World War* (Chapel Hill: University of North Carolina Press, 1999), 245; Sheila Meintjes, Anu Pillay, and Meredeth Turshen, "There is No Aftermath for Women," in *The Aftermath: Women in Post-Conflict Transformation*, ed. Sheila Meintjes, Anu Pillay, and Meredeth Turshen (London: Zed Books, 2002), 9.
9. Nelson, *Victors Divided*, 202.
10. Ibid., 75–76, 100.
11. Conan Fischer, *The Ruhr Crisis, 1923–24* (Oxford: Oxford University Press, 2003), 20.
12. Sally Marks, *The Illusion of Peace: International Relations in Europe, 1918–1933* (New York: St. Martin's, 1976; repr. London: Palgrave Macmillan, 2003), 3.
13. Nelson, *Victors Divided*, 23.
14. Ibid., 53–55, 33.
15. Vincent, *Politics of Hunger*, 80.
16. David G. Williamson, *The British in Germany, 1918–1933: The Reluctant Occupiers* (New York: Berg, 1991), 48, 49, 58–59.
17. Quoted in Vincent, *Politics of Hunger*, 80.
18. Ibid., 110–13.
19. Nelson, *Victors Divided*, 30.
20. Dickman, *Great Crusade*, 201–2.
21. *Stars and Stripes*, February 22, 1918, 4; Ibid., March 15, 1918, 1; Dickman, *Great Crusade*, 243; for a different account of the U.S. Army's occupation of the Molsberg castle, see Berton Braley, "Buddy Bosses the Boche," *Sunset* 42

(July 1919): 45–46. David M. Kennedy's *Over Here: The First World War and American Society* (New York: Oxford University Press, 1980), 212–13, discusses soldiers' views of themselves.
22. Detlev J. K. Peukert, *The Weimar Republic: The Crisis of Classical Modernity*, trans. Richard Deveson (New York: Hill and Wang, 1989), 155; Nelson, *Victors Divided*, 26–30.
23. Edwin L. James, "The Allied Armies in Germany," *Current History* 9 (January 1919), 16; Dickman, *Great Crusade*, 213, 212.
24. *Rheinisch-Westfälische Zeitung*, December 10, 1918, 2, my translation. As the American zone was later reduced in size, Trier was occupied by the French; see Nelson, *Victors Divided*, 28.
25. *Stars and Stripes*, November 22, 1918, 4.
26. *Amaroc*, June 4, 1919, 1; Nelson, *Victors Divided*, 31; Center for Military History, *United States Army in the World War*, 226.
27. Nelson, *Victors Divided*, 39, 48.
28. Both documents are reprinted in Smith, *American Military Government of Occupied Germany*, 30–32.
29. The Ordinances issued by General Pershing are reproduced and discussed fully in Center for Military History, *United States Army in the World War*, 177–90.
30. The ban is reprinted in Center for Military History, *United States Army in the World War*, 202, and discussed on pp. 202–4.
31. Nelson, *Victors Divided*, 50.
32. Elbert F. Baldwin, "The American Forces in Germany," *Outlook* 122 (August 1919): 635–36, noted that the doughboy's biggest complaint was the anti-fraternization order; Williamson, *British in Germany*, 58.
33. Enloe, *Curious Feminist*, 4–6.
34. *Stars and Stripes*, December 20, 1918, 8.
35. *Amaroc*, May 5, 1919, 1; Ibid., July 18, 1919, 1.
36. Ibid., May 5, 1919, 4.
37. Ibid., July 30, 1919, 2.
38. Quoted in ibid., July 28, 1919, 2.
39. *Amaroc*, July 11, 1919, 2; Cornebise, *Amaroc News*, 19.
40. Nelson characterized Rhinelanders as "parochial and conservative," *Victors Divided*, 27.
41. *Amaroc*, October 12, 1919, 2.
42. Ibid., May 21, 1919, 2; Theda Bara was a silent film star.
43. Ibid., June 22, 1919, 2; Ibid., June 15, 1919, 2.
44. *Stars and Stripes*, March 15, 1918, 4.
45. *Amaroc*, August 8, 1919, 2.
46. Quoted in Cornebise, *Amaroc News*, 65.
47. *Amaroc*, August 8, 1919, 2; Ibid.
48. Ibid.; *Amaroc*, July 11, 1919 (entire issue).

49. Center for Military History, *United States Army in the World War*, 205.
50. Ibid.
51. Ibid., 205–6 (emphasis mine).
52. *Amaroc*, July 18, 1919, 1 (translator unknown). Anti-American attitudes were much more common in unoccupied Germany than in the occupied zone. The Berlin *Lokal Anzeiger*, for example, called Americans "cockroaches" and "knaves," claiming that instead of bringing Germany freedom misbehaving troops had brought "Wild West manners" (quoted in Nelson, *Victors Divided*, 60).
53. Quoted in Bagby, *The American Representation in Germany*, 1920–1921, 2:46.
54. *The Nation*, 109 (July 1919): 27.
55. In addition, the groom's character had to be designated "very good," Bagby, *American Representation in Occupied Germany*, 2:46–47.
56. "Marriage Exams, Dr. Roscher," unnumbered folder, Decimal File 291.1, Entry 1367, Box 1121, RG 120, National Archives and Records Administration (hereafter NARA), College Park, Maryland, includes 52 forms filled out by Dr. Roscher certifying prospective wives' condition vis-à-vis venereal disease; all are dated 1922 (Roscher used the word "girl").
57. Bagby, *American Representation*, 2:46.
58. Ibid., 2:49. The U.S. military records includes a list of marriages that took place in 1919 and 1920, with names of husbands and their positions and the names of the women they married (unnumbered folder, Decimal File 291.1, Entry 1367, Box 1121, RG 120, NARA); 1527 soldiers applied for approval to marry between October 1, 1919, and January 1, 1922: of these, 767 were approved, Bagby, *American Representation*, 2:49.
59. Williamson, *British in Germany*, 211; Nelson, *Victors Divided*, 243.
60. "Overseas Men are Landed at Fort Moultrie," *Charleston Evening Post*, February 8, 1923, 1; Harriet H. Macdonald, "At Home with the War Brides," *Independent* 103 (September 1919): 328.
61. Carma McDonald to Dear Mother!, undated letter, copy in possession of author, courtesy of Donald Amaroc McDonald.
62. Frederick M. Strickert, *The Lorelei* (Baltimore: AmErica House, 2002), 365–66, 341–42.
63. Glenda Sluga, "Female and National Self-Determination: A Gender Re-Reading of 'The Apogee of Nationalism,'" *Nations and Nationalism* 6 (2000): 498–99.
64. See Jay Winter and Antoine Prost, *The Great War in History: Debates and Controversies, 1914 to the Present* (Cambridge: Cambridge University Press, 2005), 51–52, for a summary of economists' and historians' varying assessments of the treaty.
65. Ferdinand Czernin, *Versailles 1919: The Forces, Events and Personalities that Shaped the Treaty* (New York: Capricorn Books, 1965), 352–58, provides Count von Brockdorff-Rantzau's responses to the treaty; Nelson, *Victors Divided*, 53.

66. Nelson, *Victors Divided*, 98–104.
67. Ibid., 149.
68. Ibid., 166–68.
69. Sally Marks "Black Watch on the Rhine: A Study in Propaganda, Prejudice, and Prurience," *European Studies Review* 13 (1983): 297–334.
70. Nelson, *Victors Divided*, 214, 202.
71. Ellis Loring Dresel to Secretary of State Charles Evans Hughes, August 26, 1921, Records of the Department of State Relating to Political Relations Between the United States and Germany, 1910–29, 711.62119/5, Reel #1, M355, NARA; Unsigned editorial, "Germany and America," *Danziger Neueste Nachrichten*, January 17, 1920, Records of the Department of State Relating to Political Relations Between the United States and Germany, 1910–1929, 711.62/14, Reel #1, M355, NARA.
72. Sandra Mass, "Von der 'schwarzen Schmach' zur 'deutschen Heimat,'" *Werkstatt Geschichte*, 32 (2002): 55.
73. Jennifer D. Keene, *Doughboys, The Great War, and the Remaking of America* (Baltimore: Johns Hopkins University Press, 2001), 25; Center for Military History, *United States Army in the World War*, 204; Nancy K. Bristow, *Making Men Moral: Social Engineering During the Great War* (New York: New York University Press, 1996), 20.
74. Quoted in Cornebise, *Amaroc News*, 114.
75. Unaddressed memo from Bienhold to AFG Headquarters (translated, no German original), Coblenz, July 15, 1919, Folder 28, Decimal File no. 250.1, Box 1117, RG 120, NARA.
76. Letter from *Der Regierungspräsident* Trier to the *Herrn Oberpräsident* Coblenz, May 19, 1921, Nr. 13464, Bestände 403, *Landeshauptarchiv* Koblenz (hereafter LK), Koblenz, Germany (I have translated all of the German archival material to English); Bagby, *American Representation in Germany*, 2:69.
77. Bienhold to AFG Headquarters.
78. Memo "Instructions Relative to Control of Prostitution," from the Office of Civil Affairs to All Officers in Charge of Civil Affairs, March 11, 1920, Folder 28, Decimal File 250.1, Box 1117, RG 120, NARA; Bienhold to AFG Headquarters. There is some discrepancy in the record as to when the American military began arresting prostitutes. U.S. Army, AFG, *Digest: American Military Government of Occupied Germany, 1918–1920* (Washington: GPO, 1946), 13, indicates that a vagrancy court was established in October 1919 to try prostitutes.
79. Letter from the *Regierungspräsident* to the *Herrn Oberpräsidenten der Rhein Provinz* Coblenz, March 6, 1921, Nr. 13464, Bestände 403, LK.
80. Letter from Dr. Biesten, Deputy Mayor of the City Coblenz, to Major Flynn, AFG HQ, February 9, 1922, Folder 28, Decimal File 250.1, Box 1117, RG 120, NARA; This same folder includes lists of women convicted of vagrancy in the

Vagrancy and Juvenile Court of Coblenz, providing researchers with names, ages, and home towns of the women.
81. "Effect of Occupation on Moral Conditions in Coblenz," Annual Report of Municipal Administrations (excerpt), April 21, 1922, unnumbered folder, Decimal File 291.1, Box 1121, RG 120, NARA (translator unknown; no German original). Statistics follow on arrests made by German police and American Military Police in one year: 1,929 (395 from Coblenz) among which 539 were infected with VD.
82. Letter from *Der Regierungspräsident*, Coblenz, to the *Herrn Oberpräsidenten der Rheinprovinz*, January 21, 1921, Nr. 13464, Bestände 403, LK.
83. Letter from *Der Regierungspräsident* Trier, to the *Herrn Oberpräsident* Coblenz March 10, 1921, Nr. 13464, Bestände 403, LK (my emphasis).
84. Letter from *Der Regierungspräsident* Trier to the *Herrn Oberpräsident* Coblenz May 19, 1921, Nr. 13464, Bestände 403, LK.
85. Letter from *Regierungspräsident* Trier to *Herrn Oberpräsidenten der Rheinprovinz* Coblenz, May 9, 1921, Nr. 13464, Bestände 403, LK.
86. "Effect of Occupation on Moral Conditions in Coblenz."
87. Letter from *Der Regierungspräsident* Trier to the *Herrn Oberpräsident* Coblenz, May 19, 1921, Nr. 13464, Bestände 403, LK.
88. Bagby, *American Representation in Germany*, 2:50; Letter from B.O. Mayer, *Regierungsassessor* to Officer in Charge of Civil Affairs, early in 1920, reproduced in Bagby, *American Representation in Germany*, 2:53–55.
89. H. S. Grier, Officer in Charge of Civil Affairs, June 22, 1920, reproduced in Bagby, *American Representation in Germany*, 2:55–56 (emphasis Grier's); ibid., 50.
90. Letters from the AFG to mothers or guardians are in unnumbered folder, Decimal File 290.1, Entry 1367, Box 1121, RG 120, NARA.
91. Letter from Frau Carola Schuller to American Authorities in Coblenz, October 29, 1919, Folder 23, Decimal File 250.53, Box 1121, RG 120, NARA, translator unknown; no German original.
92. Spencer C. Tucker, ed., *The European Powers in the First World War: An Encyclopedia* (New York: Garland, 1996), 173.
93. *Amaroc*, May 8, 1919, 2.
94. "Report on Vital Statistics for *Kreis* Mayen, Germany, for the Periods 1909–1913, 1914–1918, 1919 January 1 to June 30," Entry 1369, Box 1, RG 120, NARA.
95. "Employment of Civilians," Circular #33, AFG HQ, Coblenz, March 16, 1922, Folder 116, Decimal File 230.14, Entry 1367, Box 1112, RG 120, NARA.
96. Peukert, *Weimar Republic*, 96–97.
97. Rouette, *Sozialpolitik als Geschlechterpolitik*, 33–36.
98. *Amaroc*, May 3, 1919, 2; The *Rheinisch-Westfälische Zeitung* featured many such ads; see for example December 18, 1918, 3.

99. Frau Dr. N. N., "To an American who is Fond of German Women," (1921?), Folder 4, Box 615, American Relief Administration—European Operations Records, 1919–1923, European Children's Fund, Hoover Institute Archives, Stanford University, Stanford, California.
100. "Zur Hinterbliebenenfürsorge," *Reichsbund: Neue Lebensfahrt Beilage* (May 29, 1920): n.p. (my translation).
101. Robert Weldon Whalen, *Bitter Wounds: German Victims of the Great War, 1914–1939* (Ithaca, NY: Cornell University Press, 1984), 110, quotes German activist Martha Harnoss's evaluation of women's politicization through their wartime experience.
102. "Effect of Occupation on Moral Conditions in Coblenz."
103. Regarding Schuller's request, Major J. D. White, Acting OCCA, "strongly recommended that additional space be given for the purpose named in your letter." However, he noted that fines collected could not be used for any purpose without the consent of U.S. Congress. White to *Oberbürgermeister*, Coblenz, November 13, 1919, unnumbered folder, Decimal File 291.1, Box 1121, RG 120, NARA. Lt. Col. H.S. Grier, OCCA, to Herr von Groening, *Regierungspräsident*, Coblenz, March 17, 1920, Folder 28, Box 1117, RG 120, NARA.
104. Nelson, *Victors Divided*, 252.
105. Letter from *Regierungspräsident* Trier to *Herrn Oberpräsidenten der Rheinprovinz* Coblenz, May 9, 1921, Nr. 13464, Bestände 403, LK; U.S. Army, AFG, *Digest: American Military Government of Occupied Germany, 1918–1920* (Washington: G.P.O., 1946), 13.
106. Nelson, *Victors Divided*, 256.
107. Bagby, *American Representation*, 2:42.
108. *Amaroc*, January 23, 1923, 2; The American occupation won plaudits from the German government, too; Nelson, *Victors Divided*, 251.
109. Ibid., 256.
110. Ibid., 150.
111. Researchers will find records of crimes against Germans throughout the *Akten des Oberpräsidiums der Rheinprovinz* (Bestände 403), and *der Regierungen Koblenz* (Bestände 441), LK.
112. Nelson, *Victors Divided*, 251; Edelstein, "Occupational Hazards," 85, deems the entire post-WWI occupation an overall failure.
113. David Kennedy, *Over Here*, 337–38, 342–46.
114. Edelstein, "Occupational Hazards," 87, considers the post-WWII occupation of West Germany a success.

Chapter 2

1. Keith L. Nelson, "The 'Black Horror on the Rhine': Race as a Factor in Post–World War I Diplomacy," *Journal of Modern History*, 42 (December 1970):

606–27. Sally Marks, "Black Watch on the Rhine: A Study in Propaganda, Prejudice and Prurience," *European Studies Review* 13 (1983): 297–333, Robert C. Reinders, "Racialism on the Left: E. D. Morel and the 'Black Horror on the Rhine,'" *International Review of History* 13 (1968): 1–28, and Keith L. Nelson have viewed the campaign in its diplomatic and political context; Gisela Lebzelter, "Die 'Schwarze Schmach': Vorurteile—Propaganda—Mythos," *Geschichte und Gesellschaft* 11 (1985): 37–68, and Tina Campt, Pascal Grosse, and Yara-Colette Lemke-Muniz de Fario, "Blacks, Germans, and the Politics of Imperial Imagination, 1920–60," in *The Imperialist Imagination: German Colonialism and its Legacy*, ed. Sara Friedrichsmeyer, Sara Lennox, and Susanne Zantop (Ann Arbor: University of Michigan, 1998), 205–29, view the campaign as an attempt to compensate for national anxieties produced by the defeat and occupation; Anja Schüler, "The 'Horror on the Rhine': Rape, Racism and the International Women's Movement," John F. Kennedy-Institut Für Nordamerikastudien, Abteilung für Geschichte, Working Paper No. 86 (1996), 1–19, explores the international women's movement's response to the campaign; and Christian Koller, *"Von Wilden aller Rassen niedergemetzelt": Die Diskussion um die Verwendung von Kolonialtruppen in Europa Zwischen Rassismus, Kolonial-und Militärpolitik, 1914–1930* (Stuttgart: Franz Steiner Verlag, 2001), places the campaign in its European perspective.
2. Schüler, "Horror on the Rhine," 1.
3. Nelson, "Black Horror on the Rhine," 625–26.
4. James Joll, *Origins of the First World War* (London: Longman, 1984), 148.
5. Marks, "Black Watch on the Rhine," 310.
6. Glenda Sluga, "Female and National Self-Determination: A Gender Re-Reading of 'the Apogee of Nationalism,'" *Nations and Nationalism* 6, no. 4 (2000): 496; Lloyd E. Ambrosius, "Wilson, Alliances, and the League of Nations," *Journal of the Gilded Age and Progressive Era* 5, no. 2 (April 2006): 159–60, discusses the mandates in relation to location as part of Woodrow Wilson's racism.
7. F. Walters, *A History of the League of Nations* (London: Oxford University Press, 1960), 56–58.
8. Nelson, "Black Horror on the Rhine," 626–27.
9. Quoted in Campt et al., "Blacks, Germans, and the Politics of Imperial Imagination," 211.
10. I am indebted to Manako Ogawa for my interpretation of activist women and their relationship to race and international politics. See Manako Ogawa, "The 'White Ribbon League of Nations' Meets Japan: The Trans-Pacific Activism of the Woman's Christian Temperance Union, 1906–1930," *Diplomatic History* 31, no. 1 (January 2007): 21–50.
11. Schüler, "Horror on the Rhine," 5.
12. Homer C. Davenport, "Another Old Woman Tries to Sweep Back the Sea," *New York Journal*, 1898; Joseph A. Fry, "William McKinley and the Coming of the

Spanish-American War: A Study of the Besmirching and Redemption of an Historical Image," *Diplomatic History* 3, no. 1 (Winter 1979): 77–97.
13. Erika Kuhlman, *Petticoats and White Feathers: Gender Conformity, Race, the Progressive Peace Movement, and the Debate over War, 1895–1919* (Westport, CT: Greenwood, 1997), 86–93.
14. Gail Bederman, *Manliness and Civilization: A Cultural History of Gender and Race in the United Sates, 1880–1917* (Chicago: University of Chicago Press, 1995), 184.
15. Edward J. Blum, *Reforging the White Republic: Race, Religion, and American Nationalism, 1865–1898* (Baton Rouge: Louisiana State University Press, 2005), 15–16.
16. Bederman, *Manliness and Civilization*, 113–14.
17. Ibid., 185; Theodore Roosevelt, *The Works of Theodore Roosevelt: The Strenuous Life* (New York: F. Collier & Sons, 1901), 201–2; Gerda Lerner discusses biological determinism as a justification of patriarchy in *The Creation of Patriarchy* (New York: Oxford, 1986), 6.
18. Bederman, *Manliness and Civilization*, 187–88; Roosevelt, *Strenuous Life*, 236.
19. Aileen S. Kraditor, *The Ideas of the Woman Suffrage Movement, 1890–1920* (New York: Anchor Doubleday, 1965), 52–53.
20. Roosevelt, *Strenuous Life*, 229.
21. Ibid., 241, 243–44.
22. Nuper Chaudhuri and Margaret Strobel,"Introduction," in *Western Women and Imperialism: Complicity and Resistance*, ed. Nuper Chaudhuri and Margaret Strobel (Bloomington: Indiana University Press, 1992), 3, 5.
23. Julia Clancy-Smith, "The 'Passionate Nomad' Reconsidered: A European Woman in *L'Algérie française*," Helen Callaway and Dorothy O. Helly, "Flora Shaw/Lady Lugard," and Nancy L. Paxton, "Complicity and Resistance in the Writings of Flora Annie Steel and Annie Besant," all in Chaudhuri and Strobel, *Western Women and Imperialism*, 61–78, 79–97, 158–76.
24. Gordon A. Craig, *Germany, 1866–1945* (New York: Oxford University Press, 1978), 116–18.
25. Kurt F. Reinhardt, *Germany: 200 Years*, rev. ed. (New York: Frederick Ungar, 1961), 2:624–25.
26. Alice L. Conklin, *A Mission to Civilize: The Republican Idea of Empire in France and West Africa, 1895–1930* (Stanford, CA: Stanford University Press, 1997), 1–2, 5–7; Joe Lunn, *Memoirs of the Maelstrom: A Senegalese Oral History of the First World War* (Portsmouth, NH: Heinemann, 1999), 59.
27. Berlin West Africa Conference, 1884–1885, *General Act of the Conference of Berlin: Signed February 26, 1885* (London: Harrison and Sons, 1886), n.p.
28. Robert O. Collins, *Europeans in Africa* (New York: Knopf, 1971), 77.
29. Lucy Bland, "White Women and Men of Colour: Miscegenation Fears in Britain after the Great War," *Gender & History* 17, no.1 (April 2005): 31.

30. Campt et al., "Blacks, Germans, and the Politics of Imperial Imagination," 209; Campt and her coauthors titled their work *The Imperialist Imagination*.
31. Bederman, *Manliness and Civilization*, 197.
32. Nelson, "Black Horror on the Rhine," 606.
33. Ibid., 608–9.
34. Ibid., 609–11.
35. Marks, "Black Watch on the Rhine," 297; Nelson, "Black Horror on the Rhine," 613; Lunn, *Memoirs*, 33.
36. Tyler Stovall, "Colonial Workers in France during the Great War," in *European Imperialism, 1830–1930: Climax and Contradiction*, ed. Alice L. Conklin and Ian Christopher Fletcher (New York: Houghton Mifflin, 1999), 170; Campt et al., "Blacks, Germans, and the Politics of Imperial Imagination," 209. Helene Hurwitz-Stranz's anthology of German war widows' experiences includes an anonymous entry by a widow living in German East Africa; see *Kriegerwitwen gestalten ihr Schicksal: Lebenskämpfe deutscher Kriegerwitwen nach eigenen Darstellung*, ed. Helene Hurwitz-Stranz (Berlin: Carl Heymanns Verlag, 1931), 44–49.
37. Christian Koller, "Enemy Images: Race and Gender Stereotypes in the Discussion on Colonial Troops, A Franco-German Comparison, 1914–1923," in *Home/Front: The Military, War and Gender in Twentieth-Century Germany*, ed. Karen Hagemann and Stefanie Schüler-Springorum (Oxford: Berg, 2002), 139.
38. Arthur W. Little, *From Harlem to the Rhine: The Story of New York's Colored Volunteers* (New York: Covici Friede, 1936), 328, 344.
39. Schüler, "Horror on the Rhine," 3.
40. Marks, "Black Watch on the Rhine," 298–99.
41. U.S. Congress, Senate, *Congressional Record*, 67th Congress, 3rd sess. November 27, 1922, 278.
42. Schüler, "Horror on the Rhine," 3.
43. Campt et al., "Blacks, Germans, and the Politics of Imperial Imagination," 208, 213.
44. "Vorwort zur ersten Ausgabe," *Farbige Franzosen am Rhein: Ein Notschrei deutscher Frauen* (Berlin: H. R. Engelmann, 1920), 2:6 (translation mine). Anja Schüler notes that the *Rheinische Frauenliga* operated primarily as a front for Margarethe Gärtner's efforts; see Schüler, "Horror on the Rhine," 7; Nelson, "Black Horror on the Rhine," 618–19, note 60 claims that their publications were funded by the German government.
45. Schüler, "Horror on the Rhine," 2, 6.
46. Ibid., 2; Koller, "Enemy Images," 143.
47. Cynthia Enloe, *The Curious Feminist: Searching for Women in a New Age of Empire* (Berkeley: University of California Press, 2004), 119; Cynthia Enloe, *Bananas, Beaches, and Bases: Making Feminist Sense of International Politics* (Berkeley: University of California Press, 1990), 81.

48. Tina Sideris, "Rape in War and Peace: Social Context, Gender, Power and Identity," in Sheila Meintjes, Anu Pillay, and Meredeth Turshen (eds.) *The Aftermath: Women in Post-Conflict Transformation* (London: Zed Books, 2002), 147.
49. United States Army, American Forces in Germany, *American Military Government of Occupied Germany, 1918–1920* (Washington, D.C.: G.P.O., 1943), 211–12.
50. Nelson, "Black Horror on the Rhine," 614.
51. Koller, *"Von Wilden aller Rassen niedergemetzelt,"* 211, 214.
52. Koller, "Enemy Images," 146.
53. Nelson, "Black Horror on the Rhine," 614–15.
54. Blanche Wiesen Cook, "Forword," in Helena M. Swanwick, *Builders of Peace: Being Ten Years' History of the UDC* (New York: Garland, 1924; repr. 1973), 1.
55. Schüler, "Horror on the Rhine," 3–4; Nelson, "Black Horror on the Rhine," 618; Edmund D. Morel, *The Horror on the Rhine* (London: Union of Democratic Control, 1920).
56. Nelson, "Black Horror on the Rhine," 616.
57. Koller, "Enemy Images," 143; Koller, *"Von Wilden aller Rassen niedergemetzelt,"* 248.
58. Koller., "Enemy Images," 147.
59. Koller, *"Von Wilden aller Rassen niedergemetzelt,"* 213–16.
60. Ibid., 234.
61. Schüler, "Horror on the Rhine," 10.
62. Nelson, "Black Horror on the Rhine," 615, 615n42; Nelson counted 252 pages of clippings from German newspapers relating to atrocities.
63. Michael Singer, *Colored Frenchmen on the Rhine: An Appeal of White Women to American Womanhood* (Chicago: New Press, 1920); Sandra Mass, "Von der 'schwarzen Schmach' zur 'deutschen Heimat,'" *Werkstatt Geschichte* 32 (2002): 51.
64. Schüler, "Horror on the Rhine," 5, quotes from the U.S. edition of the petition.
65. Koller, *"Von Wilden Aller Rassen Niedergemetzelt,"* 221, 224.
66. Bland, "White Women and Men of Colour," 41; Koller, "Enemy Images," 141.
67. Morel, *The Horror on the Rhine*, 9–10 (emphasis Morel's).
68. Schüler, "Horror on the Rhine," 4.
69. Quoted in Bland, "White Women and Men of Colour," 40.
70. Heinrich Distler, *Das deutsche leid am Rhein: ein buch der anklage gegen die Schandherrschaft des französischen militarismus* (Minden, Westphalia: W. Köhler, 1921), 13 (translation mine).
71. Bland, "White Women and Men of Colour," 40.
72. Marks, "Black Watch on the Rhine," 319.
73. Schüler, "Horror on the Rhine," 11.
74. Bland, "White Women and Men of Colour," 42–43.

75. Paul Löbe, "Preface," *Under the Yoke of Foreign Rule: Sufferings of the Rhineland Population* (unidentified translator) (Leipzig: K. F. Koehler, 1923), 2:4.
76. Distler, *Das deutsche leid am Rhein*, 41, translation mine.
77. Marks, "Black Watch on the Rhine," 304; Distler, *Das deutsche leid am Rhein*, 41; Marks, "Black Watch on the Rhine," 304.
78. Marks, "Black Watch on the Rhine," 303.
79. Annelise Timmermann, *Die Rheinlandbesetzung in ihrer Wirkung auf die Sozialausgaben der Städte* (Berlin: Verlag vom Reimers Hobbing, 1930), 88, translation mine.
80. Nelson, "Black Horror on the Rhine," 620.
81. Schüler, "Horror on the Rhine," 4, 6.
82. Marks, "Black Watch on the Rhine," 302.
83. Marks footnotes a State Department document that identified Beveridge as a former German Embassy employee now living in Germany, "Black Watch on the Rhine," 312.
84. Quoted in Schüler, "Horror on the Rhine," 9n32; quoted in ibid., 9.
85. Quoted in Marks, "Black Watch on the Rhine," 315.
86. Robert Zangrando, *The NAACP Crusade against Lynching, 1909–1950* (Philadelphia: Temple University Press, 1980), 3.
87. Bederman, *Manliness and Civilization*, 47; "Mob Law in Arkansas," *New York Times*, February 23, 1892, 4; Bederman, *Manliness and Civilization*, 48.
88. Michael Paul Rogin, *Ronald Reagan, The Movie, and Other Episodes in Political Demonology* (Berkeley: University of California Press, 1987), 223, 219, 222.
89. Telegram reprinted in Allen, *The Rhineland Occupation* (Indianapolis, IN: Bobbs-Merrill, 1927), 319.
90. Nelson, "Black Horror on the Rhine," 617.
91. Koller, *"Von Wilden Aller Rassen Niedergemetzelt,"* 254–55.
92. Allen, *The Rhineland Occupation*, 321.
93. Ibid., 16; see also Tyler Stovall, "Colonial Workers in France," 170.
94. Nelson, "Black Horror on the Rhine," 620; Schüler, "Horror on the Rhine," 17.
95. Nelson, "Black Horror on the Rhine," 620–21.
96. "25,000 Patriots at Garden Answer Rhine Horror Plea," *New York Times*, March 19, 1921, 1–2.
97. Bland, "White Women and Men of Colour," 41.
98. Lewis S. Gannett, "Those Black Troops on the Rhine—and the White," *Nation* 112 (May 25, 1921): 733–34.
99. "Black Troops on the Rhine," *Nation* 112 (March 9, 1921): 365.
100. Kathryn Kish Sklar, Anja Schüler, and Susan Strasser, *Social Justice Feminists in the United States and Germany: A Dialogue in Documents, 1885–1933* (Ithaca, NY: Cornell University Press, 1998), 275–86, includes reproductions of a *Fichte Bund* plea to Addams, a letter from Terrell to Addams, and the 1921 Vienna WILPF congress's resolution on colonial troops.

101. Flehinghaus to Addams, March 12, 1920, WILPF U.S. section, DG 043, microfilm #130.38, Series A,5 Literature and releases, Series C: Correspondences: General Correspondence, 1919–1924, Swarthmore College Peace Collection (hereafter SCPC), Swarthmore, Pennsylvania; Gund to Addams, June 24, 1920, ibid.
102. Schüler, "Horror on the Rhine," 12–13.
103. John Hope Franklin, *Race and History: Selected Essays, 1938–1988* (Baton Rouge: Louisiana State University Press, 1989), 17.
104. Jane Addams, "Respect the Law," *Independent* 53 (January 3, 1901): 18–20.
105. Louise W. Knight *Citizen: Jane Addams and the Struggle for Democracy* (Chicago: University of Chicago Press, 2005), 388; Bederman, *Manliness and Civilization*, 197.
106. Knight, *Citizen*, 389.
107. Bland, "White Women and Men of Colour," 43; Edmund D. Morel, "The Black Scourge in Europe: Sexual Horrors Let Loose by France on the Rhine," *London Daily Herald*, April 10, 1920, 1 (also published as a pamphlet).
108. Addams and Kittredge to Hughes, March 5, 1921, WILPF U.S. section, DG 043, microfilm #130.41, Series C, Correspondence, Box 3 Folder 35, SCPC.
109. Mercedes Randall, *Improper Bostonian: Emily Greene Balch* (Boston: Twayne, 1964), 277; WILPF, *Towards Peace and Freedom: the Women's International Congress, Zürich, May 12th to 17th, 1919*, English ed. (London: British section of WILPF), 19.
110. Addams and Kittredge to Hughes, March 5, 1921, WILPF U.S. section, DG 043, microfilm #130.41, Series C, Correspondence, Box 3 Folder 35, SCPC.
111. Document reprinted, without comment, in the *Crisis* 18 (May 1919): 16–18 (emphasis mine).
112. Joyce Blackwell, *No Peace Without Freedom: Race and the Women's International League for Peace and Freedom, 1915–1975* (Carbondale: Southern Illinois University Press, 2004), 96.
113. Terrell to Balch, July 25, 1924, WILPF Collection, DG 043, U.S. section, microfilm # 130.39, Series C, Correspondence, Box 1, General Correspondence, 1919–1924, Folder 17, SCPC.
114. Schüler, "Horror on the Rhine," 13–14.
115. Koller, *"Von Wilden Aller Rassen Niedergemetzelt,"* 220.
116. Blackwell, *No Peace Without Freedom*, 97.
117. U.S. Congress, Senate, *Congressional Record*, 67th Congress, 2nd sess., August 31, 1922, 12020.
118. Nelson, "Black Horror on the Rhine," 622–23n87, 622.
119. Schüler, "Horror on the Rhine," 19.
120. Lilli Jannasch, "Schwarze Schmach, Weisse Schmach?" *Die Frau im Staat* 2, no. 11 (November 1920): 1–4, translation mine.

121. Anna Duennebier and Ursula Scheu, *Die Rebellion ist eine Frau: Anita Augspurg und Lida G. Heymann, Das schillerndste Paar der Frauenbewegung* (Kreuzlingen/Munich: Heinrich Hugendubel, 2002), 260–62, translation mine.
122. Gertrud Baer, "Abgrunde," *Die Frau im Staat* 5, no. 2 (1923): 3–4, translation mine.
123. "Blacks Defended in German Paper," *New York Times*, January 9, 1921, Sec. 2, 10.
124. Doris Reiprich and Erika Ngambi ul Kuo, "Our Father was Cameroonian, Our Mother, East Prussian, We Are Mulattoes," in *Showing our Colors: Afro-German Women Speak Out*, ed. May Opitz, Katharina Oguntoye, and Dagmar Schultz, trans. Anne V. Adams (Amherst: University of Massachusetts Press, 1986), 56–76.
125. Lunn, *Memoirs of the Maelstorm*.
126. Nelson, "Black Horror on the Rhine," 627.
127. Sheila Meintjes, Anu Pillay, and Meredeth Turshen, "There is No Aftermath for Women," in Meintjes, Pillay, and Turshen, *The Aftermath*, 11.
128. Schüler, "Horror on the Rhine," 1.
129. Morel, *The Horror on the Rhine*, 13.
130. Ingrid Sharp, "Blaming the Women: Women's Responsibility for the First World War," in *The Women's Movement in Wartime: International Perspectives, 1914–19*, ed. Alison S. Fell and Ingrid Sharp (Basingstoke: Palgrave Macmillan, 2007), 67–87.

Chapter 3

1. Lloyd E. Ambrosius, "Wilson, Alliances, and the League of Nations," *Journal of the Gilded Age and Progressive Era* 5 no. 2 (April 2006): 139–66, 160–61.
2. Lloyd E. Ambrosius, *Wilsonian Statecraft: Theory and Practice of Liberal Internationalism During World War I* (Wilmington, DE: SR Books, 1991); Lloyd E. Ambrosius, *Woodrow Wilson and the American Diplomatic Tradition: The Treaty Fight in Perspective* (New York: Cambridge University Press, 1987); Lloyd E. Ambrosius, *Wilsonianism: Woodrow Wilson and His Legacy in American Foreign Relations* (New York: Palgrave Macmillan, 2002); G. John Ikenberry, *After Victory: Institutions, Strategic Restraint, and the Rebuilding of Order after Major Wars* (Princeton, NJ: Princeton University Press, 2001); Walter A. McDougall, *Promised Land, Crusader State: The American Encounter with the World Since 1776* (Boston: Houghton Mifflin, 1997).
3. Ambrosius, "Wilson, Alliances, and the League of Nations," 154; For works that have taken an international perspective, see Klaus Schwabe, *Woodrow Wilson, Revolutionary Germany, and Peacemaking, 1918–1919: Missionary Diplomacy and the Realities of Power*, trans. Rita Kimber and Robert Kimber (Chapel Hill: University of North Carolina Press, 1985); Sally Marks, *The*

Illusion of Peace: International Relations in Europe, 1918–1933 (New York: St. Martin's, 1976; repr. Basingstoke: Palgrave Macmillan, 2003).
4. Elizabeth McKillen, "The Unending Debate over Woodrow Wilson and the League of Nations Fight," *Diplomatic History* 27, no. 5 (November 2003) 711–14; Ambrosius, "Wilson, Alliances, and the League of Nations," 159–60; Glenda Sluga, *The Nation, Psychology, and International Politics, 1870–1919* (Basingstoke: Palgrave Macmillan, 2006), 19; Marc Gallicchio, *The African American Encounter with Japan and China: Black Internationalism in Asia, 1895–1945* (Chapel Hill: University of North Carolina Press, 2000), 23–24.
5. Rhodri Jeffreys-Jones, *Changing Differences: Women and the Shaping of American Foreign Policy, 1917–1994* (New Brunswick, NJ: Rutgers University Press, 1995), 26–27.
6. Lloyd E. Ambrosius, "Wilson, the Republicans, and French Security," *Journal of American History* 59, no. 2 (September 1972): 351; Ambrosius, *Woodrow Wilson and the American Diplomatic Tradition*, 47.
7. Annika Mombauer, *The Origins of the First World War: Controversies and Consensus* (London: Longman, 2002), 4–5, notes that the alliance system threatened to escalate any potential conflicts that might arise among the European powers.
8. Deborah Cohen, "Will to Work: Disabled Veterans in Britain and Germany after the First World War," in *Disabled Veterans in History*, ed. David A. Gerber (Ann Arbor: University of Michigan Press, 2000), 295.
9. Michael J. Hogan and Thomas G. Patterson, "Introduction," in *Explaining the History of American Foreign Relations*, 2nd ed., ed. Hogan and Thomas (New York: Cambridge University Press, 2004), 2.
10. Jill Stearns, *Gender and International Relations: An Introduction* (Cambridge: Polity Press, 1998), 2.
11. John Milton Cooper, *Breaking the Heart of the World: Woodrow Wilson and the Fight for the League of Nations* (New York: Cambridge University Press, 2001).
12. Ambrosius, "Wilson, Alliances, and the League of Nations," 154; Nathan J. Citino, "The Global Frontier: History and the Frontier-Borderlands Approach," in Hogan and Thomas, *Explaining the History of American Foreign Relations*, 194–211, suggests a comparative approach to U.S. foreign relations.
13. Jennifer D. Keene, *Doughboys, the Great War, and the Remaking of America* (Baltimore: Johns Hopkins University Press, 2001), 179–204, and Alfred E. Cornebise, *The Amaroc News: The Daily Newspaper of the American Forces in Germany, 1919–1923* (Carbondale: Southern Illinois University Press, 1981), 76–81, both discuss postwar political activism among veterans.
14. Sheldon Hackney, "Initial Shock: A Conversation with Paul Fussell," *Humanities* 17, no. 5 (November/December 1996), 6; Eugen Weber, *The Hollow Years: France in the 1930s* (New York: W. W. Norton, 1994), 12–13.
15. Paul Fussell, *The Great War and Modern Memory* (New York: Oxford University Press, 1975), 3–35.

16. Quoted in ibid., 174.
17. Quoted in Martha Hanna, *Your Death Would be Mine: Paul and Marie Pireaud in the Great War* (Cambridge: Harvard University Press, 2006), 78.
18. Edmund Blunden, *The Mind's Eye: Essays* (Freeport, NY: Books for Libraries Press, 1934; repr. 1967), 38; Fussell, *Great War and Modern Memory*, 317, notes French historian Marc Ferro's contention that the U.S. could be considered the war's only winner.
19. Mary Nolan argues that Germans took on some aspects of U.S. modernity, such as economics and technology, while eschewing others. "Imagining America, Modernizing Germany," in *Dancing on the Volcano: Essays on the Culture of the Weimar Republic*, ed. Thomas W. Kniesche and Stephen Brockmann (Columbia, SC: Camden House, 1994), 71–84.
20. Fussell, *Great War and Modern Memory*, 8; Martha Hanna, *Your Death Would be Mine*, 120.
21. For a discussion of the relevance of gender to the field of foreign relations, see Kristin Hoganson, "What's Gender Got to Do with It?" in *Explaining the History of American Foreign Relations*, 304–22.
22. "What to Do with Germany," *Public: A Journal of Democracy* (December 14, 1918): 1495–96.
23. Gail Bederman, "'The Women Have Had Charge of the Church's Work Long Enough': The Men and Religion Forward Movement of 1911–1912," *American Quarterly* 41, no. 3 (September 1989): 432–40.
24. Woodrow Wilson, "Address to the U.S. Senate, January 22, 1917," in *The Papers of Woodrow Wilson*, ed. Arthur S. Link (Princeton. NJ: Princeton University Press, 1966–1993), 40:533–39.
25. Schwabe, *Woodrow Wilson*, 52; George F. Kennan, *The Fateful Alliance: France, Russia, and the Coming of the First World War* (New York: Pantheon Books, 1984), 257, discusses nationalism and citizens' insistence that the winners' superiority in war be recognized by the losers.
26. David M. Kennedy, *Over Here: The First World War and American Society* (1980; New York, 2004), 179–84, explores the medieval theme in these works and other wartime American literature; Fussell, *Great War and Modern Memory*, 21–23, examines the same themes in English literature.
27. Unknown artist, "The Modern Knight Errant," *Current History* 9 (March 1919), 565 (reprinted from *La Baionnette*. Paris).
28. Martin E. Marty, *Modern American Religion, Volume 1: The Irony of it All, 1893–1919* (Chicago: University of Chicago Press, 1986), 301.
29. Woodrow Wilson, "An Address to a Joint Session of Congress," April 2, 1917, *The Papers of Woodrow Wilson*, 41, 527; for an analysis of the Congressional debate over intervention see Erika Kuhlman, *Petticoats and White Feathers: Gender Conformity, Race, the Progressive Peace Movement, and the Debate Over War, 1895–1919* (Westport, CT: Greenwood, 1997), 73–100.

30. Benedict Anderson, *Imagined Communities: Reflections on the Origin and Spread of Nationalism* (London: Verso, 1991), 36, 144.
31. Edward J. Blum, *Reforging the White Republic: Race, Religion, and American Nationalism, 1865–1898* (Baton Rouge: Louisiana State University Press, 2005), 4.
32. Rolf Lundén, "The Protestant Churches and the Business Spirit of the Twenties," *European Contributions to American Studies*, 10 (1986): 47, argues that the 1920s were among the most secularized and business oriented in U.S. history.
33. Blum, *Reforging the White Republic*, 10.
34. Sidney Mead, "American Protestantism: From Denominationalism to Americanism," in *Essays on the Age of Enterprise, 1870–1900*, ed. David Brody (Hinsdale, IL: Dryden, 1974), 315.
35. Ambrosius, "Woodrow Wilson, Alliances, and the League of Nations," 142–46.
36. Ann Braude, "Women's History is American Religious History," in *Religion and American Culture: A Reader*, 2nd ed., ed. David G. Hackett (New York: Routledge, 2003), 163.
37. Michael Kimmel, "Men's Responses to Feminism," *Gender & Society* 1 (September 1987): 269, claimed that at the turn of the twentieth century some men responded to feminism by seeking to dislodge women from the "private" sphere; Bederman, "'The Women Have Had Charge of the Church's Work Long Enough,'" 432–40.
38. Quoted in Kimmel, "Men's Responses to Feminism," 267.
39. Vanessa B. Beasley, "Engendering Democratic Change: How Three U.S. Presidents Discussed Female Suffrage," *Rhetoric & Public Affairs* 5 no. 1 (2002): 85.
40. Ibid., 88.
41. Woodrow Wilson, "Sixth Annual Message," in *The State of the Union Messages of the Presidents* (New York: Chelsea House, 1967), 3:2590.
42. Beasley, "Engendering Democratic Change," 89.
43. See, for example, Thomas Robert Smith, Ellen Key, and G. Lowes Dickinson, *The Woman Question* (New York: Boni and Liveright, Inc., 1919); Mary Roberts Coolidge, *Why Women Are So* (New York: Arno, 1912; repr. 1972).
44. Bederman, "'The Women Have Had Charge of the Church's Work Long Enough,'" 441, 453–54.
45. Ibid., 438.
46. Emily Greene Balch, *Approaches to the Great Settlement* (New York: B. W. Huebsch, 1918), 129.
47. George Harvey, "Beware the Peace Drive!" *North American Review* 208 (October 1918): 494.
48. James R. McGovern, "David Graham Phillips and the Virility Impulse of the Progressives," *New England Quarterly* 39 (1966) 334–55.

49. Quoted in Donald Day, *Woodrow Wilson's Own Story* (Boston: Little, Brown, 1952), 289; Schwabe, *Woodrow Wilson*, 51.
50. George Harvey, "Beware the Peace Drive!" 497.
51. Vernon Kellogg, "Unclean, Unclean," *North American Review* 208 (October 1918): 536–39.
52. Schwabe, *Woodrow Wilson*, 95–96.
53. *Outlook*, 120 (November 20, 1918) 441 (emphasis added).
54. "Congress Hails Armistice Terms," *New York Times*, November 12, 1918, 4.
55. Unsigned editorial, "Preach Modesty," *Outlook* 120 (November 20, 1918): 450–51. The *Amaroc*, the military newspaper produced during the occupation, revisited the question of the American victory repeatedly in its short history, indicating a level of doubt even in the military; Kennedy, *Over Here*, 358, however, notes with irony that the U.S. had provided the final military blow to crush the Germans, thus setting the stage for a vengeful peace that Woodrow Wilson had not wanted. Adam Gopnik, "The Big One," *New Yorker* (August 23, 2004) 84, discusses historians' sense of the U.S. contribution and concludes, with Hew Strachan and David Stevenson, that the war ended not from American intervention or technological innovations but from sheer exhaustion.
56. C. A. Bronstrup, "When Willie Comes Marching Home," *Current History* 9 (October 1918): 188 (reprinted from *San Francisco Chronicle*).
57. Raffael Scheck, "Women Against Versailles: Maternalism and Nationalism of Female Bourgeois Politicians in the Early Weimar Republic," *German Studies Review* 22, no. 1 (February 1999): 24.
58. Kenneth Stephen Zagacki, "Rhetoric, Redemption, and Reconciliation: A Study of Twentieth-Century Postwar Rhetoric," (PhD diss., University of Texas-Austin, 1986), 75–77.
59. Woodrow Wilson, "For the League of Nations," in *American Public Addresses, 1740–1952*, ed. A. Craig Baird (New York: McGraw-Hill, 1956), 239.
60. Woodrow Wilson, "Address to a Joint Session of Congress," April 2, 1917, *The Papers of Woodrow Wilson*, 41:523–26.
61. Allan M. Winkler, "The Selling of the War," *Reviews in American History* 8, no. 3 (1980): 382–85.
62. Schwabe, *Woodrow Wilson*, 51–55. In his second note to Germany regarding armistice negotiations, Wilson refused to treat with Germany while it was still ruled by an autocrat and would not agree to an armistice that was not approved by the Allied Supreme Commander, Ferdinand Foch. Schwabe claims his change in attitude was due to pressure from American public opinion and the Allies.
63. Ibid., 341.
64. Zagacki, "Rhetoric, Redemption, and Reconciliation," 78–80.
65. Albert Bushnell Hart, "Can Germany Be Regenerated?: The Coming Struggle Between the Thinking Majority and the Organized Minority," *Forum* 61 (January 1919): 4 (emphasis added).

66. *Outlook* 120 (November 20, 1918): 443.
67. Hart, "Can Germany Be Regenerated?" 6.
68. "To Shield Women in War," *New York Times*, November 11, 1918, 15.
69. Louis Graves, "Leaves from a Coblenz Diary: Fragments from the Notebook of Heinrich Scheinstutzen, Apothecary," *Atlantic Monthly* 124 (July-August 1919): 83.
70. Woodrow Wilson, "Address to a Joint Session of Congress," November 11, 1918, *The Papers of Woodrow Wilson*, 41:40.
71. Telegram quoted in the *Congressional Record*, Vol 56, Part II, 65th Congress, 2nd Session, 1918, 11571; Addams' response to the telegram recorded in "Miss Addams Knows Them," *New York Times*, November 16, 1918, 2.
72. "Defense Society Protests," *New York Times*, November 16, 1918, 2.
73. "Dr. Solf Sends Appeal," *New York Times*, November 12, 1918, 1, 2.
74. *Outlook* 120 (November 27, 1918): 481; Sally Marks and Denis Dulude note the political nature of food relief even in the eyes of German officials. "Several German leaders made a proposal to Dresel . . . to the effect that it would be most helpful politically if the Allies were to announce that no food would be sent into Germany until a responsible and stable government was guaranteed." Marks and Dulude, "German-American Relations, 1918–1921," *Mid-America: An Historical Review* 53, no. 4 (1971): 213.
75. Artist unknown, "Pity the Poor Hun!" *Independent* 96 (November 30, 1918), 276 (reprinted from the *London Evening News*).
76. "Lodge Warns against New Pro-German Move," *New York Times*, November 13, 1918, 6; "Demand Full Cost of War," *New York Times*, December 11, 1918, 2.
77. Gerald Stanley Lee, "Bloodthirsty Angels: An Inquiry into How Americans Can Get On with Germans," *Saturday Evening Post* 191 (January 4, 1919) 3.
78. Ibid., 4 (emphasis added).
79. William J. Moroney to Senator Philander Knox, April 5, 1921, Records of the Department of State Relating to Political Relations Between the United States and Germany, 1910–1929, 711.62119/P81, Reel #2, M355, RG059, National Archives and Records Administration (hereafter NARA), College Park, Maryland (emphasis added).
80. Heinrich Charles to Secretary of State Charles Evans Hughes, August 19, 1921, Records of the Department of State Relating to Political Relations Between the United States and Germany, 1910–1929, 711.62119P81/20, Reel #2, M355, NARA; Unfortunately, to date no such concurrence had developed. Scholarship determining the guilty party in instigating the Great War fills vast shelf space in libraries; the best summary of historiography is Annika Mombauer's *Origins of the First World War*, in which the author argues that Germany's imperialistic aims are indeed primarily to blame for the war and that the nation's historians and educators worked to obscure its guilt in the interwar years.

81. The German Peace Delegation's response to the Treaty of Versailles demanded a neutral inquiry by an impartial commission into the responsibility for instigating the war through research in archives of all the belligerent countries and all persons who played an important role in the coming of the war. See Count von Brockdorff-Rantzau's letter to Paris Peace Conference President Georges Clemenceau on the subject of peace terms, May 1919, in Charles F. Horne, ed., *Source Records of the Great War*, vol. 7 (Indianapolis: American Legion, 1930), 164; Heinrich Charles to Secretary of State Charles Evans Hughes.
82. Kemper Fullerton, "To the Editor," *Nation* 13 (September 7, 1921): 266.
83. Oswald Garrison Villard, "Germany, 1922: I. The Political Situation," *Nation* 115 (July 19, 1922): 61–62, and Villard, "Germany, 1922: III. In the Occupied Territory," *Nation* 115 (August 2, 1922): 117.
84. Allied and Associated Powers, *Treaties of Peace, 1919–1923* (New York: Carnegie Endowment for International Peace, 1924), 1:3–263.
85. Richard M. Gamble, *The War for Righteousness: Progressive Christianity, the Great War, and the Rise of the Messianic Nation* (Wilmington, DE: ISI Books, 2003), 230, 228–29.
86. Cooper, *Breaking the Heart of the World*, 190–91.
87. Unknown artist, "No Entangling Alliances," *Current History* 10 (April 1919): 187 (reprinted from the *Detroit News*); C. A. Bronstrup, "The Hobble Skirt," *Current History* 10 (May 1919), 373 (reprinted from *San Francisco Chronicle*).
88. Quoted in John Braeman, *Albert J. Beveridge: American Nationalist* (Chicago: University of Chicago Press, 1971), 260.
89. Quoted in Alfred E. Cornebise, *The Amaroc News: The Daily Newspaper of the American Forces in Germany, 1919–1923* (Carbondale: Southern Illinois University Press, 1981), 78–79.
90. Kennedy, *Over Here*, 387; Ambrosius, "Wilson, Alliances, and the League of Nations," 163.
91. Marks and Dulude apply the cliché "to have one's cake and eat it too" to the United States' diplomacy relating to the Treaty of Berlin. Sally Marks and Denis Dulude, "German-American Relations," 224, 220–26.
92. "Peace Treaty with Germany is Signed: We Hold Versailles Compact Rights, But Assume no League Obligations," *New York Times*, August 26, 1921, 1.
93. *Nation*, 13 (September 7, 1921), 251.
94. Lundén, "Protestant Churches," 51–52; McKillen, "Unending Debate," 711.
95. Herbert Hoover to Secretary of State Charles Evans Hughes, April 6, 1921, Records of the Department of State Relating to Political Relations Between the United States and Germany, 1910–1929, 711.62119/107, Reel #2, M355, NARA.
96. Frank N. Putnam to President Woodrow Wilson, April 15, 1921, Records of the Department of State Relating to Political Relations Between the United States and Germany, 1910–1929, 711.62119P81/1, Reel #2, M355, NARA.

97. Charles A. York, Secretary of National Disabled Soldiers' League, Indianapolis Post, to Secretary of State Charles Evans Hughes, n.d., Records of the Department of State Relating to Political Relations Between the United States and Germany, 1910–1929, 711.62119P81/4, Reel #2, M355, NARA.
98. Wilson Guthrie to President Warren G. Harding, May 18, 1921, Records of the Department of State Relating to Political Relations Between the United States and Germany, 1910–1929, 711.62119P81/13, Reel #2, M355, NARA.
99. E. F. Thompson to Secretary of State Charles Evans Hughes, April 16, 1921, Records of the Department of State Relating to Political Relations Between the United States and Germany, 1910–1929, 711.62119P81/3, Reel #2, M355, NARA.
100. Villard, "Germany, 1922: I," 61–62.
101. Villard, "Germany, 1922: II," 117.
102. Ibid.
103. Keith L. Nelson, "The 'Black Horror on the Rhine': Race as a Factor in Post–World War I Diplomacy," *Journal of Modern History* 42 (1970): 606–27.
104. Mary Lee, *It's A Great War!* (Boston: Houghton Mifflin, 1929), 460.
105. Louis Graves, "Leaves from a Coblenz Diary," 76–83; 209–15. A report issued by the thirty-second division of the American Third Army recorded the effect of the occupation on German women in a more positive light, indicating that women witnessed U.S. soldiers' respectful treatment of women and that "in some localities the women are talking of organizing in order to improve the social status of women." Major General William Lassiter, "Report of 32nd Division 3rd Army on Military Government of Germany, 1918–1920," RG 120, Entry 1368, "Reports on American Military Government and the Administration of Civilian Affairs in Occupied Germany, 1920–1921," Box 5, unnumbered folder, NARA.
106. Nelson, *Victors Divided: America and the Allies in Germany, 1918–1923* (Berkeley, CA: University of California Press, 1975), 185–88.
107. Sally Marks, *The Illusion of Peace: International Relations in Europe, 1918–1933*, 2nd ed. (Basingstoke: Palgrave Macmillan, 2003), 17.
108. Ibid.
109. Schwabe, *Woodrow Wilson*, 3.
110. Marks, *Illusion of Peace*, 18.
111. Margaret MacMillan, *Paris 1919: Six Months that Changed the World* (New York: Random House, 2002), 465–66.
112. Ibid., 394.
113. Scheck, "Women Against Versailles," 23.
114. Quoted in ibid., 24.
115. Elizabeth Harvey, "Visions of the *Volk*: German Women and the Far Right from Kaiserreich to Third Reich," *Journal of Women's History* 16, no. 3 (2004): 152.

116. Elizabeth Harvey, "Pilgrimages to the 'Bleeding Border': Gender and the Rituals of Nationalist Protest in Germany, 1919–1939," *Women's History Review* 9, no. 2 (2000): 201–29; Scheck, "Women Against Versailles," 26.
117. Scheck, "Women Against Versailles," 24, 26.
118. Ibid., 31–32.
119. Harvey, "Visions of the Volk," 157.
120. Scheck, "Women Against Versailles," 21–22.
121. Gamble, *War for Righteousness*, 235–39, 241.
122. George F. Kennan, *American Diplomacy* (Chicago: University of Chicago Press, 1951; repr. New York: New American Library, 1961), 88–89; George F. Kennan, "Morality and Foreign Policy," *Foreign Affairs* 64, no. 2 (Winter 1985/86): 205–18.

Chapter 4

1. Olaf Gulbransson, "Friedenskonferenz [Peace Conference]," *Simplicissimus* 23, no. 44 (January 28, 1919): 547, translation mine.
2. Artist unknown, "Every Day is Wash Day," *Current History* 9 no. 3 (March 1919): 558 (reprinted from *Newspaper Enterprise Association*, Cleveland).
3. Jay Norwood Darling, "Enter—The League of Nations," *Independent Weekly*, 96 (November 30, 1918): 276; Werner Hahmann, "The Peace Governess," *Current History* 14 (April–September 1921): 493 (reprinted from *Kladderadatsch*, Berlin, unknown translator).
4. Hew Strachan "War and Society in the 1920s and 1930s," in *The Shadows of Total War: Europe, East Asia, and the United States, 1919–1939*, ed. Roger Chickering and Stig Förster (Cambridge: Cambridge University Press, 2003), 43.
5. Jennifer Anne Davy, "Pacifist Thought and Gender Ideology in the Political Biographies of Women Peace Activists in Germany, 1899–1970," *Journal of Women's History* 13 no. 3 (2001): 35; Susan Zeiger, *In Uncle Sam's Service: Women Workers With the American Expeditionary Force, 1917–1919* (Philadelphia: University of Pennsylvania Press, 2004), 11–25.
6. Vellacott, "A Place for Pacifism and Trans-Nationalism in Feminist Theory: The Early Work of the Women's International League for Peace and Freedom," *Women's History Review* 2 (1993): 26.
7. Nancy F. Cott, "On Men's History and Women's History," in *Meanings for Manhood: Constructions of Masculinity in Victorian America*, ed. Mark C. Carnes and Clyde Griffen (Chicago: University of Chicago Press, 1990), 206–7.
8. "Decries Women Delegates," *New York Times*, November 17, 1918, 2; Barbara J. Steinson, *American Women's Activism in World War I* (New York: Garland, 1982), 354.
9. "Wants Men to Make Peace," *New York Times*, November 23, 1918, 13; "Women at Peace Table," *New York Times*, November 19, 1918, 2.

10. Vellacott, "A Place for Pacifism," 28; Mercedes M. Randall, *Improper Bostonian: Emily Greene Balch* (Boston: Twayne, 1964), 159.
11. Quoted in Steinson, *American Women's Activism*, 353.
12. Benedict Anderson, *Imagined Communities: Reflections on the Origin and Spread of Nationalism*, rev. ed. (London: Verso, 1991), 7; Joan C. Tronto, *Moral Boundaries: An Argument for an Ethic of Care* (New York: Routledge, 1993), 15, discusses the access-to-power conundrum in relation to women.
13. Eric J. Hobsbawm, *Nations and Nationalisms since 1780: Programme, Myth, Reality* (New York: Cambridge University Press, 1991), 131–33.
14. Julie Mostov, "Sexing the Nation/Desexing the Body: Politics of National Identity in the Former Yugoslavia," in *Gender Ironies of Nationalism: Sexing the Nation*, ed. Tamar Mayer (London: Routledge, 2000), 98–100; Martha Hanna, *Your Death Would Be Mine: Paul and Marie Pireaud in the Great War* (Cambridge: Harvard University Press, 2006), 130.
15. Tamar Mayer, "Gender Ironies of Nationalism: Setting the Stage," Mayer, *Gender Ironies of Nationalism: Sexing the Nation* (London: Routledge, 2000), 1–7; Glenda Sluga, *The Nation, Psychology, and International Politics, 1870–1919* (Basingstoke: Palgrave Macmillan, 2006), 110.
16. Glenda Sluga, "Female and National Self-Determination: A Gender Re-Reading of 'The Apogee of Nationalism,'" *Nations and Nationalism* 6, no. 4 (2000) 511–12; Dana Calise Cooper, "Informal Ambassadors: American Women, Transatlantic Marriages, and Anglo-American Marriages, 1865–1945" (PhD diss., Texas Christian University, 2006), 220–21.
17. Memo from Manton Davis to the Officer in Charge of Civil Affairs, September 25, 1919, RG 120, Entry 1367, Box 1121, dec. file 290.1, unnumbered folder, National Archives and Records Administration (hereafter NARA); Circular #5, "Regulations Governing Marriage of Soldiers," January 13, 1923, RG 120, Entry 1367, Box 1121, decimal file 290.1, unnumbered folder, NARA.
18. Since California passed woman suffrage in 1911, women married to aliens protested that because of the 1907 act they were disfranchised; Quoted in Rogers M. Smith, *Civic Ideals: Conflicting Visions of Citizenship in U.S. History* (New Haven, CT: Yale University Press, 1997), 457.
19. Otto Bauer, "The Nation" (1924), in *Mapping the Nation*, ed. Gopal Balakrishnan (London: Verso, 1996), 53.
20. Sluga, "Female and National Self-Determination," 501; Carol Miller, "'Geneva—The Key to Equality': Inter-War Feminists and the League of Nations," *Women History Review* 3 (1994): 219–20; Katharine Anthony, *Feminism in Germany and Scandinavia* (New York: H. Holt, 1915), 3–4.
21. Amira Gelblum, "Feminism and Pacifism: The Case of Anita Augspurg and Lida Gustava Heymann," *Tel Aviv Jahrbuch für Deutsche Geschichte* (1992): 212.
22. Ibid., 207.
23. Rosemary Foot, "Where are the Women? The Gender Dimension in the Study of International Relations," *Diplomatic History* 14, no. 4 (1990): 621.

24. Sluga, "Female and National Self-Determination," 502; Mary Anthony Hopkins, "Women's Ways in War," *Four Lights* (June 2, 1917) n.p.
25. Julie Mostov, "Sexing the Nation/De-Sexing the Body: Politics of National Identity in the Former Yugoslavia," in *Gender Ironies of Nationalism: Sexing the Nation*, ed. Tamar Mayer (London: Routlege, 2000), 91.
26. Frau Schuller, Chairman of the *Vereins Krippe* (Association for Orphaned Children), to American Authorities in Coblenz, October 29, 1919, RG 120, Entry 1367, Box 1121, dec file 290.1, unnumbered folder, NARA. Schuller wrote that Germany's birthrate was decreasing but that in the last quarter of 1919 the birthrate was increasing; For birth rates in the occupied zone, see RG 120, Entry 1369, Box 1, "Records Relating to the Health of the Civilian Population in the U.S. Occupied Area, 1919–1920," National Archives and Records Administration (hereafter NARA), College Park, Maryland.
27. Sluga, "Female and National Self-Determination," 515; Richard J. Evans, *The Feminist Movement in Germany, 1894–1933* (London: Sage, 1976), 236.
28. Bäumer's German original quoted in Ute Gerhard, "National oder International: Die internationalen Beziehungen der deutschen bürgerlichen Frauenbewegung," *Feministische Studien* 3 (1994): 42, translation mine.
29. U.S.-section secretary Amy Wood commended Harding for ending the U.S. occupation of the Rhineland and asked him to protest France's occupation of the Ruhr, which she believed thwarted Germany's ability to survive as a nation; Wood to Harding, January 24, 1923, WILPF Records, DG 043, Part III, U.S. section, Series C Correspondence, Box 3 Folder 34, microfilm 130.41, Swarthmore College Peace Collection (hereafter SCPC), Swarthmore, Pennsylvania.
30. For a discussion of women's roles versus the public and private spheres, see Vellacott, "A Place for Pacifism," 31.
31. "Hun Voices Sway Women's Congress," *Washington Post*, May 16, 1919, 6.
32. Quoted in Jennifer A. Davy, "'Manly' and 'Feminine' Antimilitarism: Perceptions of Gender in the Antimilitarist Wing of the Weimar Peace Movement," in *Frieden—Gewalt—Geschlecht: Friedens- und Konfliktforschung als Geschlechterforschung*, ed. Jennifer A. Davy, Karen Hagemann, Ute Kätzel (Essen: Klartext, 2005), 162.
33. My interpretation of WILPF's rhetoric and strategies has been influenced by Joan C. Tronto's book *Moral Boundaries*, especially 1–21.
34. Jane Addams, *Peace and Bread in Time of War*, ed. Blance Wiesen Cook (New York: Macmillan, 1922; repr., New York: Garland, 1972), 153–54.
35. Gelblum, "Feminism and Pacifism," 221.
36. Vellacott, "A Place for Pacifism," 33, 32.
37. Leila Rupp, "Constructing Internationalism: The Case of Transnational Women's Organizations, 1888–1945," *American Historical Review* 99 (December 1994): 1577.

38. Secretary's notes of a conversation held at Quay d'Orsay, Paris, February 13, 1919, Records of the American Commission to Negotiate Peace, RG 256, microfilm 820, reel #48, NARA II; Papers Relating to the Foreign Relations of the United States: The Paris Peace Conference (Washington, D.C., 1919), 3:1022–23; Vellacott, "Feminism As If All People Mattered: Working to Remove the Causes of War, 1919–1929," *Contemporary European History* 10, no. 3 (November 2001): 378.
39. Sluga, "Female and National Self-Determination," 508.
40. For a similar paradigm, see Caroline O. N. Moser and Fiona C. Clark, "Gender, Conflict, and Building Sustainable Peace: Recent Lessons from Latin America," in *Gender, Development, and Humanitarian Work*, ed. Caroline Sweetman (Oxford: Oxfam GB, 2001), 34.
41. Irene Cooper Willis, Honorable International Secretary, to Miss [Rosa] Manus, December 16, 1918, Series I, International Executive Committee, 1915–1978, Part F, Circular and Form Letters, microfilm 7090, reel #26, University of Arizona Library (hereafter UAL).
42. Jane Addams, "Presidential Address," in *Jane Addams on Peace, War, and International Understanding, 1899–1932*, ed. Allen F. Davis (New York: Garland, 1976), 166.
43. Jennifer D. Keene, *Doughboys, the Great War, and the Remaking of America* (Baltimore: Johns Hopkins, 2001), 113–17; see also "Our Men Mingled with Foe at End," *New York Times*, November 13, 1918, 4; Addams wrote that this phenomenon was common throughout the war, *Peace and Bread*, 69–70.
44. Annika Wilmers, "Zwischen den Fronten: Friedensdiskurse in der internationalen Frauenfriedensbewegung, 1914–1919," in *Frieden—Gewalt—Geschlecht*, 123–43.
45. Addams, "Presidential Address," 167.
46. Quoted in Mercedes M. Randall, *Improper Bostonian*, 275–76 and in Gertrude Bussey, *Women's International League for Peace and Freedom: A Record of Fifty Years' Work* (London: Allen and Unwin, 1965), 30.
47. Mary Chamberlain, "The Women at Zurich," *Survey* (June 14, 1919): 426–28; Chamberlain's article is contradicted by an unsigned letter to Matilda Widegren, president.of WILPF's Swedish branch, which notes that German women wanted to bring in a resolution expressing their horror and condemnation of German war conduct, WILPF Papers, Series I, International Exec Committee, 1915–1978, Part A, Correspondence, microfilm 7090, reel #1, UAL.
48. Quoted in Mercedes M. Randall, *Improper Bostonian*, 159.
49. WILPF, *Towards Peace and Freedom: the Women's International Congress, Zürich, May 12th to 17th, 1919*, English ed. (London: British section of WILPF), 7.
50. Vellacott, "Feminism," 384.
51. WILPF, *Towards Peace and Freedom*, 19; Aletta Jacobs presented a report on marriage and citizenship at the 1924 WILPF convention, WILPF, *Report of the*

fourth congress of the Women's international league for peace and freedom, Washington, May 1 to 7, 1924 English ed. (Washington, D.C.: WILPF U.S. section, 1924), 33–36.
52. WILPF Reports, Zurich 1919–Vienna 1921, Series I., WILPF International Executive Committee, 1915–1978, Part B, Executive Committee Records, 1915–1976, microfilm 7090, reel #9, UAL.
53. Sluga, "Female and National Self-Determination," 504.
54. Harriet Connor Brown, "America Menaced by Militarism: An Appeal to Women," 1921, WILPF Collection, DG 043, Part III, U.S. Section, Series A,5 Box 1, reel 130.33, SCPC.
55. Gail Bederman, *Manliness and Civilization: A Cultural History of Gender and Race in the United States, 1880–1917* (Chicago: University of Chicago, 1995), 188.
56. "World Disarmament," Hearings before the Committee on Military Affairs, House of Representatives, 66th Congress, 3rd session, January 11, 1921 (Washington, D.C.: Government Printing Office, 1921), 4–5, 28.
57. Ibid., 41.
58. For a discussion of the impact of woman suffrage in the U.S., see Kristi Andersen, *After Suffrage: Women in Partisan and Electoral Politics before the New Deal* (Chicago: University of Chicago Press, 1996), 6–7.
59. Brown was joined by three other WILPF members in the 1923 hearings. "War Appropriations Bill, 1923," Hearings before the subcommittee of the Committee on Appropriations. United States Senate, Sixty-Seventh Congress, second session, on H.R. 10871 (Washington D.C.: Government Printing Office, 1923), 663.
60. Hull to Hon. Frank B. Kellogg, July 7, 1924, WILPF Collection, DG043, Part III U.S. Section, Series A,5 Literature, Box 1, reel 130.33, SCPC (emphasis added); "Impressions of the Women's Conference," Hannah Clothier Hull, undated, WILPF Collection, DG043, Part III U.S. Section, Series A,5 Literature, Box 1, reel 130.33, SCPC.
61. Gelblum, "Feminism and Pacifism," 216, 209–11.
62. Ibid., 210, 216.
63. Auguste Kirchhoff, "Unserer Kinder Land," in *Ein Weib Wie Wir?!: Auguste Kirchhoff: Ein Leben für den Frieden und für die Rechte der Frauen*, ed. Hannelore Cyrus and Verena Steinecke (Bremen:Verlag in der Sonnonstrasse, 1989), 105–6, translation mine.
64. Gertrud Baer, "Merkblatt" Berlin section, 1924, WILPF Swarthmore College Peace Collection Accession, 32–38, Archives, University of Colorado at Boulder Libraries (hereafter UCBL), n.p., translation Dr. Joan Birch.
65. WILPF German section, *Völkerversöhnende Frauenarbeit*, November 1918–December 1920, Part 2 (Stuttgart: Verlag "Friede Durch Recht," GMBH, 1921), 9, translation Dr. Joan Birch.
66. Statement from Württemberg branch of German WILPF, March 14, 1920, WILPF Paper, Series I, International Executive Committee, 1915–1978, Part A

Correspondence, 1915–1978, reel #1, microfilm 7090, UAL, translator unknown; no German original.
67. Gelblum, "Feminism and Pacifism," 225.
68. Ibid., 220.
69. WILPF German section, *Völkerversöhnende Frauenarbeit*, 11–12, Dr. Joan Birch translator.
70. Gelblum, "Feminism and Pacifism," 219; see German section's criticisms of their government's foreign policy "Meisterstücke Deutscher Diplomatie," *Die Frau im Staat* 6, no. 3 (March 1924): 1–3.
71. WILPF German section, *Völkerversöhnende Frauenarbeit*, 11, Dr. Joan Birch translator; emphasis mine.
72. Addams, *Peace and Bread*. 199; Addams quotes from the British Labour Party's recommendations of three measures: (1) a complete raising of the blockade; (2) granting credits to liberated countries and enemy countries to enable them to obtain food and raw materials sufficient to put them in a position where they can begin to help themselves; (3) measures for the special relief of children everywhere without regard to the political allegiance of their parents; ibid., 209–10.
73. Lida Gustava Heymann, "Völkerverständigung—Volksverständigung," *Die Frau im Staat* 3, no. 2 (1921): 5, translation mine.
74. "10 Gebote" 1924, WILPF Swarthmore College Peace Collection Accession, 32–38, UCBL, my translation.
75. "Resolution," German section to David Lloyd George, January 3, 1921, WILPF Swarthmore College Peace Collection Accession, 32–37, UCBL.
76. WILPF German section, *Völkerversöhnende Frauenarbeit*, 21–22, translation Dr. Joan Birch.
77. Gertrude Baer, "Merkblatt," n.p., translation Dr. Joan Birch.
78. *Kinder Zeitung*, 1922, WILPF Swarthmore College Peace Collection Accession, 36–38, UCBL, translation mine.
79. "Friede auf Erden! Herausgeben von der IFFF, Christmas 1921," n.p., WILPF Swarthmore College Peace Collection, 36–38, UCBL, translation mine; WILPF German section, *Völkerversöhnende Frauenarbeit*, 24, translation Dr. Joan Birch.
80. Philip Haxall Bagby, "Weekly Bulletin of Military Information," December 10, 1919, United States Army, American Forces in Germany, Miscellaneous records, 1919–1923, 4087614.1, Box 1, Hoover Institute Archives (hereafter HIA), Stanford, California; Jane Addams confirmed that Germany fostered militarism in its education system, *Peace and Bread*, 226.
81. Christiane Henke, *Anita Augspurg* (Hamburg: Reinbek bei Hamburg, 2000), 110.
82. Baer, "Merkblatt," n.p., translation by Dr. Joan Birch.
83. Lucy Biddle Lewis, "The Last Word from Europe," report dated February 12, 1923, U.S. section WILPF, reel 130.33, SCPC.
84. "Pax Altra/Ruhrbesetzung," *Die Frau im Staat* 5, no. 4 (April 1923): 1–4.

85. WILPF, *Report of the Fourth Congress of the Women's International League for Peace and Freedom, Washington, D.C., 1924*, English ed. (Washington, D.C.: WILPF), 30–33; Andrée Jouve's letter to "German comrades," October 25, 1923, WILPF Swarthmore College Peace Collection Accession, 32–36, Archives, UCBL, translation Dr. Pamela Park.
86. Gertrud Baer, "Merkblatt," n.p., translation Dr. Joan Birch.
87. Gelblum, "Feminism and Pacifism," 212, 215.
88. Davy, "Pacifist Thought," 36; Rupp, "Constructing Internationalism," 1589.
89. Davy, "Pacifist Thought," 36.
90. R. M. Whitney, "Peace at Any Old Price," Beckwith Press, 1923?, WILPF Collection, DG 043, Part III, US section, Series C Correspondence, Box 1, General Correspondence, 1919–1924, reel 130.39, SCPC (emphasis added). Folder contains many accusations linking WILPF with communism.
91. Harriet Hyman Alonso, *Peace as a Women's Issue: a History of the U.S. Movement for World Peace and Women's Rights* (Syracuse: Syracuse University Press, 1993), 83.
92. Carrie Chapman Catt, "Poison Propaganda," *The Woman Citizen* (May 31, 1924): 14, 32–33; WILPF records also contain the "slacker oath," poem, and correspondence; Maude Wood Park to Hon. John W. Weeks, April 2, 1924, WILPF Collection, DG 043, Part III. US section, Series C Correspondence, Box 1, General Correspondence, 1919–1924, Folder 13, 130.39, SCPC.
93. WILPF German section, *Völkerversöhnende Frauenarbeit*, cover; Gertrude Baer, "Merkblatt," back page.
94. Addams, *Peace and Bread*, 166.
95. WILPF, *Towards Peace and Freedom*, 8.
96. Vellacott, "A Place for Pacifism," 41.
97. Vellacott, "Feminism," 385–86.
98. For a discussion of women pacifists' positions on wartime work, see Erika Kuhlman, *Petticoats and White Feathers: Gender Conformity, Race, the Progressive Peace Movement, and the Debate over War, 1895–1919* (Westport CT: Greenwood, 1997), 114–16; Gelblum, "Feminism and Pacifism," 211, 223.
99. Kittredge to Addams, October 31, 1920, WILPF Collection, DG 043, Part III. US section, Series C, Correspondence, 1919–1924, Box 1, reel 130.38, SCPC.
100. "History of the U.S. section of WILPF," WILPF Collection, DG043, Part III, US section, Series A,5 Literature, Box 1, 130.33, SCPC; Steinson, *American Women's Activism*, 369.
101. Vellacott, "Feminism," 385.
102. J. G. Randall and David Donald, *The Civil War and Reconstruction* 2nd ed. (Boston: D. C. Heath and Company, 1961), 488.
103. Marian Baldwin, *Canteening Overseas, 1917–1919* (New York: Macmillan, 1920), 182.
104. Hamilton Holt, "The American Watch on the Rhine," *Independent* 104 (December 4, 1920): 348; W.C. Gregg, "Unscathed and Unrepentant," *Outlook*

127 (March 16, 1921) 422; Harry A. Franck, *Vagabonding Through Changing Germany* (New York: Harper & Brothers, 1920), 140.
105. Weekly Digest of Censorship Information, No. 20, November 20, 1919, 5, United States Army, American Forces in Germany, Miscellaneous records, 1919–1923, 4087614.1, Box 7, HIA.
106. Frank M. Surface and Raymond L. Bland, *American Food in the World War and Reconstruction Period: Operations of the Organizations Under the Direction of Herbert Hoover, 1914–1924* (Stanford, CA: Stanford University Press, 1931), 5–6.
107. C. Paul Vincent, *The Politics of Hunger: the Allied Blockade of Germany, 1915–1919* (Athens: Ohio University Press, 1985), 70, 71, 78.
108. Nick Cullather, "The Foreign Policy of the Calorie," *American Historical Review*, 112, no. 2 (April 2007): 350–51.
109. Robert H. Van Meter, Jr., "Herbert Hoover and the Economic Reconstruction of Europe, 1918–1921," in *Herbert Hoover: The Great War and its Aftermath*, ed. Lawrence E. Gelfand (Iowa City: University of Iowa Press, 1979), 145–54.
110. David Burner, *Herbert Hoover, a Public Life* (New York: Knopf, 1979), 296, claims that Hoover was not a pacifist in the Quaker sense of rejecting all war.
111. Vincent, *Politics of Hunger*, 77–78.
112. Ibid., 66.
113. Bliss to The American Peace Commission, February 26, 1919, Tasker H. Bliss Papers, 4086358.1, HIA.
114. Vincent, *Politics of Hunger*, 93, 110.
115. Ibid., 110, 113, 117.
116. Jane Addams and Alice Hamilton, *Report to the American Friends Service Committee on the Situation in Germany*, AFSC Bulletin 25 (Philadelphia: AFSC, 1919), available from AFSC, 1501 Cherry Street, Philadelphia, Pennsylvania AFSC, 19101.
117. Addams, *Peace and Bread*, 199–201; for more on the politics of care, see Joan C. Tronto, *Moral Boundaries: A Political Argument for an Ethic of Care* (New York: Routledge, 1993).
118. Addams, *Peace and Bread*, 172–73, 208.
119. Allen F. Davis, *American Heroine: The Life and Legend of Jane Addams* (Chicago: Ivan R. Dee, 2000), 260; Christian A. Herter, Office of Secretary, Dept of Commerce, to Charles Nagel, April 4, 1921, American Relief Administration European operational records, 1919–1923, Washington Office Correspondence, 4087618.1, Box 466, Folder 2, HIA.
120. Addams, *Peace and Bread*, 225.
121. Quoted in Jennifer A. Davy, "'Manly' and 'Feminine' Antimilitarism," 162.
122. Susan Grayzel, *Women's Identities at War: Gender, Motherhood, and Politics in Britain and France during the First World War* (Chapel Hill: University of North Carolina Press, 1999), 246.

123. Unattributed quote in Jane Addams, "The Revolt Against War," in *Women at the Hague: The International Congress of Women and Its Results*, ed. Jane Addams, Emily G. Balch, and Alice Hamilton (New York: Garland, 1972), 65–66.
124. Ibid., 55–81.
125. Vincent, *Politics of Hunger*, 110.

Chapter 5

1. *Outlook*, 120 (November 27, 1918) 511. I use the word "boy" instead of "man" because that is the word that appears most frequently in contemporary literature. For example, a Hudson Motor Car Company advertisement in the *New York Times*, November 13, 1918, 9, uses much the same language as the *Outlook* ad; the headline of the ad copy reads: "The Boys Are Coming Back." See also Raymond Fosdick. "When the Boys Come Home," *Independent* 96 (December 28, 1918) 430–31.
2. *Outlook*, 511.
3. Karen Hagemann, "Home/Front: The Military, Violence and Gender Relations in the Age of the World Wars," in *Home/Front: The Military, War and Gender in Twentieth-Century Germany*, ed. Hagemann and Stefanie Schüler-Springorum (London: Berg, 2002), 2; Elise Cleveland Mead, "A Woman's War: An Account of the Work of the Women's Division of the YMCA During the World War," unpublished, undated manuscript, World War I-related records, Y.USA.4–1, Box 65, Folder 1, 5, Kautz Family YMCA Archives, Social Welfare History Archives, Elmer L. Andersen Library, University of Minnesota, Minneapolis. Mead distinguishes the U.S. women's YMCA work from that of their British counterparts by noting that "American women went much nearer the front than the English 'Y' women." See also Susan Zeiger, *In Uncle Sam's Service: Women Workers with the American Expeditionary Force, 1917–1919* (Ithaca, NY: Cornell University Press, 1999), 74. For the same pattern in Britain, see Jeffrey S. Reznick, *Healing the Nation: Soldiers and the Culture of Care-giving in Britain During the Great War* (Manchester: Manchester University Press, 2004), 56.
4. Martha Hanna, *Your Death Would be Mine: Paul and Marie Pireaud in the Great War* (Cambridge: Harvard University Press, 2006), 17–18.
5. Susan Zeiger, *In Uncle Sam's Service*; Kennedy, *Over Here: The First World War and American Society* (New York: Oxford University Press, 1980); Ute Daniel, *The War From Within: German Working-Class Women in the First World War* (New York: Berg, 1997); Susanne Rouette, *Sozialpolitik als Geschlechterpolitik: die Regulierung der Frauenarbeit nach dem Ersten Weltkrieg* (Frankfurt: Campus, 1993); Karin Hausen, "Die Sorge der Nation für ihre 'Kriegsopfer': Ein Bereich der Geschlechterpolitik während der Weimarer Republik," in *Von der Arbeiterbewegung zum modernen Sozialstaat*, ed. Jürgen Kocka (Munich: Saur Verlag, 1994), 719–39.

6. Sultan Barakat, "Post-War Reconstruction and Development: Coming of Age," in *After the Conflict: Reconstruction and Development in the Aftermath of War*, Sultan Barakat (London: I. B. Tauris, 2005), 25.
7. Jay Winter, *Remembering War: The Great War Between Memory and History in the Twentieth Century* (New Haven: Yale University Press, 2006), 136; Winter himself borrows the term from Carol Gluck.
8. Dora Apel, "'Heroes' and 'Whores': The Politics of Gender in Weimar Antiwar Imagery," *Art Bulletin* 79, no. 3 (September 1997): 367; George L. Mosse, *Fallen Soldiers: Reshaping the Memory of the World Wars* (Oxford: Oxford University Press, 1993), 70–106.
9. Colin Nicolson, *The Longman Companion to the First World War* (New York: Longman, 2000), 248; Hausen, "Sorge," 725; U.S. statistics on Great War veterans and their widows can be found in U.S. Congress, *Pensions—World War widows: Pensions to widows and children of World War veterans: Hearings before the Committee on Pensions, House of Representatives, Seventy-fifth Congress, third session, on H.R. 8690 (now known as H.R. 9285) a bill granting a pension to widows and dependent children of World War veterans. January 25 and 28, 1938* (Washington, D.C.: GPO, 1938), 37.
10. Martha Harnoss, "Die Organisation der Kriegerwitwen," in *Kriegerwitwen gestalten ihr Schicksal: Lebenskämpfe deutscher Kriegerwitwen nach eigenen Darstellung*, ed. Helene Hurwitz-Stranz (Berlin: Carl Heymanns Verlag, 1931), 117 (my translation). Gertrude Bäumer makes similar remarks in her forward to *Kriegerwitwen*, 9.
11. Susanne Rouette, "Mothers and Citizens: Gender and Social Policy in Germany after the First World War," *Central European History*, 30 (1997): 48.
12. Leonhard Frank, *Der Mensch ist gut* (Zürich: M. Rascher, 1918), 43, translation mine.
13. Dora Hansen-Blancke, "Review of Helene Hurwitz-Stranz, *Kriegerwitwen gestalten ihr Schicksal*," *Die Frau* 39 (1931/32): 112, questions Hurwitz-Stranz's use of the *gestalten*: can one really *determine* "fate"? Rouette, "Mothers," 49.
14. Anna Fischer-Dückelmann, "Häusliche Krankenpflege in Kriegszeiten: Was lehrte uns der Krieg?" (Stuttgart: Süddeutsches Verlags: Institut Julius Müller, 1916), 7–9; Renata Bridenthal, Atina Grossmann, and Marion Kaplan, eds., *When Biology Became Destiny: Women in Weimar and Nazi Germany* (New York: Monthly Review, 1984), 7; Rouette, "Mothers," 51.
15. Bridenthal, et al., *When Biology*, 7; Rouette, *Sozialpoltik als Geschlechterpolitik: Die Regulierung der Frauenarbeit nach dem Ersten Weltkrieg* (Frankfurt: Campus), 34; Raffael Scheck, "German Conservatism and Female Political Activism in the Early Weimar Republic," *German History* 15, no. 1 (1997): 52.
16. Ute Frevert, *Women in German History from Bourgeois Emancipation to Sexual Liberation*, trans. Stuart McKinnon-Evans (New York: Berg, 1989), 170; Harnoss, "Die Organisation," 117.

17. Rouette, "Mothers and Citizens," 48; Ute Frevert, *Women in German History*, 171; Nancy Woloch, *Women and the American Experience* (New York: Knopf, 1984), 355.
18. Susan Grayzel, *Women's Identities at War: Gender, Motherhood, and Politics in Britain and France during the First World War* (Chapel Hill: University of North Carolina Press, 1999), 245.
19. Lynn Abrams and Elizabeth Harvey, "Introduction," in *Gender Relations in German History: Power, Agency and Experience from the sixteenth to the twentieth Century*, ed. Lynn Abrams and Elizabeth Harvey (Durham, NC: Duke University Press, 1997), 21; Irene Stoehr, "Housework and Motherhood: Debates and Policies in the Women's Movement in Imperial Germany and the Weimar Republic," in *Maternity and Gender Policies: Women and the Rise of the European Welfare States, 1880s-1950s*, ed. Gisela Bock and Pat Thane (London: Routledge, 1991), 213–32; Harnoss, in *Kriegerwitwen*, also says that women's educational role in children's lives should be acknowledged through higher pensions, 120.
20. Whalen, *Bitter Wounds*, 95.
21. Tagung des Hauptausschusses der Kriegerwitwen-und-Waisenfürsorge, *Frauenerwerb und Kriegswitwe: Referate erstattet auf der 2. Tagung des Hauptausschusses der Kriegerwitwen- und -Waisenfürsorge am 27. November 1915 im Reichstagsgebäude in Berlin* (Berlin: Carl Heymanns, 1916).
22. Ute Daniel, *The War From Within*, 38. Daniel drew her statistics about female employment during the war from the Factory Inspector's reports, which did not include all German employers; Doris Obschernitzki, *"Der Frau ihre Arbeit!": Lette Verein: Zur Geschichte einer Berliner Institution, 1866 bis 1986* (Berlin: Hentrich, 1987), 137.
23. Levy-Rathenau, "Berufsberatung und Kriegshinterbliebene," in Tagung, *Frauenerwerb*, 1; Rouette, *Sozialpolitik*, notes the government's plans to dismiss them before the war ended, 35–36.
24. Karin Hausen, "The German Nation's Obligations," in *Behind the Lines: Gender and the Two World Wars*, ed. Margaret Randolph Higonnet, Sonya Michel, Jane Jenson, and Margaret Collins Weitz (New Haven, CT: Yale University Press), 130–31, notes that Gertrud Hanna, Käthe Gäbel, and Helene Simon each argued that mothers—even unwed mothers—should be paid for their work.
25. Rouette, "Mothers and Citizens," 53–54. Hedwig Dransfeld, leading member of the German Catholic women's movement, offered a class-based analysis of the problem of working women in German society. Dransfeld portrayed widows as upholders of their social class as she outlined the roles that they could play in the German state and in churches to help maintain Germany's class system; see Deutschen Verein für Armenpflege und Wohltätigkeit, *Soziale Fürsorge für Kriegerwitwen und Kriegerwaisen* (Muenchen und Leipzig: Duncker und Humboldt, 1915), 51–52.

26. Levy-Rathenau, "Berufsberatung und Kriegshinterbliebene," in Tagung, *Frauenerwerb*, 1–3; Hurwitz-Stranz, *Kriegerwitwen*, 94–95; other examples of industrious widows follow on pp. 96 and 98.
27. Dr. Shrup-Gleiwitz, "Die Kriegswitwe in Fabrik, Handwerk, und Hausgewerbe," in Tagung, *Frauenerwerb*, 9; John R. McDill, *Lessons from the Enemy: How Germany Cares for her War Disabled* (Philadelphia: Lea & Febiger, 1918), x.
28. Shrup-Gleiwitz, "Die Kriegswitwe," 9; Compare Rouette, "Mothers and Citizens," 62, where she notes that the German government placed "lower value . . . on women's labor" judging by the lower wages paid to women, the lower benefit rates for unemployed.
29. Schlusstagung des Hauptausschusses, *Stand und Künftige Entwicklung der Kriegerwitwen und Kriegswaisenfürsorge* (Berlin: Carl Heymanns, 1918), 8 (translation mine).
30. Hermann Geib, "Einführung," in Hurwitz-Stranz, *Kriegerwitwen*, 6–7 (translation mine).
31. Richard Bessel, *Germany After the First World War* (Oxford: Oxford University Press, 1993), 141.
32. Rouette, "Mothers," 58–59; Else Dregos, "Arbeitsbeschaffung für Kriegerwitwen in der Praxis," in *Soziale Praxis und Archiv für Volkswohlfahrt* 32, (1923), 84–85.
33. Ute Daniel, *The War from Within*, 276–77.
34. Young-Sun Hong, "Gender, Citizenship, and the Welfare State: Social Work and the Politics of Femininity in the Weimar Republic," *Central European History* 30, no. 1 (1997): 14–15.
35. Bessel, *Germany after the First World War*, 49, 69.
36. Barakat, "Post-War Reconstruction and Development," 256.
37. Bessel, *Germany after the First World War*, 274.
38. Quoted in Whalen, *Bitter Wounds*, 107.
39. Whalen, *Bitter Wounds*, 110–11, 124–25.
40. Frau M. Goetting, "Vom Wollen und Wirken," 1926, R 43 I 708, microfiche #6, Bundesarchiv (hereafter BA), Berlin.
41. Quoted in Bessel, *Germany After the First World War*, 278.
42. Letter, from the Reichsbund, Ortsgruppe Landberg am Werther, December 18, 1918, to the Oberpräsident der Provinz Brandenburg RAM 3901, film #36072, BA.
43. Hermann Geib, Staatssekretär des Reichsarbeitsministeriums October 24, 1919, R 43 I 706 microfilm reel #3, BA.
44. Whalen, *Bitter Wounds*, 136–38.
45. Karl Nau, *Die Wirtschaftliche und soziale Lage von Kriegshinterbliebenen: Eine Studie auf Grund von Erhebungen über die auswirkung der versorgung von Kriegshinterbliebenen in Darmstadt* (Leipzig: Lühe, Kommissionsverlag, 1930), 48. Hausen, "Sorge," shows that widows received from 30 to 50 percent of what their dead husbands would have gotten as "severely damaged" pensions

in 1920 (that percentage rose to 40 to 60 by 1924), 732–33. See also Hurwitz-Stranz, *Kriegerwitwen*, 64.
46. Bessel, *Germany after the First World War*, 226.
47. Hurwitz-Stranz, *Kriegerwitwen*, 78–79; Eine Hauptmannswitwe, "Was leistet das Reich für die Kriegsbeschädigten und Kriegerhinterbliebenen?" *Neue Lebensfahrt: Mitteilungen für Kriegerhinterbliebene, Beilage zum Reichsbund*, 3, no. 21 (November 1, 1920), n.p., translation mine.
48. Rouette, "Mothers and Citizens," 50.
49. Whalen, *Bitter Wounds*, 143.
50. Quoted in Hausen, "The German Nation's Obligations," 127.
51. Whalen, *Bitter Wounds*, 141–47.
52. Eine Hauptmannswitwe, "Was leistet das Reich," n.p.; Hausen, "The German Nation's Obligations," 136.
53. Ingrid Sharp, "Blaming the Women: Women's Responsibility for the First World War," in *The Women's Movement in Wartime: International Perspectives, 1914–19*, ed. Alison Fell and Ingrid Sharp (Basingstoke: Palgrave Macmillan, 2007), 67.
54. Bianca Schönberger, "Motherly Heroines and Adventurous Girls: Red Cross Nurses and Women Army Auxiliaries in the First World War," in *Home/Front: The Miltiary, War and Gender in Twentieth-Century Germany*, ed. Karen Hagemann and Stefanie Schüler-Springorum (New York: Berg, 2002), 91, 89; Ute Daniel, *War From Within*, 94, provides comparative statistics on men's and women's wartime wages in Germany.
55. The *Reichsbund* journal called upon women to end their "quiet devotion of their fate," and join the protest against the inadequacy of the RVG in a street protest from September 5 through 12, 1920, "Die Aufgaben der Hinterbliebenen im Kampfe [sic] um ausreichende Versorgung und Fürsorge," *Neue Lebensfahrt: Mitteilungen für Kriegerhinterbliebene, Beilage zum Reichsbund* 3, no. 17 (September 4, 1920): n.p.
56. Whalen, *Bitter Wounds*, 162; Hausen, "Sorge," 728.
57. "Brauchen die Hinterbliebenen einen Rechtsausspruch auf Heilbehandlung und Berufsausbildung?" *Neue Lebensfahrt: Mitteilungen für Kriegerhinterbliebene, Beilage zum Reichsbund* 3, no. 7 (April 17, 1920): n.p.; Daniel, *The War From Within*, 98.
58. Quoted in Hausen, "Sorge," 719, translation mine.
59. Paul Allenberger, "Zur Hinterbliebenenfürsorge," *Neue Lebensfahrt: Mitteilungen für Kriegerhinterbliebene, Beilage zum Reichsbund* 3, no. 9/10 (May 29, 1920) n.p.
60. Kameradin Dr. Thürnagel, "Die Hinterbliebenen und das neue Gesetz," *Neue Lebensfahrt: Mitteilungen für Kriegerhinterbliebene, Beilage zum Reichsbund* 3, no. 18 (September 18, 1920), n.p.; Hausen, "Sorge," 731.
61. Hurwitz-Stranz, *Kriegerwitwen*, 27, 41, 77, 83, 91–92.
62. Quoted in Bessel, *Germany after the First World War*, 231(emphasis mine).

63. Karl Kuetti, "Zahlenergebnis," in *Kriegshinterbliebenenfürsorge in Preussen: Ergebnis einer Umfrage bei den Fürsorgestellen* (Berlin: Carl Heymanns, 1919), 9.
64. Hans Harmsen, *Der Einfluß der versorgungsgesetzlichen Regelung auf die wirtschaftliche und soziale Lage der Kriegerwitwen: eine soziologische und bevölkerungspolitische Untersuchung, zugleich der Versuch einer sozialhygienischen Beurteilung und Kritik unserer heutigen Versorgungsgesetzgebung* (Berlin: Schoetz, 1926), 35; French historians viewed France's low birthrate as a weakness; see Eugen Weber, The Hollow Years: France in the 1930s (New York: W. W. Norton, 1994), 12–13.
65. Harmsen, *Der Einfluß der versorgungsgesetzlichen Regelung auf die wirtschaftliche und soziale Lage der Kriegerwitwen*, 32, 52, 60–62.
66. Bessel, *Germany after the First World War*, 40–41.
67. Helene Hurwitz-Stranz, "8 Jahre Beisitzerin an Reichsversorgungsgericht" *Die Frau* 38 (1930/31): 264–71.
68. Sweet-Orr & Company, *To Managers of Factories, Machine Shops, Ammunition Plants and Other Industries Where Women are Employed* (New York: Sweet-Orr, 1918), 8.
69. Maurine Weiner Greenwald, *Women, War, and Work: The Impact of World War I on Women Workers in the United States* (Westport, CT: Greenwood, 1980; repr. Ithaca, NY: Cornell University Press, 1990), 13; Kennedy, *Over Here*, 285–86; Eric Foner, *Women and the American Labor Movement from WWI to the Present* (New York: Free Press, 1980), 124.
70. Janet F. Davidson, "Women and the Railroad: The Gendering of Work During the First World War Era, 1917–1920" (PhD dissertation, University of Delaware, 1999), 11, 334–43.
71. U.S. Women's Bureau, *The New Position of Women in American Industry* (Washington, D.C.: GPO, 1920), 25–34, 137.
72. Davidson, "Women and the Railroad," 379.
73. Paul Anthony Samuelson and Everett Einar Hagen, *After the War, 1918–1920: Military and Economic Demobilization of the United States* (Washington, D.C.: G.P.O, 1943), 9.
74. Vye Smeigh Thompson, *History of the National American Legion Auxiliary* (Pittsburgh: Jackson-Remlinger, 1926), 3:17, 32–33.
75. Women's Trade Union League, *Women and Reconstruction: Being the Report of the Committee on Social and Industrial Reconstruction of the National Women's Trade Union League of America, Meeting in New York, December 9–12, 1918* (Chicago: The League), n.p.
76. Ibid.
77. Elizabeth Payne, *Reform, Labor, and Feminism: Margaret Dreier Robins and the Women's Trade Union League* (Urbana: University of Illinois Press, 1988), 143–44.
78. Bessel, *Germany After the First World War*, 30; Martha Hanna, *Your Death Would Be Mine*, 53–57.

79. William H. Glasson, *Federal Military Pensions in the United States* (New York: Oxford University Press, 1918), 283–92.
80. See Jennifer D. Keene's chapter on the Bonus Army in *Doughboys, the Great War, and the Remaking of America* (Baltimore: Johns Hopkins University Press, 2001), 179–204.
81. Zeiger, *In Uncle Sam's Service*, 168–72.
82. George L. Mosse, *Fallen Soldiers: Reshaping the Memory of the World Wars*, (Oxford: Oxford University Press, 1990), 105.
83. Richard Bessel, "The Great War in German Memory: The Soldiers of the First World War, Demobilization, and Weimar Political Culture," *German History* 6, no. 1 (1988): 21.
84. Apel, "'Heroes' and 'Whores,'" 368.
85. Bianca Schönberger, "Motherly Heroines," 91–96, 103.
86. Apel, "'Heroes' and 'Whores,'" 372; *Der Stahlhelm: halbmonatsschrift des Bundes der Frontsoldaten* 4, no. 1 (January 1, 1922), n.p.
87. Apel, "'Heroes' and 'Whores,'" 367, 368.
88. Sabine Keinitz, "Body Damage: War Disability and the Constructions of Masculinity in Weimar Germany," in *Home/Front: The Military, War and Gender in Twentieth-Century Germany*, ed. Karen Hagemann and Stefanie Schüler-Springorum (Oxford: Berg, 2002), 181.
89. Whalen, *Bitter Wounds*, 24.
90. Michael Geyer, "The Stigma of Violence, Nationalism, and War in Twentieth-Century Germany," special issue, *German Studies Review* (Winter 1992): 85; Apel, "'Heroes' and 'Whores,'" 368–69.
91. G. Kurt Piehler, *Remembering the War in the American Way* (Washington and London: Smithsonian Institution Press, 1995), 187; George L. Mosse, *Fallen Soldiers: Reshaping the Memory of the World Wars* (Oxford: Oxford University Press, 1990), 105.
92. Richard J. Evans, *The Feminist Movement in Germany, 1894–1933* (London: Sage, 1976), 236; Hans Harmsen, *Der Einfluß der versorgungsgesetzlichen Regelung auf die wirtschaftliche und soziale Lage der Kriegerwitwen*, 35.
93. Dora Apel, "'Heroes' and 'Whores,'" 366, 378, 368
94. Michael Geyer, "The Stigma of Violence," 88.
95. David A. Bell, *The First Total War: Napoleon's Europe and the Birth of Warfare as We Know It* (Boston: Houghton Mifflin, 2007), 294, 299.
96. "Gedenkfeier des Deutschen Volkes zu Ehren der Opfer des Weltkrieges, Programm," R 43 I 710 microfilm reel #4, BA, translation mine.
97. Whalen, *Bitter Wounds*, 33–34.
98. Letter from the Volksbund Deutsche Kriegsgräberfürsorge to Herren Reichskanzler, February 17, 1922, R 43 I 710 #1, BA includes signatures of leaders of the various women's organizations.

99. Anne-Marie Claire Hughes, "The Significance of the Death and Mourning of Edith Cavell in Britain," *European Review of History* 12, no. 3 (November 2005): 425–26.
100. Hausen, "Sorge," 726; "Die Aufgaben der Hinterbliebenen im Kampfe [sic]," *Neue Lebensfahrt: Mitteilungen für Kriegerhinterbliebene, Beilage zum Reichsbund*, n.p.
101. Frau Bahersdorff, "Karmerad! Kameradin!" *Neue Lebensfahrt: Mitteilungen für Kriegerhinterbliebene, Beilage zum Reichsbund* 3, no. 8 (May 1, 1920): n.p.; Carroll Smith-Rosenberg asked whether a minority group within in a society can ever challenge the power held by the dominant group if they co-opt the language used by the dominant; see Smith-Rosenberg, "Writing History: Language, Class and Gender," in *Feminist Studies/Critical Studies*, ed. Teresa deLauretis (Bloomington: Indiana University Press, 1986), 32–54.
102. Helene Hurwitz-Stranz, *Kreigerwitwen Gestalten ihre Schicksal*.
103. David M. Kennedy, *Over Here*, 205–6.
104. Quoted in ibid., 212.
105. Willa Cather, *One of Ours* (New York: Knopf, 1922); Kennedy, *Over Here*, 214.
106. Kennedy, *Over Here*, 217.
107. Ibid., 219–25; John Dos Passos, "Against American Literature," *New Republic* 8 (October 14, 1916): 270.
108. Cather, *One of Ours*, 209–10.
109. Mary Lee, *It's a Great War!* (Boston: Houghton, 1929).
110. Harry Hansen, *New York World*, October 25, 1929, 17; A. H. Gibbs, *New York Times*, January 26, 1930, 16.
111. Katherine Anne Porter, *Pale Horse, Pale Rider: Three Short Novels* (New York: Harcourt, Brace, 1939).
112. Frank Edwin Peat and Lee Orean Smith, *Legion Airs: Songs of "Over There" and "Over Here"* (New York: L. Feist, 1932).
113. Clemens Work, *Darkest before Dawn: Sedition and Free Speech in the American West* (Albuquerque: University of New Mexico Press. 2005), 3.
114. Kim E. Nielsen, *Un-American Womanhood: Antiradicalism, Antifeminism, and the First Red Scare* (Columbus: Ohio State University Press, 2001), 14–16; quoted in Christy Jo Snider, "Patriots and Pacifists: The Rhetorical Debate about Peace, Patriotism, and Internationalism, 1914–1930," *Rhetoric & Public Affairs* 8, no. 1 (2005): 69.
115. Records of the Women's International League for Peace and Freedom, U.S. section, 130.39 Series C Correspondence, Box 1, General Correspondence, Folder 13, Attacks and Criticisms, SCPC.
116. Kennedy, *Over Here*, 217–18.
117. *Constitution and by-laws of the Women's Auxiliary of the American Legion, Kansas Department: As Adopted by the First Annual Department Convention, Newton, Kan., Jan. 10–11, 1921* (Topeka: Kansas State Printing Plant, 1921), n.p.
118. Vye Smeigh Thompson, *History of the Women's Auxiliary*, 33.

119. Ibid., 191 (emphasis mine).
120. American War Mothers, *Constitution and By-Laws* (Chicago: American War Mothers, 1939); Committees on the Judiciary, 68th Congress, 1st session (1924), "To Incorporate the American War Mothers," joint hearing on H.R. 8980 and H.R. 9095 (Washington, D.C.: GPO, 1924), 1–12, emphasis mine.
121. Quoted in Sharp, "Blaming the Women," 69–70.
122. Leonhard Frank, *Der Mensch ist Gut* (Zurich: Max Rascher, 1918), 26.
123. William March, Company K (New York: H. Smith and R. Haas, 1933), 101–2.
124. Rouette, "Mothers," 65–66.
125. Constance Potter, "World War I Gold Star Mothers Pilgrimages, Part I," *Prologue: Quarterly of the National Archives and Records Administration* 31, no. 2 (Summer 1999): 142–43; John W. Graham, *The Gold Star Mothers Pilgrimages of the 1930s: Oversees Grave Visitations by Mothers and Widows of the Fallen U.S. WWI Soldiers* (Jefferson, NC: McFarland, 2005), 15. During WWI, it became customary to place a "service flag" in the window of a home that had a person serving in the military during the war. If the person died during the war, the blue star was replaced with a gold star.
126. Quoted in Hausen, "Sorge," 721, translation mine.

Epilogue

1. Kristi Andersen, *After Suffrage: Women in Partisan and Electoral Politics before the New Deal* (Chicago: University of Chicago Press, 1996), 2–5.
2. Shawn Meghan Burn, *Women Across Cultures: A Global Perspective* (New York: McGraw-Hill, 2005), 227.
3. United Nations, *The World's Women: Trends and Statistics, 2000* (New York: United Nations, 2000), 85.
4. Lezak Shallat, "Democracy in the Nation, but Not at Home: Domestic Violence and Women's Reproductive Health in Chile," in *No Paradise Yet: The World's Women Face the New Century*, ed. Judith Mirsky and Marty Radlett (London: PANOS/Zed, 2000), 137, 140.
5. United Nations, *The World's Women*, 31, 34, 151, 164.
6. Anne Armstrong, *Unconditional Surrender: The Impact of the Casablanca Policy Upon World War II* (New Brunswick: Rutgers University Press, 1961), 64–65.
7. Paul Kecskemeti, *Strategic Surrender: The Politics of Victory and Defeat* (New York: Atheneum, 1964), 217; Armstrong, *Unconditional Surrender*, 64–65, 93–100.
8. Eric W. Osborne, "Casualties," in *Encyclopedia of World War II*, ed. Spencer Tucker (Santa Barbara: ABC-CLIO, 2005), 1:300–301; Lance Janda, "Casualties, Combatant and Noncombatant," in *The Encyclopedia of World War I*, ed. Spencer C. Tucker (Santa Barbara: ABC-CLIO, 2005), 1:272–73. Both writers confirm that civilian casualties (for either war) are nearly impossible to provide. Eric Hobsbawm, "War and Peace in the Twentieth Century," in Geir

Lundestad & Olav Njølstad, eds. *War and Peace in the Twentieth Century and Beyond: Proceedings of the Nobel Centennial Symposium* (London: World Scientific, 2002), 25; Alan Kramer, *Dynamic of Destruction: Culture and Mass Killing in the First World War* (Oxford: Oxford University Press, 2007) regards the two world wars as a single destructive entity.
9. Christy Jo Snider, "The Influence of Transnational Peace Groups on U.S. Foreign Policy Decision-Makers During the 1930s: Incorporating NGOs into the UN," *Diplomatic History* 27, no. 3 (2003): 377–404; Dorothy B. Robins, *Experiment in Democracy: the Story of U.S. Citizen Organizations in Forging the Charter of the United Nations* (New York: Parkside, 1971), ix–xi.
10. WILPF, *Towards Peace and Freedom: the Women's International Congress, Zürich, May 12th to 17th, 1919*, English ed. (London: British section of WILPF), 18–19.
11. Foreign Policy Association, *. . . And Justice For All: The Universal Declaration of Human Rights at 50* (New York: Foreign Policy Association, 1998), 6–7.
12. Allen F. Davis, *American Heroine: Life and Legend of Jane Addams* (Chicago: Ivan R. Dee, 1973; repr. 2000), 5, 164; Hebe Spaull, *Women Peace-Makers* (London: G. C. Harrup, 1924), 40.
13. Cynthia Enloe, *Bananas, Beaches, and Bases: Making Feminist Sense of International Politics* (Berkeley: University of California Press, 1990).
14. Swanee Hunt and Cristina Posa, "Women Waging Peace: Inclusive Security," *Foreign Policy* 124 (2001): 39–40.
15. Julie Mertus, *Bait and Switch: Human Rights and U.S. Foreign Policy* (New York: Routledge, 2004), 184–85.
16. Camille Pampell Conaway, *The Role of Women in Stabilization and Reconstruction* (Washington, D.C.: U.S. Institute of Peace, 2006), 3.
17. Donald K. Steinberg, *Conflict, Gender, and Human Rights: Lessons Learned from the Field* (San Diego: University of San Diego Joan B. Kroc Institute for Peace & Justice, 2004), 14.
18. Mertus, *Bait and Switch*, 186.
19. Aaron D. Pina, *Women in Iraq: Background and Issues for U.S. Policy* (Washington, D.C.: Congressional Research Service, 2006), 6, 7, 10.
20. Steinberg, *Conflict, Gender, and Human Rights*, 16–17; Hunt and Posa, "Women Waging Peace," 38.
21. Sheila Meintjes, Anu Pillay, and Meredeth Turshen, "There is no Aftermath for Women," in *The Aftermath: Women in Post-Conflict Transformation*, ed. Sheila Meintjes, Anu Pillay, and Meredeth Turshen (London: Zed Books, 2002), 4.

Bibliography

Contemporary Newspapers and Journals

The Amaroc
Charleston Evening Post
Chicago Tribune
The Crisis
Current History
Danziger Neueste Nachrichten
Kladderadatsch (Berlin)
Lokal Anzeiger (Berlin)
London Daily Herald
New York Times
Reichsbund: Mitteilungen fur Kriegshinterbliebene
Rheinisch-Westfälische Zeitung
Simplicissimus (Munich)
Der Stahlhelm
Stars and Stripes
Washington Post

Addams, Jane. "Respect the Law." *Independent* 53 (January 3, 1901): 18–20.
Baldwin, Elbert F. "The American Forces in Germany." *Outlook* 122 (August 1919): 635–36.
Braley, Berton. "Buddy Bosses the Boche." *Sunset* 42 (July 1919): 45–46.
Catt, Carrie Chapman. "Poison Propaganda." *Woman Citizen* (May 31, 1924): 14, 32–33.
Chamberlain, Mary. "The Women at Zurich." *Survey* (June 14, 1919): 426–28.
Dos Passos, John. "Against American Literature." *New Republic* 8 (October 14, 1916): 269–71.
Fullerton, Kemper. "To the Editor." *Nation* 13 (September 7, 1921): 266.

Gannett, Lewis S. "Those Black Troops on the Rhine—and the White." *Nation* 112 (May 25, 1921): 733–34.

Graves, Louis. "Leaves from a Coblenz Diary: Fragments from the Notebook of Heinrich Scheinstutzen, Apothecary." *Atlantic Monthly* 124 (July–August 1919): 76–83, 209–15.

Gregg, W. C. "Unscathed and Unrepentant." *Outlook* 127 (March 16, 1921) 422–27.

Hamilton, Alice, and Jane Addams. "After the Lean Years: Impressions of Food Conditions in Germany when Peace Was Signed." *Survey* (September 6, 1919): 793–97.

Hart, Albert Bushnell. "Can Germany Be Regenerated? The Coming Struggle Between the Thinking Majority and the Organized Minority." *Forum* 61 (January 1919): 1–11.

Harvey, George. "Beware the Peace Drive!" *North American Review* 208 (October 1918): 493–97.

Holt, Hamilton. "The American Watch on the Rhine." *Independent* 104 (December 4, 1920): 347–49.

Hopkins, Mary Anthony. "Women's Ways in War." *Four Lights* (June 2, 1917): n.p.

James, Edwin L. "The Allied Armies in Germany." *Current History* 9 (January 1919): 16.

Kellogg, Vernon. "Unclean, Unclean." *North American Review* 208 (October 1918): 536–39.

Lee, Gerald Stanley. "Bloodthirsty Angels: An Inquiry into How Americans Can Get On with Germans." *Saturday Evening Post* 191 (January 4, 1919): 1–4, 26, 28.

Macdonald, Harriet H. "At Home with the War Brides." *Independent* 103 (September 1919): 328–29, 337.

Villard, Oswald Garrison. "Germany, 1922: I. The Political Situation." *Nation* 115 (July 19, 1922): 61–62.

———. "Germany, 1922: III. In the Occupied Territory." *Nation* 115 (August 2, 1922): 116–18.

"What to Do with Germany." *Public: A Journal of Democracy* (December 14, 1918): 1495–96.

Archives

American Friends Service Committee Archives, Philadelphia, Pennsylvania.

Bundesarchiv, Berlin: Reichskanzlei.

Elmer L. Andersen Library, University of Minnesota, Minneapolis: Kautz Family YMCA Archives, Social Welfare History Archives.

Hoover Institute Archives, Stanford University, Stanford, California: Records of the United States Army, the American Relief Administration, and the Tasker H. Bliss Papers.

Landeshauptarchiv Koblenz, Germany: Records of the Oberpräsidium der Rheinlande, Besatzungszeit.

McDonald, Carma. Letter. From the files of Donald Amaroc McDonald.
National Archives Records Administration, College Park, Maryland: War Department Records and State Department Records.
Stiftung Archiv der deutschen Frauenbewegung, Kassel, Germany.
Swarthmore College Peace Collection, Swarthmore, Pennsylvania: Women's International League for Peace and Freedom Collection.
University of Colorado Boulder Libraries, Boulder, Colorado: Collection of the Women's International League for Peace and Freedom, 2nd Accession (1915–1998).
University of Colorado Boulder Libraries, Boulder, Colorado: Women's International League for Peace and Freedom (WILPF) Swarthmore College Peace Collection Accession (1915–2000).
University of Arizona Library, Tucson, Arizona: Women's International League for Peace and Freedom Papers, 1915–1978 Collection.

Published Sources

Abrams, Lynn, and Elizabeth Harvey, eds. *Gender Relations in German History: Power, Agency and Experience from the Sixteenth to the Twentieth Century* (Durham, NC: Duke University Press, 1997).
Addams, Jane. *Peace and Bread in Time of War*. Edited by Blance Wiesen Cook. New York: Garland, 1972.
Addams, Jane, and Alice Hamilton, *Report to the American Friends Service Committee on the Situation in Germany*. AFSC Bulletin 25. Philadelphia: AFSC, 1919.
Addams, Jane, Emily G. Balch, and Alice Hamilton, *Women at The Hague: The International Congress of Women and Its Results*. New York: Garland, 1972.
Allen, Henry T. *My Rhineland Journal*. Boston: Houghton Mifflin, 1923.
———. *The Rhineland Occupation*. Indianapolis, IN: Bobbs-Merrill, 1927.
Allied and Associated Powers, *Treaties of Peace, 1919–1923*, Vol. 1. New York: Carnegie Endowment for International Peace, 1924.
Alonso, Harriet Hyman. *Peace as a Women's Issue: A History of the U.S. Movement for World Peace and Women's Rights*. Syracuse, NY: Syracuse University Press, 1993.
Ambrosius, Lloyd E. "Wilson, Alliances, and the League of Nations," *Journal of the Gilded Age and Progressive Era* 5, no. 2 (April 2006): 139–66.
———. *Wilsonian Statecraft: Theory and Practice of Liberal Internationalism During World War I*. Wilmington, DE: SR Books, 1991.
———. *Wilsonianism: Woodrow Wilson and His Legacy in American Foreign Relations*. New York: Palgrave Macmillan, 2002.
———. *Woodrow Wilson and the American Diplomatic Tradition: The Treaty Fight in Perspective*. New York: Cambridge University Press, 1987.
American War Mothers. *Constitution and By-Laws*. Chicago: American War Mothers, 1939.

Anderson, Benedict. *Imagined Communities: Reflections on the Origin and Spread of Nationalism*. London: Verso, 1991.

Andersen, Kristi. *After Suffrage: Women in Partisan and Electoral Politics before the New Deal*. Chicago: University of Chicago Press, 1996.

Anderson, Shelley. "Women's Many Roles in Reconciliation." In *People Building Peace: 35 Inspiring Stories from Around the World*, edited by European Centre for Conflict Prevention, 230–36. Maastricht: European Centre for Conflict Prevention, 1999.

Anthony, Katharine. *Feminism in Germany and Scandinavia*. New York: H. Holt, 1915.

Apel, Dora. "'Heroes' and 'Whores': The Politics of Gender in Weimar Antiwar Imagery." *Art Bulletin* 79, no. 3 (September 1997): 366–84.

Aristophanes, *Lysistrata/The Acharnians the Clouds*. Introduction and translation by Alan H. Sommerstein. New York: Penguin Classics, 1974.

Armstrong, Anne. *Unconditional Surrender: The Impact of the Casablanca Policy upon World War II*. New Brunswick, NJ: Rutgers University Press, 1961.

Bagby, Philip H. *The American Representation in Germany, 1920–1921*. Vols. 1 and 2. Coblenz, Germany: United States Army, American Forces in Germany, 1922.

Baird, A. Craig, ed. *American Public Addresses, 1740–1952*. New York: McGraw-Hill, 1956.

Balakrishnan, Gopol, ed. *Mapping the Nation*. London: Verso, 1996.

Balch, Emily Greene. *Approaches to the Great Settlement*. New York: B. W. Huebsch, 1918.

Baldwin, Marian. *Canteening Overseas, 1917–1919*. New York: Macmillan, 1920.

Barakat, Sultan. "Post-War Reconstruction and Development: Coming of Age." In *After the Conflict: Reconstruction and Development in the Aftermath of War*, edited by Sultan Barakat, 7–32. London: I. B. Tauris, 2005.

Beasley, Vanessa B. "Engendering Democratic Change: How Three U.S. Presidents Discussed Female Suffrage." *Rhetoric & Public Affairs* 5 no. 1 (2002): 79–103.

Bederman, Gail. *Manliness and Civilization: A Cultural History of Gender and Race in the United Sates, 1880–1917*. Chicago: University of Chicago Press, 1995.

———. "'The Women Have Had Charge of the Church's Work Long Enough': The Men and Religion Forward Movement of 1911–1912." *American Quarterly* 41, no. 3 (September 1989): 432–65.

Bell, David A. *The First Total War: Napoleon's Europe and the Birth of Warfare as We Know It*. Boston: Houghton Mifflin, 2007.

Bessel, Richard. *Germany After the First World War*. Oxford: Oxford University Press, 1993.

———. "The Great War in German Memory: The Soldiers of the First World War, Demobilization, and Weimar Political Culture." *German History* 6, no. 1 (1988): 20–34.

Blackwell, Joyce. *No Peace Without Freedom: Race and the Women's International League for Peace and Freedom, 1915–1975*. Carbondale: Southern Illinois University Press, 2004.

Bland, Lucy. "White Women and Men of Colour: Miscegenation Fears in Britain after the Great War." *Gender & History* 17, no. 1 (April 2005): 29–61.

Blum, Edward J. *Reforging the White Republic: Race, Religion, and American Nationalism, 1865–1898*. Baton Rouge: Louisiana State University Press, 2005.

Blunden, Edmund. *The Mind's Eye: Essays*. Freeport, NY: Books for Libraries, 1934; reprinted 1967.

Braeman, John. *Albert J. Beveridge: American Nationalist*. Chicago: University of Chicago Press, 1971.

Bridenthal, Renata, Atina Grossmann, and Marion Kaplan, eds. *When Biology Became Destiny: Women in Weimar and Nazi Germany*. New York: Monthly Review, 1984.

Bristow, Nancy K. *Making Men Moral: Social Engineering During the Great War*. New York: New York University Press, 1996.

Brody, David, ed. *Essays on the Age of Enterprise, 1870–1900*. Hinsdale, IL: Dryden, 1974.

Burn, Shawn Meghan. *Women Across Cultures: A Global Perspective*. New York: McGraw-Hill, 2005.

Burner, David. *Herbert Hoover, a Public Life*. New York: Knopf, 1979.

Bussey, Gertrude. *Women's International League for Peace and Freedom: A Record of Fifty Years' Work*. London: Allen and Unwin, 1965.

Campt, Tina, Pascal Grosse, and Yara-Colette Lemke-Muniz de Fario. "Blacks, Germans, and the Politics of Imperial Imagination, 1920–60." In *The Imperialist Imagination: German Colonialism and its Legacy*, edited by Sara Friedrichsmeyer, Sara Lennox, and Susanne Zantop. Ann Arbor: University of Michigan, 1998.

Carnes, Mark C., and Clyde Griffen, eds. *Meanings for Manhood: Constructions of Masculinity in Victorian America*. Chicago: University of Chicago Press, 1990.

Cather, Willa. *One of Ours*. New York: Knopf, 1922.

Center for Military History. *United States Army in the World War, 1917–1919: American Occupation of Germany*, Vol. 11. Washington: G.P.O., 1948.

Chaudhuri, Nuper, and Margaret Strobel. "Introduction." In *Western Women and Imperialism: Complicity and Resistance*, edited by Nuper Chaudhuri and Margaret Strobel, 1–15. Bloomington: Indiana University Press, 1992.

Chickering, Roger and Stig Förster, eds. *The Shadows of Total War: Europe, East Asia, and the United States, 1919–1939*. Cambridge: Cambridge University Press, 2003.

Collins, Robert O. *Europeans in Africa*. New York: Knopf, 1971.

Conaway, Camille Pampell. *The Role of Women in Stabilization and Reconstruction*. Washington, D.C.: U.S. Institute of Peace, 2006.

Conklin, Alice L. *A Mission to Civilize: The Republican Idea of Empire in France and West Africa, 1895–1930*. Stanford, CA: Stanford University Press, 1997.

Constitution and by-laws of the Women's Auxiliary of the American Legion, Kansas Department: As Adopted by the First Annual Department Convention, Newton, Kan., Jan. 10–11, 1921. Topeka: Kansas State Printing Plant, 1921.

Coolidge, Mary Roberts. *Why Women Are So.* New York: Arno, 1912; reprinted 1972.

Cooper, John Milton. *Breaking the Heart of the World: Woodrow Wilson and the Fight for the League of Nations.* New York: Cambridge University Press, 2001.

Cornebise, Alfred. *The Amaroc News: the Daily Newspaper of the American Forces in Occupied German 1919–1923.* Carbondale: Southern Illinois University Press, 1981.

Craig, Gordon A. *Germany, 1866–1945.* New York: Oxford University Press, 1978.

Cullather, Nick. "The Foreign Policy of the Calorie," *American Historical Review*, 112, no. 2 (April 2007): 337–64.

Czernin, Ferdinand. *Versailles 1919: The Forces, Events and Personalities that Shaped the Treaty.* New York: Capricorn Books, 1965.

Daniel, Ute. *The War From Within: German Working-Class Women in the First World War.* New York: Berg, 1997.

Davis, Allen F. *American Heroine: Life and Legend of Jane Addams.* Chicago: Ivan R. Dee, 1973; reprinted 2000.

Davy, Jennifer Anne. "Pacifist Thought and Gender Ideology in the Political Biographies of Women Peace Activists in Germany, 1899–1970." *Journal of Women's History* 13, no. 3 (2001): 34–45.

Day, Donald. *Woodrow Wilson's Own Story.* Boston: Little, Brown, 1952.

Dickman, Joseph T. *The Great Crusade: A Narrative of the World War.* New York, London: D. Appleton, 1927.

Edelstein, David M. "Occupational Hazards: Why Military Occupations Succeed or Fail." *International Security* 29 (2004): 49–91.

Enloe, Cynthia. *Bananas, Beaches, and Bases: Making Feminist Sense of International Politics.* Berkeley: University of California Press, 1990.

———. *The Curious Feminist: Searching for Women in a New Age of Empire.* Berkeley: University of California Press, 2004.

Evans, Richard J. *The Feminist Movement in Germany, 1894–1933.* London: Sage, 1976.

Fischer, Conan. *The Ruhr Crisis, 1923–24.* Oxford: Oxford University Press, 2003.

Foner, Eric. *Women and the American Labor Movement from WWI to the Present.* New York: Free Press, 1980.

Foot, Rosemary. "Where are the Women? The Gender Dimension in the Study of International Relations." *Diplomatic History* 14, no. 4 (1990): 615–22.

Foreign Policy Association. . . . *And Justice For All: The Universal Declaration of Human Rights at 50.* New York: Foreign Policy Association, 1998.

Franck, Harry A. *Vagabonding through Changing Germany.* New York: Harper & Brothers, 1920.

Franklin, John Hope. *Race and History: Selected Essays, 1938–1988*. Baton Rouge: Louisiana State University Press, 1989.
Frevert, Ute. *Women in German History: From Bourgeois Emancipation to Sexual Liberation*. Translated by Stuart McKinnon-Evans. New York: Berg, 1989.
Friedrichsmeyer, Sara, Sara Lennox, and Susanne Zantop, eds. *The Imperialist Imagination: German Colonialism and its Legacy*. Ann Arbor: University of Michigan, 1998.
Fry, Joseph A. "William McKinley and the Coming of the Spanish-American War: A Study of the Besmirching and Redemption of an Historical Image." *Diplomatic History* 3, no. 1 (Winter 1979): 77–97.
Fussell, Paul. *The Great War and Modern Memory*. New York: Oxford University Press, 1975.
Gallicchio, Marc. *The African American Encounter with Japan and China: Black Internationalism in Asia, 1895–1945*. Chapel Hill: University of North Carolina Press, 2000.
Gamble, Richard M. *The War for Righteousness: Progressive Christianity, the Great War, and the Rise of the Messianic Nation*. Wilmington, DE: ISI Books, 2003.
Gelblum, Amira. "Feminism and Pacifism: the case of Anita Augspurg and Lida Gustava Heymann." *Tel Aviv Jahrbuch für Deutsche Geschichte* (1992): 207–24.
Gelfand, Lawrence E., ed. *Herbert Hoover: The Great War and its Aftermath*. Iowa City: University of Iowa Press, 1979.
Gerber, David A. ed. *Disabled Veterans in History*. Ann Arbor: University of Michigan Press, 2000.
Geyer, Michael. "The Stigma of Violence, Nationalism, and War in Twentieth-Century Germany." Special issue, *German Studies Review* (Winter 1992): 75–110.
Glasson, William H. *Federal Military Pensions in the United States*. New York: Oxford University Press, 1918.
Goebel, Stefan. *The Great War and Medieval Memory: War, Remembrance and Medievalism in Britain and Germany, 1914–1940*. Cambridge: Cambridge University Press, 2007.
Gopnik, Adam. "The Big One." *New Yorker*, August 23, 2004, 78–85.
Graham, John W. *The Gold Star Mothers Pilgrimages of the 1930s: Oversees Grave Visitations by Mothers and Widows of the Fallen U.S. WWI Soldiers*. Jefferson, NC: McFarland, 2005.
Grayzel, Susan R. *Women's Identities at War: Gender, Motherhood, and Politics in Britain and France during the First World War*. Chapel Hill: University of North Carolina Press, 1999.
Greenwald, Maurine Weiner. *Women, War, and Work: The Impact of World War I on Women Workers in the United States*.Westport, CT: Greenwood, 1980; reprinted, Ithaca, NY: Cornell University Press, 1990.
Hackett, David G., ed. *Religion and American Culture: A Reader*, 2nd ed. New York: Routledge, 2003.

Hackney, Sheldon. "Initial Shock: A Conversation with Paul Fussell." *Humanities* 17, no. 5 (November/December 1996): 4–9.
Hagemann, Karin. "Home/Front: The Military, Violence and Gender Relations in the Age of the World Wars." In *Home/Front: The Military, War and Gender in Twentieth-Century Germany*, edited by Karin Hagemann and Stefanie Schüler-Springorum, 1–41. London: Berg, 2002.
Hanna, Martha. *Your Death Would Be Mine: Paul and Marie Pireaud in the Great War*. Cambridge: Harvard University Press, 2006.
Harvey, Elizabeth. "Visions of the *Volk*: German Women and the Far Right from Kaiserreich to Third Reich." *Journal of Women's History* 16, no. 3 (2004): 152–67.
———. "Pilgrimages to the 'Bleeding Border': Gender and the Rituals of Nationalist Protest in Germany, 1919–1939," *Women's History Review* 9, no. 2 (2000): 201–29.
Hemingway, Ernest. *A Farewell to Arms*. New York: Charles Scribner's Sons, 1929; reprinted 1993.
Hobsbawm, Eric J. *Nations and Nationalism since 1780: Programme, Myth, Reality*. New York: Cambridge University Press, 1992.
———. "War and Peace in the Twentieth Century." In *War and Peace in the Twentieth Century and Beyond: Proceedings of the Nobel Centennial Symposium*, edited by Geir Lundestad & Olav Njølstad, 25–40. London: World Scientific, 2002.
Hogan, Michael J. and Thomas G. Patterson, eds. *Explaining the History of American Foreign Relations*, 2nd ed. New York: Cambridge University Press, 2004.
Hong, Young-Sun. "Gender, Citizenship, and the Welfare State: Social Work and the Politics of Femininity in the Weimar Republic." *Central European History* 30, no. 1 (1997): 1–23.
Horne, Charles F., ed. *Source Records of the Great War*, Vol. 7. Indianapolis: American Legion, 1930.
Hughes, Anne-Marie Claire. "The Significance of the Death and Mourning of Edith Cavell in Britain." *European Review of History* 12, no. 3 (November 2005): 425–644.
Hunt, Swanee, and Cristina Posa, "Women Waging Peace: Inclusive Security." *Foreign Policy* 124 (2001): 38–47.
Ikenberry, G. John. *After Victory: Institutions, Strategic Restraint, and the Rebuilding of Order after Major Wars*. Princeton, NJ: Princeton University Press, 2001.
Iriye, Akira. "The United States as an Occupier." *Reviews in American History* 16, no. 1 (1988): 65–72.
Jeffreys-Jones, Rhodri. *Changing Differences: Women and the Shaping of American Foreign Policy, 1917–1994*. New Brunswick: Rutgers University Press, 1995.
Joll, James. *Origins of the First World War*. London: Longman, 1984.
Kaplow, Larry. "2 Soldiers Defy Order, Marry Baghdad Women." *Chicago Tribune*, August 28, 2003, 8.

Kecskemeti, Paul. *Strategic Surrender: The Politics of Victory and Defeat*. New York: Atheneum, 1964.
Keene, Jennifer D. *Doughboys, The Great War, and the Remaking of America*. Baltimore: Johns Hopkins University Press, 2001.
Kennan, George F. *American Diplomacy*. Chicago: University of Chicago, 1951; reprinted New York: New American Library, 1961.
———. *The Fateful Alliance: France, Russia, and the Coming of the First World War*. New York: Pantheon Books, 1984.
———. "Morality and Foreign Policy," *Foreign Affairs* 64, no. 2 (Winter 1985/86): 205–18.
Kennedy, David M. *Over Here: The First World War and American Society*. New York: Oxford University Press, 1980.
Kimmel, Michael, "Men's Responses to Feminism." *Gender & Society* 1 (September 1987): 261–83.
Knight, Louise W. *Citizen: Jane Addams and the Struggle for Democracy*. Chicago: University of Chicago Press, 2005.
Kraditor, Aileen S. *The Ideas of the Woman Suffrage Movement, 1890–1920*. New York: Anchor Doubleday, 1965.
Kramer, Alan. *Dynamic of Destruction: Culture and Mass Killing in the First World War*. Oxford: Oxford University Press, 2007.
Kuhlman, Erika. *Petticoats and White Feathers: Gender Conformity, Race, the Progressive Peace Movement, and the Debate over War, 1895–1919*. Westport, CT: Greenwood, 1997.
Lee, Mary. *It's A Great War!* Boston: Houghton Mifflin, 1929.
Lerner, Gerda. *The Creation of Patriarchy*. Oxford: Oxford University Press, 1986.
Link, Arthur S., ed. *The Papers of Woodrow Wilson*, Vol. 40. Princeton, NJ: Princeton University Press, 1966–1993.
Little, Arthur W. *From Harlem to the Rhine: The Story of New York's Colored Volunteers*. New York: Covici Friede, 1936.
Löbe, Paul. *Under the Yoke of Foreign Rule: Sufferings of the Rhineland Population*, Vol. 2, unidentified translator. Leipzig: K. F. Koehler, 1923.
Lundén, Rolf. "The Protestant Churches and the Business Spirit of the Twenties." *European Contributions to American Studies*, 10 (1986): 47–62.
Lunn, Joe. *Memoirs of the Maelstrom: A Senegalese Oral History of the First World War*. Portsmouth, NH: Heinemann, 1999.
MacMillan, Margaret. *Paris 1919: Six Months that Changed the World*. New York: Random House, 2002.
Marks, Sally. "Black Watch on the Rhine: A Study in Propaganda, Prejudice, and Prurience." *European Studies Review* 13 (1983): 297–334.
———. *The Illusion of Peace: International Relations in Europe, 1918–1933*. New York: St. Martin's, 1976; reprinted Basingstoke: Palgrave Macmillan, 2003.
Marks, Sally, and Denis Dulude. "German-American Relations, 1918–1921." *Mid-America: An Historical Review* 53, no. 4 (1971): 211–26.

Marty, Martin E. *Modern American Religion, Volume 1: The Irony of it All, 1893–1919*. Chicago: University of Chicago Press, 1986.

May, Henry F. *The End of American Innocence: A Study of the First Years of Our Own Time, 1912–1917*. New York: Alfred A. Knopf. 1959.

Mayer, Arno J. *Politics and Diplomacy of Peacemaking: Containment and Counterrevolution at Versailles, 1918–1919*. New York: Knopf, 1967.

Mayer, Tamar, ed. *Gender Ironies of Nationalism: Sexing the Nation*. London: Routledge, 2000.

McDill, John R. *Lessons from the Enemy: How Germany Cares for Her War Disabled*. Philadelphia: Lea & Febiger, 1918.

McDougall, Walter A. *Promised Land, Crusader State: The American Encounter with the World Since 1776*. Boston: Houghton Mifflin, 1997.

McGovern, James R. "David Graham Phillips and the Virility Impulse of the Progressives," *New England Quarterly* 39 (1966): 334–55.

McKillen, Elizabeth. "The Unending Debate over Woodrow Wilson and the League of Nations Fight," *Diplomatic History* 27, no. 5 (November 2003): 711–15.

Meintjes, Sheila, Anu Pillay, and Meredeth Turshen, eds. *The Aftermath: Women in Post-Conflict Transformation*. London: Zed Books, 2002.

Mertus, Julie. *Bait and Switch: Human Rights and U.S. Foreign Policy*. New York: Routledge, 2004.

Miller, Carol, "Geneva—The Key to Equality': Inter-War Feminists and the League of Nations." *Women History Review* 3 (1994): 219–45.

Mombauer, Anika. *The Origins of the First World War: Controversies and Consensus*. London: Longman, 2002.

Morel, Edmund D. *The Horror on the Rhine*. London: Union of Democratic Control, 1920.

Mosse, George L. *Fallen Soldiers: Reshaping the Memory of the World Wars*. Oxford: Oxford University Press, 1993.

Nelson, Keith L. "The 'Black Horror on the Rhine': Race as a Factor in Post–World War I Diplomacy." *Journal of Modern History* 42 (December 1970): 606–27.

———. *Victors Divided: America and the Allies in Germany, 1918–1923*. Berkeley: University of California Press, 1975.

Nicolson, Colin. *The Longman Companion to the First World War: Europe, 1914–1918*. New York: Longman, 2000.

Nielsen, Kim E. *Un-American Womanhood: Antiradicalism, Antifeminism, and the First Red Scare*. Columbus: Ohio State University Press, 2001.

Ogawa, Manako. "The 'White Ribbon League of Nations' Meets Japan: The Trans-Pacific Activism of the Woman's Christian Temperance Union, 1906–1930." *Diplomatic History* 31, no. 1 (January 2007): 21–50.

Opitz, May, Katharina Oguntoye, and Dagmar Schultz, eds. *Showing our Colors: Afro-German Women Speak Out*. Translated by Anne V. Adams. Amherst: University of Massachusetts Press, 1986.

Payne, Elizabeth. *Reform, Labor, and Feminism: Margaret Dreier Robins and the Women's Trade Union League.* Urbana: University of Illinois Press, 1988.

Peat, Frank Edwin, and Lee Orean Smith. *Legion Airs: Songs of "Over There" and "Over Here."* New York: L. Feist, 1932.

Peukert, Detlev J. K. *The Weimar Republic: The Crisis of Classical Modernity.* Translated by Richard Deveson. New York: Hill and Wang, 1989.

Piehler, G. Kurt. *Remembering the War in the American Way.* Washington, D.C.: Smithsonian Institution Press, 1995.

Pina, Aaron D. *Women in Iraq: Background and Issues for U.S. Policy.* Washington, D.C.: Congressional Research Service, 2006.

Porter, Katherine Anne. *Pale Horse, Pale Rider: Three Short Novels.* New York: Harcourt, Brace, 1939.

Potter, Constance. "World War I Gold Star Mothers Pilgrimages, Part I." *Prologue: Quarterly of the National Archives and Records Administration* 31, no. 2 (Summer 1999): 140–45.

Randall, J. G., and David Donald, *The Civil War and Reconstruction,* 2nd ed. Boston: D. C. Heath, 1961.

Randall, Mercedes. *Improper Bostonian: Emily Greene Balch.* Boston: Twayne, 1964.

Randolph, Margaret Higgonet, Sonya Michel, Jane Jenson, and Margaret Collins Weitz, eds. *Behind the Lines: Gender and the Two World Wars.* New Haven, CT: Yale University Press, 1987.

Reinders, Robert C. "Racialism on the Left: E. D. Morel and the 'Black Horror on the Rhine.'" *International Review of History* 13 (1968): 1–28.

Reinhardt, Kurt F. *Germany: 200 Years,* Vol. 2, revised ed. New York: Frederick Ungar, 1961.

Reznick, Jeffrey S. *Healing the Nation: Soldiers and the Culture of Care-giving in Britain During the Great War.* Manchester: Manchester University Press, 2004.

Rich, Norman. *The Age of Nationalism and Reform, 1850–1890,* second edition. New York: W. W. Norton, 1977.

Rickards, Maurice. *Posters of the First World War.* New York: Walker, 1968.

Robins, Dorothy B. *Experiment in Democracy: The Story of U.S. Citizen Organizations in Forging the Charter of the United Nations.* New York: Parkside, 1971.

Rogin, Michael Paul. *Ronald Reagan, The Movie, and Other Episodes in Political Demonology.* Berkeley: University of California Press, 1987.

Roosevelt, Theodore. *The Works of Theodore Roosevelt: The Strenuous Life.* New York: P. F. Collier & Sons, 1901).

Rouette, Susanne. "Mothers and Citizens: Gender and Social Policy in Germany after the First World War." *Central European History* 30 (1997): 48–67.

Rupp, Leila. "Constructing Internationalism: The Case of Transnational Women's Organizations, 1888–1945." *American Historical Review* 99 (December 1994): 1571–1600.

Samuelson, Paul Anthony, and Everett Einar Hagen. *After the War, 1918–1920: Military and Economic Demobilization of the United States*. Washington, D.C.: G.P.O, 1943.
Scheck, Raffael. "German Conservatism and Female Political Activism in the Early Weimar Republic." *German History* 15, no. 1 (1997): 34–55.
———. "Women Against Versailles: Maternalism and Nationalism of Female Bourgeois Politicians in the Early Weimar Republic." *German Studies Review* 22, no. 1 (February 1999): 21–42.
Schüler, Anja. "The 'Horror on the Rhine': Rape, Racism and the International Women's Movement." John F. Kennedy-Institut Für Nordamerikastudien, Abteilung für Geschichte, Working Paper No. 86 (1996): 1–19.
Schwabe, Klaus. *Woodrow Wilson, Revolutionary Germany, and Peacemaking, 1918–1919: Missionary Diplomacy and the Realities of Power*. Translated by Rita and Robert Kimber. Chapel Hill: University of North Carolina Press, 1985.
Shallat, Lezak. "Democracy in the Nation, but Not at Home: Domestic Violence and Women's Reproductive Health in Chile." In *No Paradise Yet: The World's Women Face the New Century*, edited by Judith Mirsky and Marty Radlett, 137–56. London: PANOS/Zed, 2000.
Sharp, Ingrid. "Blaming the Women: Women's Responsibility for the First World War." In *The Women's Movement in Wartime: International Perspectives, 1914–19*, edited by Alison Fell and Ingrid Sharp, 67–87. Basingstoke: Palgrave Macmillan, 2007.
Sklar, Kathryn Kish, Anja Schüler, and Susan Strasser. *Social Justice Feminists in the United States and Germany: A Dialogue in Documents, 1885–1933*. Ithaca, NY: Cornell University Press, 1998.
Sluga, Glenda. "Female and National Self-Determination: A Gender Re-Reading of 'The Apogee of Nationalism.'" *Nations and Nationalism* 6, no. 4 (2000): 495–522.
———. *The Nation, Psychology, and International Politics, 1870–1919*. Basingstoke: Palgrave Macmillan, 2006.
Smith, Rogers M. *Civic Ideals: Conflicting Visions of Citizenship in U.S. History*. New Haven, CT: Yale University Press, 1997.
Smith, Thomas Robert, Ellen Key, and G. Lowes Dickinson, *The Woman Question*. New York: Boni and Liveright, 1919.
Smith, Truman. *The American Military Government of Occupied Germany, 1918–1920: Report of the Officer in Charge of Civil Affairs, Third Army and American Forces in Germany*. Washington: G.P.O., 1943.
Smith-Rosenberg, Carroll. "Writing History: Language, Class and Gender." In *Feminist Studies/Critical Studies*, ed. Teresa deLauretis, 32–54. Bloomington: Indiana University Press, 1986.
Snider, Christy Jo. "The Influence of Transnational Peace Groups on U.S. Foreign Policy Decision-Makers During the 1930s: Incorporating NGOs into the UN." *Diplomatic History* 27, no. 3 (2003): 377–404.

———. "Patriots and Pacifists: The Rhetorical Debate about Peace, Patriotism, and Internationalism, 1914–1930." *Rhetoric & Public Affairs* 8, no. 1 (2005): 59–83.

The State of the Union Messages of the Presidents, Vol. 3. New York: Chelsea House, 1967.

Stearns, Jill. *Gender and International Relations: An Introduction*. Cambridge: Polity, 1998.

Steinberg, Donald K. *Conflict, Gender, and Human Rights: Lessons Learned from the Field*. San Diego: University of San Diego Joan B. Kroc Institute for Peace & Justice, 2004.

Steinson, Barbara J. *American Women's Activism in World War I*. New York: Garland, 1982.

Stoehr, Irene. "Housework and Motherhood: Debates and Policies in the Women's Movement in Imperial Germany and the Weimar Republic." In *Maternity and Gender Policies: Women and the Rise of the European Welfare States, 1880s-1950s*, edited by Gisela Bock and Pat Thane, 213–32. London: Routledge, 1991.

Strickert, Frederick M. *The Lorelei*. Baltimore: AmErica House, 2002.

Sullivan, Julie. "Joined by Love and War." *Sunday Oregonian*, July 23, 2006, A1.

Surface, Frank M., and Raymond L. Bland. *American Food in the World War and Reconstruction Period: Operations of the Organizations Under the Direction of Herbert Hoover, 1914–1924*. Stanford, CA: Stanford University Press, 1931.

Swanwick, Helena M. *Builders of Peace: Being Ten Years' History of the UDC*. London: Swarthmore Press, 1924; reprinted New York: Garland, 1973.

Sweetman, Caroline, ed. *Gender, Development, and Humanitarian Work*. Oxford: Oxfam GB, 2001.

Sweet-Orr & Company, *To Managers of Factories, Machine Shops, Ammunition Plants and Other Industries Where Women are Employed*. New York: Sweet-Orr, 1918.

Thompson, Vye Smeigh. *History of the National American Legion Auxiliary*, Vol. 1. Pittsburgh: Jackson-Remlinger, 1926.

Tickner, J. Ann. *Gender in International Relations: Feminist Perspectives on Achieving Global Security*. New York: Columbia University Press, 1992.

Tronto, Joan C. *Moral Boundaries: An Argument for an Ethic of Care*. New York: Routledge, 1993.

Tucker, Spencer C., ed. *The Encyclopedia of World War I*, Vol. I. Santa Barbara: ABC-CLIO, 2005.

———, ed. *The European Powers in the First World War: An Encyclopedia*. New York: Garland, 1996.

Under the Yoke of Foreign Rule: Sufferings of the Rhineland Population, Vol. 1. Leipzig: K. F. Koehler, 1923.

United Nations. *The World's Women: Trends and Statistics, 2000*. New York: United Nations, 2000.

United States Army, American Forces in Germany, *American Military Government of Occupied Germany, 1918–1920*. Washington, D.C.: G.P.O., 1943.

United States Congress. *Pensions—World War widows: Pensions to widows and children of World War veterans: Hearings before the Committee on Pensions, House of Representatives, Seventy-fifth Congress, third session, on H.R. 8690 (now known as H.R. 9285) a bill granting a pension to widows and dependent children of World War veterans. January 25 and 28, 1938.* Washington, D.C.: GPO, 1938.

United States Women's Bureau, *The New Position of Women in American Industry.* Washington, D.C.: GPO, 1920.

Vellacott, Jo. "Feminism As If All People Mattered: Working to Remove the Causes of War, 1919–1929." *Contemporary European History* 10, no. 3 (November 2001): 375–94.

———. "A Place for Pacifism and Trans-Nationalism in Feminist Theory: The Early Work of the Women's International League for Peace and Freedom." *Women's History Review* 2 (1993): 23–56.

Vincent, C. Paul. *The Politics of Hunger: the Allied Blockade of Germany, 1915–1919.* Athens: Ohio University Press, 1985.

Walters, F. P. *A History of the League of Nations.* London: Oxford University Press, 1960.

Weber, Eugen. *The Hollow Years: France in the 1930s.* New York: W. W. Norton, 1994.

Whalen, Robert Weldon. *Bitter Wounds: German Victims of the Great War, 1914–1939.* Ithaca, NY: Cornell University Press, 1984.

Winkler, Allan M. "The Selling of the War." *Reviews in American History* 8, no. 3 (1980): 382–85.

Williamson, David G. *The British in Germany, 1918–1933: The Reluctant Occupiers.* New York: Berg, 1991.

Willoughby, John. *Remaking the Conquering Heroes: The Social and Geopolitical Impact of the Post-War American Occupation of Germany.* New York: Palgrave, 2001.

———. "The Sexual Behavior of American GIs During the Early Years of the Occupation of Germany." *Journal of Military History* 62, no. 1 (1998): 155–74.

Winter, Jay. *Remembering War: The Great War Between Memory and History in the Twentieth Century.* New Haven, CT: Yale University Press, 2006.

Winter, Jay, and Antoine Prost. *The Great War in History: Debates and Controversies, 1914 to the Present.* Cambridge: Cambridge University Press, 2005.

Woloch, Nancy. *Women and the American Experience.* New York: Knopf, 1984.

Women's International League for Peace and Freedom. *Towards Peace and Freedom: the Women's International Congress, Zürich, May 12th to 17th, 1919.* English edition. London: British section of WILPF, 1919.

Women's Trade Union League, *Women and Reconstruction: Being the Report of the Committee on Social and Industrial Reconstruction of the National Women's Trade Union League of America, Meeting in New York, December 9–12, 1918.* Chicago: The League, 1918.

Work, Clemens P. *Darkest before Dawn: Sedition and Free Speech in the American West.* Albuquerque: University of New Mexico Press. 2005.

Zangrando, Robert. *The NAACP Crusade Against Lynching, 1909–1950*. Philadelphia: Temple University Press, 1980.

Zeiger, Susan. *In Uncle Sam's Service: Women Workers With the American Expeditionary Force, 1917–1919*. Philadelphia: University of Pennsylvania Press, 2004.

German Language Publications

Baer, Gertrud. "Abgrunde," *Die Frau im Staat* 5, no. 2 (1923): 3–4.

Cyrus, Hannelore, and Verena Steinecke, eds. *Ein Weib Wie Wir?!: Auguste Kirchhoff: Ein Leben für den Frieden und für die Rechte der Frauen*. Bremen:Verlag in der Sonnonstrasse, 1989.

Davy, Jennifer A., Karen Hagemann, and Ute Kätzel, eds. *Frieden—Gewalt—Geschlecht: Friedens- und Konfliktforschung als Geschlechterforschung*. Essen: Klartext Verlag, 2005.

Deutschen Verein für Armenpflege und Wohltätigkeit. *Soziale Fürsorge für Kriegerwitwen und Kriegerwaisen*. Muenchen und Leipzig: Duncker und Humboldt, 1915.

Distler, Heinrich. *Das deutsche Leid am Rhein: ein Buch der Anklage gegen die Schandherrschaft des franzosischen Militarismus*. Minden, Westphalia: W. Köhler, 1921.

Dregos, Else. "Arbeitsbeschaffung für Kriegerwitwen in der Praxis." In *Soziale Praxis und Archiv für Volkswohlfahrt* 32 (1923): 84–85.

Duennebier, Anna, und Ursula Scheu. *Die Rebellion ist eine Frau: Anita Augspurg und Lida G. Heymann, Das schillerndste Paar der Frauenbewegung*. Kreuzlingen/Munich: Heinrich Hugendubel Verlag, 2002.

Farbige Franzosen am Rhein: Ein Notschri deutscher Frauen, Vol. 2. Berlin: H. R. Engelmann, 1920.

Fischer-Dückelmann, Anna. *Häusliche Krankenpflege in Kriegszeiten: Was lehrte uns der Krieg?* Stuttgart: Süddeutsches Verlangs: Institut Julius Müller, 1916.

Frank, Leonhard. *Der Mensch ist gut*. Zürich: M. Rascher, 1918.

Gerhard, Ute. "National oder International: Die internationalen Beziehungen der deutschen bürgerlichen Frauenbewegung." *Feministische Studien* 3 (1994): 34–52.

Hansen-Blancke, Dora. "Buchbesprechung von Helene Hurwitz-Stranz, *Kriegerwitwen gestalten ihr Schicksal*." *Die Frau* 39 (1931/32): 112.

Harmsen, Hans. *Der Einfluß der versorgungsgesetzlichen Regelung auf die wirtschaftliche und soziale Lage der Kriegerwitwen: eine soziologische und bevölkerungspolitische Untersuchung, zugleich der Versuch einer sozialhygienischen Beurteilung und Kritik unserer heutigen Versorgungsgesetzgebung*. Berlin: Schoetz, 1926.

Hausen, Karin. "Die Sorge der Nation für ihre 'Kriegsopfer': Ein Bereich der Geschlechtspolitik während der Weimarer Republik." In *Von der Arbeiterbewegung zum modernen Sozialstaat*, edited by Jürgen Kocka, 719–39. Munich: Saur, 1994.

Henke, Christiane. *Anita Augspurg*. Hamburg: Reinbek bei Hamburg, 2000.

Hurwitz-Stranz, Helene. *Kriegerwitwen gestalten ihr Schicksal: Lebenskämpfe deutscher Kriegerwitwen nach eigenen Darstellung*. Berlin: Carl Heymanns, 1931.

Jannasch, Lilli. "Schwarze Schmach, Weisse Schmach?" *Die Frau im Staat* 2, no. 11 (November 1920): 1–4.

Koller, Christian. *"Von Wilden aller Rassen niedergemetzelt": Die Diskussion um die Verwendung von Kolonialtruppen in Europa zwischen Rassismus, Kolonial-und Militärpolitik, 1914–1930*. Stuttgart: Franz Steiner, 2001.

Lebzelter, Gisela. "Die 'Schwarze Schmach': Vorurteile—Propaganda—Mythos." *Geschichte und Gesellschaft* 11 (1985): 37–68.

Mass, Sandra. "Von der 'schwarzen Schmach' zur 'deutschen Heimat,'" *Werkstatt Geschichte* 32 (2002): 44–57.

Nau, Karl. *Die Wirtschaftliche und soziale Lage von Kriegshinterbliebenen: Eine studie auf grund von erhebungen über die auswirkung der versorgung von kriegshinterbliebenen in Darmstadt*. Leipzig: Lühe, 1930.

Obschernitzki, Doris. *"Der Frau ihre Arbeit!": Lette Verein: Zur Geschichte einer Berliner Institution, 1866 bis 1986*. Berlin: Hentrich, 1987.

Peters, Otto, ed. *Kampf um den Rhein: Beiträge zur Geschichte des Rheinlandes und seiner Fremdherrschaft, 1918–1930*. Mainz: Mainzer Verlagsanstalt, 1930.

Rouette, Susanne. *Sozialpolitik als Geschlechterpolitik: Die Regulierung der Frauenarbeit nach dem Ersten Weltkrieg*. Frankfurt: Campus, 1993.

Schlusstagung des Hauptausschusses. *Stand und Künftige Entwicklung der Kriegerwitwen und Kriegswaisenfürsorge*. Berlin: Carl Heymanns, 1918.

Tagung des Hauptausschusses der Kriegerwitwen-und-Waisenfürsorge. *Frauenerwerb und Kriegswitwe: Referate erstattet auf der 2. Tagung des Hauptausschusses der Kriegerwitwen-und-Waisenfürsorge am 27. November 1915 im Reichstagsgebäude in Berlin*. Berlin: Carl Heymanns, 1916.

Timmermann, Annelise. *Die Rheinlandbesetzung in ihrer Wirkung auf die Sozialausgaben der Städte*. Berlin: Reimers Hobbing, 1930.

Unpublished Manuscripts

Cooper, Dana Calise. "Informal Ambassadors: American Women, Transatlantic Marriages, and Anglo-American Marriages, 1865–1945." PhD dissertation, Texas Christian University, 2006.

Davidson, Janet F. "Women and the Railroad: The Gendering of Work During the First World War Era, 1917–1920." PhD dissertation, University of Delaware, 1999.

Zagacki, Kenneth S. "Rhetoric, Redemption, and Reconciliation: a Study of Twentieth Century Postwar Rhetoric," PhD dissertation, University of Texas at Austin, 1986.

Index

Addams, Jane, 6, 87, 106, 109, 111, 132, 135–36, 176; and League of Nations, 133–34; and Lusk Committee, 126; and Rhineland horror, 62–65; and WILPF, 62, 112, 114, 115, 123, 128, 166, 169
A Farewell to Arms, 1–2
Africa, 41, 42, 46–51, 55, 63, 67, 72, 173, 175
African Americans, 42, 44, 49, 50, 58–59, 61, 63, 64–65, 67
African colonial soldiers, 3, 8, 30, 31, 38, 51, 55, 60–62, 68, 110, 112; and sexuality, 41–42, 49, 52, 56–57, 63–64, 67, 96
Allen, General Henry T., 27, 29, 30, 35, 41, 60, 65, 69
alliance system, 72, 93
Allied forces, 6, 9, 12, 25, 39, 52, 54, 83, 88, 91, 94, 96, 110, 113, 115, 130–31, 133, 155; and occupation, 9, 14, 16, 20, 29, 51, 87, 91, 94, 96, 103. *See also individual countries*
Amaroc, The, xiii, 18, 23–26, 27–28, 31, 33, 34, 93, 103
Ambrosius, Lloyd E., 71–73
American exceptionalism, 3, 4, 8, 59, 72, 73, 75–80, 99, 103, 165
American Federation of Labor, 118, 154

American Forces in Germany (AFG), 29, 33, 60, 98–99. *See also* U.S. Army
American Friends Service Committee, 127, 128, 132–33
American Legion, 8, 61, 155, 164, 166, 168
American Legion Women's Auxiliary, 6, 10, 142, 155, 166–68, 170
American Peace Commission. *See* Versailles Treaty
American Relief Administration, 16, 34, 127, 128, 130–31
American War Mothers, 167–68, 170
Anderson, Benedict, 77, 107
Anderson, Mary, 154–55
anniversaries of war's outbreak and end in Germany, 142, 161, 163
Anthony, Katharine, 108
anti-immigration legislation, 142, 165
Antiwar Museum (Berlin), 160
Apel, Dora, 160–61
Aristophanes, xiii, 6
Armenian genocide (1915), 72
armistice, 3, 6, 7, 12, 15, 49–50, 71, 75–76, 82–88, 93, 96, 99, 100, 103
Army of Occupation. *See* American Forces in Germany (AFG)
art, 127, 159, 160–61
Augspurg, Anita, 67–68, 122, 125, 128

Baer, Gertrud, 67, 122, 124, 125
Bagby, Philip H., 129

237

Baker, Newton, 91
Balch, Emily Greene, 64–65, 81, 112, 126, 128, 165–66
Baldridge, C. LeRoy, 17
Baldwin, Elbert F., 183n32
Baldwin, Marian, 129
Balfour, Arthur, 113–14
Bauer, Otto, 109
Bäumer, Gertrude, 86–87, 125, 211n10
Belgium, 17–18, 20, 28, 44, 48, 54, 58, 66, 67, 74, 82, 87, 96
Berlin Act (1885), 48
Berlin Treaty, 71, 93–99, 103, 165
Bessel, Richard, 148
Beveridge, Albert J., 93
Beveridge, Ray, 42, 51, 57–58, 64
Bikaner, Maharaja, 113
binary opposites, 7, 8, 136, 141. *See also* "separate spheres"
Birth of a Nation, 59, 62
birthrates, 33–34, 74, 108, 110, 134
Bismarck, Otto von, 46–47
Bland, Lucy, 62, 63
Bliss, Tasker H., 131
blockade against Germany, 6, 15, 16, 52, 86–87, 115, 129–30, 131–32, 134, 143, 153, 207n72
Blum, Edward J., 78
Blunden, Edmund, 74
Bolshevism, 16, 24, 82, 100, 105, 126, 130, 166
Bonus Army March (U.S.), 158
Borah, William, 98–99
Bosnian War, 176
Boyd, Alex, and Elisabeth Ternes Boyd, 28
Brest-Litovsk Treaty, 112
British Labour Party, 123, 207n72
British Union for Democratic Control, 53, 117
Brockdorff-Rantzau, Count von, 29, 187n65, 199n81
brothels, 27, 31, 51–52, 54, 56–57, 67, 97
Brown, Harriet Connor, 118, 119, 126, 128, 134–35

Bund Deutscher Frauenvereine (BDF), 9, 54, 67, 84, 110, 125, 162

Caldwell, Charles, 119
Calvinism, 79
camp-followers. *See* prostitution
Cather, Willa, 163, 164
Catholic Church, 15, 18, 60–61, 62, 161
Catt, Carrie Chapman, 64, 106, 176
Cavell, Edith, 81, 85
cease-fire. *See* armistice
censorship. *See under* War
Center for Military History, 183n30
Central Powers, 86, 106, 111, 112
Chamberlain, Mary, 115, 128
Charles, Heinrich, 89–90
Chemical Warfare Service, 120, 126
child labor, 156
child support laws, 32–33
Chile, 173–74
citizenship, 4, 48, 57–58, 78, 108–9, 110, 141, 158, 166, 170, 173
Civil War (U.S.), 44, 58, 59, 65, 78, 129
Clansman, The, 59
class, social and economic, 25–26, 42, 72, 73, 78, 100–102, 112, 150, 157, 164, 176
Clemenceau, Georges, 14–15, 50, 113, 131
Coblenz, 14, 17–18, 29, 31–37, 86, 91
Coffin, Henry Sloane, 102–3
Colby, Bainbridge, 59–60
Cologne, 15–16, 22, 53
colonization, 40, 42, 46–49
commemoration, 141–42, 158–59, 161–62, 166–68
Commission for International Labour Legislation, 113
Commission on Training Camp Activities, 158
Committee for the Protection of Women Under Law, 85–86
Committee on Public Information, 85, 139
comparative history, 4, 5, 7, 10

comradeship: among soldiers, 22, 139, 161–62, 166; and fraternal, 107–8
Conklin, Alice L., 47
Cooper, John Milton, 73
Cornebise, Alfred E., 195*n*13
Council of Ten. *See under* Versailles Treaty
Crowdy, Dame Rachel, 117, 176
"cult of the fallen hero," 3, 142, 159, 160–61, 163
Cuno, Wilhelm, 35, 37
custody laws, 108
Czechoslovakia, 100

Daniel, Ute, 141, 147, 151
darwinism, 44
Davidson, Janet F., 154, 155
Dawes, Charles G., and the Dawes Plan, 37, 94, 121
Dayton Peace Accords, 176
defeat in war, 1–3, 4, 6, 19, 48, 50, 52, 73, 75–6, 81–84, 87, 97–98, 102, 105, 107, 114, 116, 122, 129, 131–32, 141–43, 148, 150, 157, 159, 160, 174. *See also* military conquest
democracy and self-determination for states, 18–20, 21, 24, 41, 47, 72, 74, 85, 97, 99, 107–10, 116–17, 125, 134, 156, 173
Deutschnationale Volkspartei (DNVP), 102
Dickman, Joseph T., 16–18
disillusionment, with war, 2, 103, 142, 163–64
Distler, Heinrich, 55, 56–57
Dix, Otto, 159, 160
Dos Passos, John, 163–64
Doty, Madeline, 107
Doughboy. *See* U.S. Army
Dransfeld, Hedwig, 221*n*25
Dresel, Ellis Loring, 30, 60, 61, 94
Dyer, Leonidas C., 168

Ebert, Friedrich, 30, 52, 159
economic relations. *See* trade relations
Edelstein, David M., 13
Enloe, Cynthia, 12, 21, 34, 176

equality, sexual, 3–4, 5, 9, 42, 44, 67, 72, 112, 117, 134, 143, 156–57, 170, 175, 178
Espionage and Sedition Acts (U.S.), 165
Etappenhelferinnen, 150, 159
European Children's Fund, 132
Expatriation Act (U.S.), 108–9

Fawcett, Millicent Garrett, 112, 113
Federal Council of Churches, 91
female paid labor, 34, 109–10, 117, 141–42, 144–47, 150, 151–56, 167, 174
female self-determination, 9, 108–10, 117
femininity, 4, 10, 16, 24, 101, 110–11
feminism, 73, 108–10, 126–27, 143, 157; and essentialism, 109, 111, 118, 123–24, 136; and pacifism, 109, 122, 126, 136; and universalism, 109, 123, 134
fertility rates. *See* birthrates
First World War. *See* Great War
Foch, Ferdinand, 20, 29, 53, 96, 198*n*62
Foner, Eric, 154
Foot, Rosemary, 109
foreign policy, 5–6, 9–10, 71–73, 78–79, 83–84, 91, 93–103; and women's involvement in, 6, 9–10, 75, 100–103, 107–11, 115–17, 121, 124, 130–37, 174–78
France, 14–15, 16–17, 28, 29–30, 32, 48, 72, 73, 74, 81–82, 100, 102, 108, 114, 115, 123, 124–25, 131, 162, 163;and *mission civilisatrice*, 47–48; and Rhineland Horror campaign, 3, 6–7, 30, 39–40, 49, 50–53, 55, 57, 65–66, 68–69, 96
Franck, Harry A, 129
Francke, Ernest, 144–45
Frank, Leonhard, 143, 169
Frankfurt, 30, 53–54, 55, 132
Fraternal Aid for the Children of the Ruhr, 125
fraternization, xiii, 11–12, 14, 20–22, 25–26, 27, 29, 30, 31, 37; and the

British Army, 21; and the treatment of fraternizing women, 21–22, 97–98
Frauenausschuss zur Bekämpfung der Schuldlüge, 101
Frauenpolitik, 122–23
Fräuleins, xiii, 4, 11, 13–14, 17, 25–28, 34–35, 62
Frevert, Ute, 143–44
Friedrich, Ernst, 160
Fussell, Paul, 74, 179n2, 195n18, 196n26

Gannett, Lewis, 62
Gärtner, Margarete, 42, 54
Geib, Hermann, 147
Gelblum, Amira, 123
gender, 2, 4–5, 8, 13, 28, 42–44, 67, 74–75, 79–80, 87–89, 91–93, 97–98, 101–2, 105–6, 109–11, 118–27, 133–34, 136–37, 140–44, 146, 158–60, 169–71, 177–78. *See also* masculinity; femininity
Geneva, Switzerland, 79, 128
George, David Lloyd, 16, 53, 74, 90, 132
German Americans, 60
German communist party. *See Kommunistische Partei Deutschlands*
German League for Private Charity, 144
German military, 66–67, 82–83, 84, 87, 89
German Women's Association. *See Bund Deutscher Frauenvereine*
Germany, 3–4, 7, 15–16, 20–21, 22, 26–27, 28–30, 32, 37–38, 40, 41, 53–55, 64–65, 105, 109, 123, 128–36, 144–53, 158–62, 170, 174; and defeat, 73, 75–76, 84–85, 88, 94–96, 98–102, 142; and economy, 15, 30, 32, 35; and Imperial Germany, 46–47, 48, 50; and occupation of Belgium and France, 66–67, 112, 124–25; and responsibility for starting war, 89–90, 199n80, 200n81; women's peace movement in, 122–25. *See also* Weimar Republic
German youth, 121, 124–25, 132–33, 136, 159
Geyer, Michael, 160–61
Glasson, William H., 157
Gold Star Mothers Association, 170
Graves, Louis, 86, 98
Grayzel, Susan R., 13, 135, 144
Great Britain, 21, 37, 40, 48, 50, 53, 73, 96, 124, 129, 162. *See also* British Labour Party; British Union for Democratic Control; George, David Lloyd
Great War, 3–4, 17, 40, 43, 50, 72–75, 99, 112, 139, 163, 169; and historiography, 4–7, 135, 141, 144; and trench warfare, 1–2; and women's roles in, 104–6, 108, 122, 127, 144–47, 153–54, 171
Greenwald, Maurine Weiner, 154
Gregg, W. C., 129
Griffith, D. W. *See Birth of a Nation*

Hague, The, 111, 112, 116, 121, 125, 135
Hall, Stanley G., 44
Hamilton, Alice, 132
Hanna, Martha, 74, 141
Harding, Warren G., 29, 30, 60, 79, 83, 93, 94, 98–99, 103
"Harlem Hell-Fighters," 50
Harmsen, Hans, 152
Harnoss, Martha, 142–43, 187n101, 212n19
Hart, Albert Bushnell, 85–86, 87, 89, 97
Harvey, George, 74, 81–82, 87, 89
Hausen, Karin, 141, 162, 212n24, 213n45
Hemingway, Ernest, 1–2, 163
heroes and heroism, 4, 6–7, 77, 141, 144, 158–62, 167, 170–71
Herron, George D., 79
Heymann, Lida Gustava, 67–68, 109, 115, 122–24, 125, 128
Hindenburg, Paul von, 159

Hitchcock, Sen. Gilbert, 65
Hobsbawm, Eric, 10, 107
Holt, Hamilton, 129
home front, 2, 7, 80, 102, 105, 137, 141, 159
homosexuality, 181–82n2
Hong, Young-Sun, 147
Hoover, Herbert, 16, 95, 128, 130–32, 133, 136, 209n110. *See also* American Relief Administration
Horror on the Rhine, The, 53
Hughes, Ann-Marie Claire, 162
Hughes, Charles Evans, 30, 35, 94–95, 118
Hull, Cordell, 174
Hull, Hannah Clothier, 121–22
Hull, Harry E., 120
humanitarian relief, 5–7, 107, 109, 127–34
human rights, 3–5, 7, 9, 72, 109, 122, 124, 175–76
Hunt, Swanee, 176–77
Hurwitz-Stranz, Helene, 142, 153

illegitimate births, 32–34, 35, 37
immigration, 10, 38, 78, 142, 165
imperialism, 40, 42–9, 53, 59, 78, 118; and women, 45–46
Independent Social Democratic Party of Germany (USPD), 52–53
Industrial Workers of the World, 165
International Committee of Women for Permanent Peace (ICWPP), 111–12
International Congress of Women, 111–12, 135
Internationaler Bund, 150–51
international relations, 3–4, 7, 13, 30, 39, 91–92, 107, 130, 133; and "ordinary" people, 71–79, 100–103, 108–14
Iraq, xiii, 177, 181n1
Iriye, Akira, 12
isolationism, 10, 13, 25, 29, 37–38, 74–75, 78–79, 93, 102–3, 142, 165

Jacobs, Aletta, 135, 205n51
Jannasch, Lilli, 42, 54, 66–68

Japan, 72, 113, 119
Jews, 53, 102
Johnson, Sen. Hiram, 98
Jouve, Andrée, 125
Junger, Ernst, 160
Jünger, Karl, 169

Kahn, Julius, 119
Kaiser Wilhelm, 75–76, 83, 84, 101, 102
Kamerad/Kameradin, 161–62
Kearns, Charles C., 119–20
Keene, Jennifer D., 195n13, 215n80
Kellogg, Frank B., 121
Kellogg, Vernon, 82
Kempf, Rosa, 102
Kennan, George F., 103, 196n25
Kennedy, David M., 5, 93, 141, 154, 163, 182–83n21, 196n26, 198n55
Key, Ellen, 108
Kimmel, Michael, 197n37
Kipling, Rudyard, 45
Kirchhoff, Auguste, 122, 124
Kittredge, Mabel, 63, 128
Knight, Louise W., 63
Knox, Philander C., 72, 93
Knox-Porter Resolution, 93–94
Koblenz. *See* Coblenz
Koller, Christian, 51
Kollwitz, Käthe, 127, 160
Köln. *See* Cologne
Kommunistische Partei Deutschlands, 54
Köster, Adolf, 53–54
Kriegerwitwen, 142–43, 144–53, 162, 166
Kriegsopfer, 151, 162, 169–71
Kuetti, Karl, 152
Ku Klux Klan, 59
Kultur, 22, 69, 82, 88, 95–96, 98

La Follette, Suzanne, 157
Langstein, Leo, 147
language co-optation by minority groups, 162, 217n101
Lansing, Robert, 59–60
League of Nations, 25, 28–29, 40–41, 54–55, 72, 78–79, 80, 91–93, 99, 105, 109, 113, 116, 117, 118, 175;

Addams on, 132–34; and Covenant, 41, 48, 79, 92, 116; and mandates, 41, 63, 72, 92, 110
Lee, Gerald Stanley, 74, 88–89, 90, 97
Lee, Mary, 97–98, 99, 103, 164
Lenin, Vladimir, 100
Lerner, Gerda, 12
Levy-Rathenau, Josephine, 144–46, 147, 151, 152, 154
Lewis, Lucy Biddle, 125
Lille (France), 66, 102, 124–25
Löbe, Paul, 56
Lodge, Sen. Henry Cabot, 29, 61, 71–72
"lost generation," 72–73, 143
Lundén, Rolf, 196n32
Luxembourg, 16–17
lynching, 58–59, 62–63, 67
Lysistrata, xiii, 6

MacKaye, Jessie Hardy, 118–19, 120
Madison Square Garden, 60–61
manhood. *See* masculinity
Marks, Sally, 5, 40, 50, 57, 94, 99–100, 192n83, 199n74, 200n91
Marriage, xi, xiii, 4, 7, 11–12, 25–8, 34–37, 48–49, 60, 62, 74, 108, 117, 124, 152
Marshall, Catherine E., 128
Marxists, 100
masculinity, 4, 12, 13, 58, 43–46, 57–58, 79–80, 88, 89–90, 92–93, 107, 123, 145, 154, 158; and chivalry, 2, 17, 165, 171
maternity. *See* motherhood
Maxwell, Lucia R., 126–27
May Day, 130–31
McCluer, Margaret N., 167–68
McDill, John Rich, 146
McDonald, Alva L., Carma, and Donald, 27–28
McGovern, James R., 81
McKay, Claude, 56
Meintjes, Sheila, 5, 13, 177–78
Mélin, Jeanne, 115
"memory activists" 10, 141

Men and Religion Forward Movement, 75, 79–90, 102
Michener, Earl C., 168
militarism, 54, 69, 82, 83, 88, 98, 118, 131, 144, 159, 207n80
military conquest, 4, 9, 14, 17, 18, 20, 44, 46, 47–49, 57, 73–74, 76, 111, 116, 117, 125, 157; and questionable nature of U.S. victory in WWI, 82–83, 198n55
Mombauer, Annika, 195n7, 199n80
Monroe Doctrine, 116
"Moorish cafes." *See* brothels
morality, 14, 18, 25, 30–33, 35, 37, 38, 47–49, 53–54, 65, 75, 76–77, 79, 89, 101, 102–3. *See also under* U.S. foreign policy
Morel, Edmund Dene, 44, 53–56, 63
Moroney, William J., 89–90, 103
Mosse, George L., 158–59
Mostov, Julie, 110
motherhood, 110, 122, 144, 156–57; and war remembrance, 170–71. *See also* birthrates
multilateralism. *See* U.S. foreign policy

National American Woman Suffrage Association, 106. *See also* suffrage
National Assembly (Germany), 52–53
National Association for the Advancement of Colored People, 55, 59, 62
National Association to Oppose Woman Suffrage, 106. *See also* suffrage
National Council of Catholic Women, 61
National Disabled Soldiers League, 95–96
Nationaler Frauenausschuss zum Kampf gegen Versailles, 101
Nationaler Frauendienst, 105–6
national interest. *See under* U.S. foreign policy
nationalism, 3–4, 7, 10, 46, 72, 73, 75, 77–79, 100–102, 107–8, 131, 133, 136, 142, 144, 160–61; and women,

46, 75, 101–2, 108–15. *See also* American exceptionalism
national self-determination, 5, 29–30, 41, 72, 74–75, 107–8, 110, 116–17, 125, 134
National Socialist Party (Nazi Party), 53, 125
Nelson, Keith L., xiv, 5, 12, 29, 49, 68
Neuwied, Germany, 18, 21–22
New Position of Women in American Industry, 154–55
New York Committee Against the Horror on the Rhine, 62
Nolan, Mary, 196n19
nongovernmental organizations (NGOs), 175

occupation (postwar), xiii, 4, 5, 7, 8, 9, 11–21, 25–26, 28–37, 75, 86, 90–91, 99; and Rhineland horror, 39–40, 49–53, 56–57, 62, 64, 66, 68–69, 96–98
Ogawa, Manako, 188n10
Opfer auf den Altar des Vaterlandes, 169
Ottoman Empire, 41, 72
Owen, Wilfred, 74

patriarchy, 2, 5, 7–8, 10, 12–14, 21, 34, 37, 67, 143, 177–78
Paul, Alice, 157
peace, xi–xii, 2–3, 4, 6, 8, 11, 13, 26, 36, 39–41, 76, 77, 80–93, 95–103, 109–12, 117, 119–20, 123–24, 127, 139, 143; and peacemakers, 5–6, 18, 29, 72–74, 82–83, 93–94, 105–7, 113–16, 129, 135; and representations of, 43, 105
Pennsylvania Rail Road, 154
pensions, 148–51, 156, 158, 211n9, 212n19, 213n45
Permanent Committee for the Promotion of Female Workers' Interests, 151
Pershing, General John J., 12, 16, 17, 20–21, 37, 61, 64, 65
Peukert, Detlev J. K., 34,
Philippine American War, 45

Piehler, Kurt, 160
Pillay, Anu, 5, 13, 77–78
Pireaud, Paul, 74
Plumer, Herbert, 132, 136
Poland, 101
Porter, Katherine Anne, 164
pragmatism, 93–94
Prohibition, 24
propaganda, 6, 8, 16, 69, 75, 85, 87, 129, 139; and Rhineland horror, 39, 42, 51–53, 55–56, 57, 59–62
prostitution, 11, 30–32, 35–36, 37, 56–57, 67, 79, 81–82, 97, 108, 127, 150, 159, 171, 185n78
protective legislation, 144–46, 156–57
Protestantism, 44, 77–80, 95, 161. *See also* religion
Prussia, 29–30, 50, 98

Quakers, 130, 132, 209n110

racism, 8, 26–27, 39–67, 72, 119
rape, 49–52, 54–56, 58–60, 63–64, 68–69, 85–86, 87, 96, 127
realism. *See* U.S. foreign policy
Red Cross, 106
Red Scare, 133, 142, 165–66
Reichsbund der Kriegsbeschaedigten, Kriegsteilnehmer und Kriegshinterbliebenen, 148–49, 150–51
Reichsbund journal, 149, 150, 162
Reichstag, 54, 56, 123, 144, 159, 170
Reichsverband, 150–51
Reichsversorgungsgesetz (RVG), 149–50
relief. *See* humanitarian relief
religion, 76–80, 91, 95. *See also* Catholic Church; Protestantism; Social Gospel movement
Remarque, Erich Maria, 163, 164
reparations, 3, 9, 14–15, 28, 37, 63, 65, 91, 94, 99, 100, 110, 121–22, 125, 131, 151
Republican Party, 72, 88, 95
returning soldiers. *See* veterans
Reznick, Jeffrey S., 179n6, 210n3
Rhenish Women's League, 39, 51, 54, 62, 69

244 Index

Rhineland, 5, 7, 11, 13–15, 17–18, 20–23, 25–31, 33–35; and separatism, 15, 16, 29; and U.S. withdrawal from, 36–38. *See also* Coblenz; Cologne; occupation; Rhineland Horror campaign; Trier
Rhineland Horror campaign, 39–42, 48–57, 60, 62, 65–69
Richtofen, Manfred von, 162
Robins, Margaret Dreier, 156–57
Roosevelt, Eleanor, 175–76
Roosevelt, Franklin D., 174
Roosevelt, Theodore, 43–46, 49, 59, 63, 81, 118
Root, Elihu, 72
Rost, Ida, 152
Roth, Amélie, 102
Rouette, Susanne, 5, 13, 141, 145–46, 170, 212n23, 213n28
Ruhr Crisis, 3, 36, 53, 66, 100, 125, 128, 136

Salomon, Alice, 86–87
Samuelson, Paul Anthony, 155
Schirmacher, Käthe, 54
Schleswig-Holstein, 135–36
Schüler, Anja, 51
Schuller, Carola, 33, 35, 187n103, 203–4n26
Schwabe, Klaus, 5, 81, 196n25, 198n62
Second World War. *See* World War II
"Secret Information Concerning Black Troops," 64
"separate spheres," 9–10, 79–80, 102, 110–11, 135
separatist movement. *See under* Rhineland
sexuality, 11–13, 26–27, 30–35, 37, 51–52, 117, 123; and nationalism, 108–9; and race, 41–42, 48–49, 51–52, 55–57, 60, 62–63, 66–67
Shaw, Anna Howard, 106
Shaw, Flora, 46, 49
Sheepshanks, Mary, 128
Simon, Helene, 144–45, 212n24
"slacker oath," 126–27
Sluga, Glenda, 110

Social Democratic Party (SPD), 53–54, 147, 151–52, 161
Social Gospel movement, 80
soldiers. *See* U.S. Army; veterans
Solf, Wilhelm, 15, 49–50, 87
Somme, Battle of, 74
Sonnino, Sidney, 113
sovereignty, 29, 48, 71–72, 92–93, 99–100
Spanish American War, 43, 61, 90
"spider-web chart," 126
"stab-in-the-back" theory, 102, 143, 150
Stars and Stripes, 17, 18, 21, 24
Steghagen, Emma, 155–56
Steinberg, Donald K., 177
Steuben Society, 60
Stöcker, Helene, 122
Strachan, Hew, 198n55
suffrage, 8–9, 72, 79–80, 106–7, 108, 120–21, 122–23, 144–45, 156, 173; as an international policy issue, 113–14, 117, 177
Sunday, Billy, 79
Supreme Council of Supply and Relief, 131
Swanwick, Helena, 42, 63, 128

Taubles, Mildred, 158
Terrell, Mary Church, 42, 64–65
Third Army. *See* U.S. Army
Thompson, Vye Smeigh, 155, 166–67
Timmermann, Annelise, 57
"total" war, 73, 105–6, 144
trade relations, 30, 37, 75, 93–94, 95, 123–24, 141, 147
trade unions, 118, 147, 148, 154, 155–56
transnationalism, xi–xii, 3–7, 39–40, 42, 103, 112–14, 116, 119, 125–26, 127–28, 134–36, 142, 165, 175–76
Treaty of Berlin. *See* Berlin Treaty
Treaty of Versailles. *See* Versailles Treaty
Trier, 18, 21–22, 32, 35
Tronto, Joan C., 202n12, 204n33
"turnip winter," 146–47

Turshen, Meredeth, 5, 13, 77–78
unilateralism. See under U.S. foreign policy
United Nations, 175–77
U.S. Army, 16–21, 29–30, 50, 52, 83, 93, 98–99, 129, 131, 139–140, 158, 169; and fraternization order, 21–25; German women employed by, 34; and marriage, 11–12, 25–28, 31–36 women in, 106, 158, 168. See also American Forces in Germany (AFG)
U.S. Bureau of Investigation, 165
U.S. Department of Labor, 154–55
U.S. foreign policy, 71–73, 78, 91, 93–95, 130–32, 174; and morality, 74–75; and multi- and unilateralism, 71–72; and national interest, 73, 111, 136; and realism in, 72–73, 103
U.S. House Committee on Military Affairs, 118–120
U.S. Navy, 158
U.S. Senate, 3, 29, 51, 52, 65, 71–73, 76, 88, 91–93, 118–20, 126, 167–68, 170
U.S. State Department, 59–60
U.S. War Department, 27, 29–30, 126, 158

Vellacott, Jo, 112, 116, 135
venereal disease, 11–12, 27, 30–32, 35, 57, 159
Versailles Treaty, 2–3, 5, 15, 26–28, 30, 32, 54, 72, 79, 96, 98–101, 105–7, 112, 156, 159, 174, 176, 177 and Council of Ten, 49–50, 113–14, 132; provisions of, 40–41, 48–49, 94, 110–11; and U.S. rejection of, 91–93; and WILP F, 112–17, 128, 132–34, 136
veterans, 3, 23, 147–48, 150, 158–61, 168
victims. See war victims
victory. See military conquest
Villard, Oswald Garrison, 90–91, 96–97
Vincent, C. Paul, 130, 131, 132

Völkerversöhnende Frauenarbeit, 127
Volksbund Rettet die Ehre, 39, 54
Volkskörper, 53–54
Volkstrauertag, 161, 162
voting. See suffrage

Wadsworth, Alice Hay, 106, 111
Walderdorff, Countess von, 17
Walsh, Frank, 99
war, 1–2, 105–6, 135–36, 140–41; and censorship, 20, 74; how interpreted, 1–2, 4–6, 8, 73–74, 76, 152–53, 160; and religion, 19, 77, 91; and trench warfare, 2, 73–74, 76, 90. See also Great War; World War II
war brides, xiii, 11–12, 26–28, 37
War Department Appropriation Bill (H. R. 10871), 120–21
War Insurance Law, 157–58
war pensions. See pensions
war victims, 73–74, 161–62, 169; and organizations in Germany, 148–53
war widows. See Kriegerwitwen
Weimar Republic, 3, 15–16, 34, 40–41, 54, 75–76, 100–101, 122, 143, 145–46, 160–61, 170; and Constitution, 143, 152; and veterans, 148–50, 158
welfare, 54, 67, 72–73, 144–53, 157–58, 160, 169
Whalen, Robert Weldon, 139, 160, 187n101
Willoughby, John, 12
WILPF, British section, 55–56, 128
WILPF, German section, 65–68, 122–25
WILPF, U.S. section, 118–121
Wilson, Edith, 86–87
Wilson, Woodrow, 25, 50, 59–60, 64, 79–80, 82–83, 84–85, 87, 89, 93, 101, 106–7, 130, 139, 154, 157; and the Council of Ten, 113–14; and League of Nations, 15, 28–29, 91, 100, 115–16; and Wilsonian statecraft, 5, 71–78, 95, 99–100, 103
Winter, Jay, 141–42
woman suffrage. See suffrage

Woman Voters' Anti-Suffrage Party, 106
women, 3–7, 16–17, 21–28, 30–35, 46, 48–49, 73–74, 76, 79–80, 85–87, 97–98, 132–34, 170–71, 173–78; as peacemakers, xiii, 6–7, 11–12; and Rhineland horror, 41–43, 51–52, 54–57, 62–65, 66–69; and wartime service, 105–8, 128; and work, 141–42, 144–46, 150–57, 166–69. *See also* birthrates; femininity; foreign policy; sexuality; Women's International League for Peace and Freedom
Women's Bureau, 154–55
Women's Committee to Combat the War Guilt Lie (Germany), 101–2
Women's International League for Peace and Freedom (WILPF), 7, 109–11, 125–27, 165–66, 169, 175, 204*n*33; and humanitarian relief, 127–29, 131–32; and organization principles, 112–13;, and Rhineland Horror campaign, 42, 62–65; and Women's Charter, 116–17, and Zurich conference, 112–17. *See also individual branches*

"women's issues" in foreign policy, 177
women's labor. *See* female paid labor
Women's National Committee of the American Defense Society, 87
Women's Overseas Service League, 158
Women's Peace Society, 118–19
Women's Peace Union, 126
women's rights. *See* equality; gender; suffrage
Women's Service Section, 154
Women's Trade Union League, 155–57
Wood, Carolena, 132
World Trade Center, September, 11, 2001; bombings of, 71
World War I. *See* Great War
World War II, 37–38, 174–75
Württemberg branch of German WILPF, 122–23

Young Men's Christian Association, 79, 105–6, 129, 141, 164, 210n3

Zagacki, Kenneth S., 2
Zeiger, Susan, 141, 158
Zentralverband, 148, 150–51
Zietz, Luise, 54